PIG LATIN

PIG LATIN

A SERIOUSLY FUNNY TRUE STORY
OF A FORMER POLICE OFFICER

ERIC TANSEY

with Nick Palmisciano

ATRIA BOOKS

New York   Amsterdam/Antwerp   London
Toronto   Sydney/Melbourne   New Delhi

ATRIA
BOOKS

An Imprint of Simon & Schuster, LLC
1230 Avenue of the Americas
New York, NY 10020

First Atria Books hardcover edition August 2025

ATRIA B O O K S and colophon are trademarks of Simon & Schuster, LLC

For information about special discounts for bulk purchases, please contact Simon &
Schuster Special Sales at 1-866-506-1949 or business@simonandschuster.com.

The Simon & Schuster Speakers Bureau can bring authors to your live event. For more
information or to book an event, contact the Simon & Schuster Speakers Bureau at
1-866-248-3049 or visit our website at www.simonspeakers.com.

Interior design by Jill Putorti

Manufactured in the United States of America

1 3 5 7 9 10 8 6 4 2

Library of Congress Cataloging-in-Publication Data has been applied for.

ISBN 978-1-6680-6795-6
ISBN 978-1-6680-6797-0 (ebook)

AUTHOR'S INTRODUCTION

My name is Eric Tansey, and after eight years as a police officer patrolling one of the toughest neighborhoods in the United States—Raleigh, North Carolina's Southeast District—I was presented with a lifesaving award and was fired on the same day.

Spoiler Alert: That's how my police journey ends, and if that sounds like a wild juxtaposition, then just wait until you hear about everything that led up to that moment. As a cop, I did my job the same way I do everything: full-throated, unapologetically, and with everything I have. That led me to many amazing and terrible adventures as an officer, from gunfights, to car crashes, to being nicknamed Leroy Jenkins (after the famous *World of Warcraft* video where the guy ruins the plan by jumping into a fight too early), to becoming a sommelier, to talking people off ledges, and to everything in between. I routinely vacillated between hating my job and loving what I did, almost as if I were two officers playing as one.

To be honest, though, my life kind of rolls that way. In high school, I was the football player who was also a surfer, where neither group was fond of the other and I was stretched in between. I went to Bible Club but I wore all black, grew my hair out, and played punk rock. I loved the social aspect of school but hated sitting in a chair all day and dreamed of dirt-biking, skateboarding, surfing, or really anything other than sitting there and looking at a chalkboard.

After I graduated, I lived on the beach in St. Augustine, Florida, with my girlfriend and my buddy, working a fishing charter and loving life.

And then one day I heard the Battle of Fallujah livestreaming over a radio.

I knew then that I had to leave my idyllic life and do something more, so I enlisted in the National Guard, as a cavalry scout. (They sold me on the idea that I would ride dirt bikes. Surprisingly, I never saw one the entire time I was in.)

At nineteen years old, I went straight to Afghanistan and was immediately split off from my platoon and into a six-man recon element that was used to run missions from in and around Jalalabad, in Nangarhar Province, all the way to Bagram and the capital, Kabul. I was the youngest guy in the squad and was wildly immature. I literally volunteered for every mission, every convoy, and every foot patrol. I just felt it was my destiny to be there and so I was determined to do it all and go the distance.

A few months into the deployment, a Green Beret Operational Detachment Alpha (ODA) spent the night at our forward operating base and requested for one of us to join them as a gunner on one of their gun trucks. My sergeant decided I was the one going with them on their extended mission. I stayed with them for six months, and had no choice but to grow up or die.

Two years later I would attend the Special Forces assessment and selection process to become a Green Beret. I made it through the grueling three-week ordeal and I got selected. I then attended the Special Forces Qualification Course, graduating in BLC and BNOC (Basic Leadership Course and Basic Non-Commissioned Officer Course), Small Unit Tactics, SERE (Survival, Evasion, Resistance, and Escape), Airborne School, and the basic waterborne operation course.

The only thing I had left to pass was language school. While attending these schools, typically a few guys pool their resources and live in a house to save money. A couple of my roommates got caught up in some kind of investigation for allegedly defrauding the government by double-billing rent or something, and everyone in the house got sucked into the investigation.

While I wasn't involved, was never suspected of anything, and didn't get into any kind of trouble, the Army played it safe. I couldn't become a Green Beret until the investigation was over. That took over a year.

During that time I attended an advanced land navigation course, various shooting courses, and a lot of swamp-based tactics training exercises, since my group was located in the swamps of Florida and operated mainly in South America. Most importantly, I met a beautiful girl whom I instantly knew was the one. We dated for a while, and she told me that she couldn't marry a Green Beret with all the baggage the job entailed.

Because of the long delay, my enlistment was up, and I had a choice: either reenlist, go to language school, and finally become a Green Beret, or chase the girl. Without telling her, asking her, or anything else, I left the military and showed up at her doorstep. To say she was flummoxed would be an understatement. Fourteen years and five kids later, I know I made the right decision, even though I abandoned the dream of earning the coveted Green Beret.

But now I was in a new place and needed a job. I wanted to continue to serve, so becoming a cop made perfect sense. And after all, after spending time in combat with special operations, how hard could it be being a cop?

Real hard. Real. Fucking. Hard!

Truth be told, I had no idea what I was getting into. My military training prepared me for some of what I was about to see, but the only way to truly understand the challenges of being a police officer is to live it.

The job almost broke me many times, and if it were not for the support and mentorship from my fellow officers, it would have. Nevertheless, the longer I served, the more I found I needed to find catharsis outside the job to keep my sanity. One way I did this was to jot down stories of my worst (and occasionally best) days, so I could unload the emotions onto my laptop and not bring them home with me.

There the stories sat, in an emotional cocoon, trapped away for me and my wife alone, until that same woman encouraged me to share them with people who might be able to help me get them published. She told me the stories were good enough, and even though I wasn't sure she was right, I trusted her.

Through mutual friends, I met up with Nick Palmisciano, who had just written the *New York Times* bestselling book *Scars and Stripes* with Tim Kennedy, and I told him some of the stories. He was crying laughing as I relived my past, so I asked him if he would read my collection.

"I've never seen stories like this before," he told me. I was surprised, so I asked him if that was good or not. His reply got me fired up. "I've read cop books where the cops are perfect in every way, and I didn't believe them. I've read the cop hate books where every cop is corrupt and the criminals are the real victims, and I didn't believe them at all. But this is real. It's honest. I believe it. This made me understand in a way that no other explanation could."

And with that, *Pig Latin* was born.

My goals with this book are pretty straightforward.

First and foremost, I want to put you in the shoes of a new police officer and watch my journey. I want you to feel my stress, be pissed at me when I fuck up, cry with me when I encounter loss, and ask me what the fuck is wrong with me over and over again as I try my best to protect my community. Whether you agree with what I did or how I did it, I want you to understand how hard the job can be. I don't want you to revere cops any more than I want you to hate cops, but I do want you to empathize with the challenges officers face. The only way I know to do this is to be honest with you, for better or worse.

Second, I want you to understand that there is nothing sexy or cool about gangs, regardless of what Hollywood movies and television shows tell you. We've done a fantastic job of mocking white-trash racists in our society as being nothing to aspire to, but for some reason, we've gone the other direction with gangs. Gangs ruin communities. They ruin kids. They bring nothing but violence, rape, fear, and death.

Third, I want you to empathize with the communities that have to deal with gangs. Life is hard for everyone, no matter who you are. Life is harder still if you were born poor. It's hard as fuck if you're born poor and gangs are actively trying to keep you from getting out from beneath their heel.

Fourth, even though I don't use their real names, I want to tell you about the amazing officers who shaped me, supported me, and worked with me. They are the best of us (except the assholes, whom I will tell you about too), and I want you to see their sacrifices.

Finally, I want to make you laugh. Being a cop is a wild ride. You're either dealing with bad people or good people on their worst day. A lot of crazy stuff happened to me during my ten years in uniform, and most of it (if you're not the one it was happening to) is pretty damn funny.

As you read my book, please keep a few things in mind:

1. Gang members use the "N-word." No one wants to use it, let alone put it in their book, and I removed it anywhere it was not necessary, but the word has incredible power and knocks people off their feet. When I was at the police academy, they shared stories about how the use of that word can unbalance officers of all races and force them to lose focus in key situations. As such, working with my editor, I chose a few critical moments to retain the word and eliminated it elsewhere.

2. The "fog of war" is a real thing in both the military and police work. So I looked back at police reports, newspaper articles, and interviews with my fellow officers to help corroborate some of the stories I tell in this book. The dialogue is largely reconstructed based on my recollections.

3. I wrote most of the stories in this book when I was still a police officer. I resisted the desire to change "how I felt" in the book to reflect how I now feel about certain situations with the benefit of time and space. This is not a book that is meant to be from the perspective of an older, reflective man, but rather a man who is still in the fight, hence why I opted to use the first-person present tense for most of the book.

Thank you very much for taking the time to read my book. Please take it easy on yourself (and me) as you read it. These stories will make you laugh, and they will make you cry. Some will probably piss you off, while others will have you giving thanks. They will bring you anxiety, and maybe even some adrenaline dumps of your own. I did my absolute best to be honest and raw in my telling, and I hope you enjoy it, feel the emotion in it, and in the end, I hope that brings us closer together.

Enjoy your first lesson in my language: Pig Latin.

1

THE DEEP END OF THE POOL

Hovering above me, perched at the top of a short set of stairs and framed like a goddess by the early morning sun, stands a rather large woman. When I say large, I want to be really clear about exactly what I'm staring at. I don't mean "big-boned." I don't mean "plus-sized." I mean this lady is four hundred pounds—the same weight as a large male lion or, you know . . . a bear. She has an American flag wrapped around her head like a turban and she is draped by a long sundress that is flowing just a little at the bottom as the wind blows past her. If someone started playing the theme song to *The Good, the Bad, and the Ugly* right now, it would be oddly appropriate.

But that's not what's worrying me twelve whole minutes into my first-ever shift in the Southeast District of the Raleigh Police Department. Nor is it her death stare, as if she's looking right through me.

It's that right after I showed her the department-recommended steepled-fingers pose and calmly delivered the lines "Hello, ma'am. My name is Officer Tansey of the Raleigh Police Department. Your son is worried about you. How are you today?" she raised her hands into tight fists and assumed a boxing stance, daring me to climb farther up.

I'm not new to violence. I spent years in special operations in the military. I've trained in martial arts. I've been around. And because I've been around, I do not like the fact that her boxing stance looks legit.

Her elbows are locked in tight. Her right hand is protecting her chin. Her left hand is just a little away from her body so that the jab can flow freely. More than that, though, she is rocking back and forth, from her left foot to her right, like an athlete. You know that opening screen of every fighting video game where you toggle from one character to another and they're just kind of bouncing a little? Well, I am apparently playing *Street Fighter, Raleigh Edition*, because this lady is ready to go.

Visions of getting knocked the fuck out by a woman on my first day on the job dance through my head. I know I'm the rookie, and I know there'd be nothing funnier than me getting starched by this lady. I know I'd never live it down. Hazing, like it was in the military, is a critical part of being welcomed into an elite police force. There'd be nicknames, photos, reminders in PowerPoint presentations. It would never go away. I was also raised to never hit a woman, and I don't want to start now. More important, I don't want to overreact and hurt this lady if I have to roll up my sleeves and go to work. *What the fuck do I do now?*

I look over to my training officer, Jayce, as I round out my thirteenth minute on the force.

Jayce has his arms crossed and looks bored. Fingers facing the ground, he extends his arm a little and flicks his wrist at me in the "get on with it" motion.

Well, thanks a pantload, Jayce.

As I turn back to the lady, she reaches into her mouth with her sausage fingers and proceeds to remove some big white object from it. I squint. *Mother of God, those are her teeth!* As she calmly places them on the railing of the staircase, she locks right back into her fighting stance.

Who takes out their fucking teeth before they fight? Someone who has lost their teeth fighting before, that's who.

I take one last desperate look at Jayce. Surely he sees this is about to go south, and for the benefit of both me, the rookie under his charge, and her, the lady shadowboxing like she's Apollo Creed at the top of the stairs, he will now get involved to provide guidance and wisdom.

Nope. Now he looks even more pissed at me, spits on the ground, and gives me another limp-wristed flurry of get-on-with-it. I take a deep breath and turn back to the lady. My eyes go wide and my body tenses in fight-or-flight mode.

In the moment that I took to look at Jayce, she decided to charge me. And by God, she is lightning-fast. I now know what elk feel like before they get run down and eaten alive by a grizzly bear. They look over and see this giant creature and probably think, *Even if it does try something, I'm so quick that I will easily be able to get away. I'm gonna keep munching on this grass.*

Wrong.

She's so close that I can feel the static electricity of her body about to connect with mine, and I throw myself to the side with everything I have, narrowly avoiding a major impact with this force of nature the way a matador avoids the charge of a bull . . . or at least that's how I think I look. Jayce would later describe my actions as "jumping back like a scared child," but I'm going with "deftly maneuvered like a skilled matador."

Her momentum carries her way past me and for a brief moment she takes in Jayce's presence. She quickly realizes he's not getting involved, and huffing and puffing from her explosive assault attempt, she turns her eyes back to me. But something changes. Her eyes soften. Her muscles relax. She unfurls the American flag wrapped around her head, snakes it between her legs, and while making eye contact with me, starts grinding on it.

"You want some of this, baby?" she asks as she breaks out Shakira levels of hip gyrations on that poor flag. *I'm gonna have to have that thing donated to the Boy Scouts to be disposed of, because there is no coming back from that.*

"No, ma'am, I do not," I say, steepling my fingers so hard that they hurt. "Can we just talk?"

"You like that, Daddy? You want to arrest me?" she beckons.

"Not really, ma'am. I just want to talk. Can we please talk?" I plead.

But she has other ideas. She lies down on the flag belly first and begins to grind and hump it, thrusting her hips into it sensually. I'm mesmerized by her rhythmic hip thrusts. *How does a woman that size move so gracefully?* She looks up at me, still twerking on the flag, and whispers, "You like this, big boy?"

I did not sign up for this. I look back at Jayce helplessly, albeit for much less time than last time, just in case she tries to charge me again. I'm so overwhelmed. I want this to end so badly. I would do anything for just a little bit of help but Jayce looks like he's about to pour himself a glass of tea and do the crossword or some shit. Actually no, now there is a little smirk, like he's enjoying himself. *Fuck!*

I have no idea what to say or what to do, but since no one is coming to help, I remember my time in the military. *When in charge, be in charge.*

With my background driving me, I finally muster up the intestinal fortitude to speak. I deepen my voice and bellow, "Ma'am, I'm going to need you to stand up and calmly walk over to the police car so we can have a discussion, or else I will have no choice but to take you in." My delivery is powerful and masculine. *That should do it.*

Drinking me in with those deep brown eyes, barely visible with those fat cheeks peeking over the edge of them, she rolls onto her side, brings her top knee to her chest, and props her head up, while resting on one hand, also known as the "come and get me" pose. The same pose every man who is even a little bit lucky has seen once or twice in his life, and the same pose I hope to get from my wife if I make it through this shitpot of a day. She adds a sexy come-hither look motion with her finger. *Oh God. I've somehow made it worse.*

She rolls her tongue across her lips and says, "Come here, big boy. You know you want me. You gonna arrest me?" As she delivers that line, she pops up on one elbow so her whole body is in a one-armed push-up position and pulls her dress up. She is not wearing underwear, which was a little gift I didn't expect to be receiving at 6 a.m. With some minor struggle, her large belly frees itself from the trappings of the dress, but she can't quite clear the dress over her bosom in this position. With a grunt, she yanks with her arm and straightens her body, clearing the dress completely, and tosses it aside. She is now completely naked. *It's now a whole lot worse.*

I know better than to look at Jayce. It's me versus her. I am going to prevail.

"Now, you gonna arrest me, baby?" she moans.

"Yeah sure, ma'am. For lewd and lascivious acts, I guess . . ."

I take one step toward her. With a feat of athleticism I generally would only expect from professional athletes or elite CrossFitters, this lady burpees to her feet. The instant those pudgy toes hit the ground, she jumps, spins in the air, and lands in a perfect 180, so that her ass is facing me and she is now looking over her shoulder. The fat jiggles down her body like a wave.

Then I hear something. A grunt. *I know that sound.*

I had been trying very hard not to make direct visual contact with her. You don't want to stare at the naked body of a person in this condition. It gives you that uncomfortable feeling, like when you're thirteen and your weird uncle brings you to Hooters. But I have to look, and as I do, I see the result of the grunt. There is a turtle head poking out of this woman's ass. She is twerking in my direction and she is trying to shit. *Oh my God, she's shitting on me!* She relaxes and the shit goes back inside.

She grunts again and the turtle head reappears and makes it a little farther out. This time it doesn't go back in. She hops backward toward me with the poo still protruding from her ass. I am in a sheer panic. Fight-or-flight kicks in again and I choose flight. I attempt to maneuver past her to get closer to Jayce, but she matches my every move, hopping in circles, wincing and groaning, as she tries to cover me in shit. Just then, I hear the sound I've been waiting for—my training officer!

"Put some handcuffs on her!" Jayce offers.

"She's shitting on me!" I scream back as her dancing, shitting ass moves at me to the beat of some music that only she can hear. Then, with one more grunt, she leaves a small piece of shit in the grass and takes off at a dead sprint, back toward the stairs we started from.

"Go get her!" Jayce screams in my eighteenth minute as a peace officer. He seems mad. I don't give a fuck. I'm mad. I wanted a nice first day. I wanted coffee and a donut with a mentor who welcomed me into the thin blue line with stories and lessons. But here I am, losing a footrace to a four-hundred-pound lady who is trying to shit on me.

She flies up the stairs like a cat, waves of cellulite dancing with each bound. I don't know what this chick used to do, but she should not be able to move like this. She hits the doorway of her house and sprints in, just as I hit the top of the stairs.

I look to Jayce. In the military, you never go into a building alone. "You better go get her!" he screams at me, even more perturbed than he was a minute ago. I do as I'm told and open the door.

She explodes out, leaping into the air. To me it's all happening in slow motion. I don't know how high she got, but in my mind, she's hovering in the air at least three feet above me, like she's descending from the heavens. As she reaches the apex of her jump, she screams, "My president is black, muthafucka!" and with perfect timing, as she delivers the final syllable on "muthafucka," she brings down the full weight of her power and proceeds to smash an extremely large portrait of President Barack Obama over my face, head, and shoulders, so that I'm left wearing a picture frame like a goddamn Bugs Bunny cartoon.

I'm done. I've been a cop for nineteen minutes and it's the worst nineteen minutes of my fucking life. Obviously, I'm not cut out to be a cop. And then it happens.

Just as I'm wondering if, after multiple tours to the Middle East, I'm going to die at the hands of a large, naked, flag-humping lady with shit stains running down her leg, a SWAT officer the size of the Incredible Hulk sprints past me, palms her face like it's a basketball, and bends her backward over the railing with one hand while brandishing pepper spray with the other, screaming, "You wanna get sprayed?"

She calmly replies, "Nah, I'm good."

"Put your hands behind your back," he says gruffly.

She does. He cuffs her.

"Was that so hard?" this nameless superhero asks me.

"No," I respond.

"She almost shit on you, man," he says, reminding me. I resist the urge to say, "No shit," and instead meekly say, "I know."

"You can't be scared of them, man, or you'll end up hurt," Mr. SWAT says as he walks away in slow motion. I can almost see fiery explosions begin to burst around him. He refuses to look at them because he is too busy emanating cool. If I wasn't married and straight, I might've proposed at that moment.

I take over, walking her down the stairs and to the police car.

"Ma'am, I'm going to put you in the car now." Surprisingly, she lets me do it without a fight. *Finally, some respect.*

As I close the door to the back of the car, I let out a deep breath. *Holy shit, I am glad that's over.*

And there I meet Jayce's eyes. He has finally moved from his perch. "You gonna bring her to the jail like that or are you going to try to put her dress back on?"

"I'm going to put her dress back on," I mumble.

I walk back onto the grass toward her dress, careful to sidestep the pieces of shit she left there, and gather it in my hands. I then return to the vehicle and open the door as SWAT drives away.

Expecting the same calm rational attitude she offered to Mr. SWATTY McHulkMan, I am surprised when I eat a kick from one of her giant legs. "Get away from me, you son of a bitch!" she screams. I slam the door and sprint to the other side while she's completely committed to kicking where I just was. I open the door on the other side of the vehicle and see her head, and instantly and victoriously throw the dress over it. But as I start to try to pull it down her body, she somehow completely flips toward me, lashing out with her meaty hooves once more. I slam the door again. After four or five attempts at this, where I run back and forth around the back of the car trying to outmaneuver this lady, I come to the conclusion that a dress necklace will have to do.

I am twenty-four minutes into my first shift—which, incidentally, I started twenty-four minutes early, so I'm really at minute zero—when Jayce walks over and says, "You better get her to the jail."

I get back into my police car and Jayce gets into the passenger seat. Two dozen minutes ago, getting into this car was the coolest thing I had done in a long time. Right now, sweating through my uniform from the antics of trying to be a cop for the first time, feeling Jayce's judgmental eyes on me, and hearing the occasional "You can't have none of this no more, you son of a bitch!" from the back of the car make it markedly less cool. I radio in that 421 David (our vehicle) is on its way to the jail, and head out.

———

"You know, you don't have to strip them down before you bring them in, rookie," the stern jailer says to me.

"I know that. She wasn't cooperating. I tried to get it back on," I sheepishly reply.

"Mmmm . . . hmmmm . . ." she answers, filling those syllables with more judgment than even a tribunal of Italian, Jewish, and Asian grandmothers could. I don't know what to say, so I just stand there until Jayce points me to a row of computers. "Go over there and type up an affidavit," he says, emotionless.

"Absolutely," I reply confidently. As I walk in the direction of the computers, I realize I have two problems. First, I have no way of logging into the system since this is my first time at the jail, and I haven't been given credentials yet. Second, I have no idea what an affidavit is or what it looks like. Nevertheless, I've failed so many times today that I cannot bring myself to tell Jayce I suck once again, so I wing it.

There's only one other cop sitting there—a state trooper who is cranking out about a thousand words per minute. I plop down next to him and pray to the gods that he is cooler than Jayce. "Hey, man, is there any chance you can help me?" "Sure, what's up, man?" comes the reply. "I've been a cop for thirty-three minutes and I need to do an affidavit and I have never done one and I don't know how to get on the system and I have the training officer from hell."

He smiles and takes pity on me, logging me in, sifting through all the forms to show me where the affidavit is, and showing me exactly what and where to type. *Thank God.*

As I get to the meat of the document, I realize I can only fit four or five sentences in the allowed space. How do I possibly explain what just happened in five sentences? But as I'm about to ask the nice trooper that very question, Jayce appears behind me like the Phantom of the fucking Opera. I prepare myself for the deluge of insults and the mockery of my typing speed that I am sure are about to occur. Instead I hear something much more low-key: "You gonna do something about that?"

As I look to where Jayce is nodding I realize that the "that" which he is asking me to do something about is my nemesis, the lady who brained me with President Obama and shit-twerked me while other officers laughed, has climbed onto the bench, is once again naked, and is dropping soft-serve ice cream–style shit cakes all over the jail floor.

I rocket my chair back, forgetting Jayce is there, hitting him in the nuts. He groans and says, "You're lucky she's not throwing it at you." In that moment, I realize that having shit thrown at me seems to be a real part of this job, and that Jayce would have happily let that happen in the name of "teaching me." I approach the lady once again, with no idea how to stop this, and with no member of SWAT to back me up.

I didn't need it. This time I am saved by a jailer who is maybe five feet tall. Her size doesn't affect the booming in her voice as she proclaims, "Ohhhhh hell no! You best not be shitting on my floor. Bitch, you gotta be crazy if you think Imma let that fly!" In a blink this tiny woman was on the bench, retrieving my nemesis by the hair, and dragging her into a holding cell.

"Get somebody in here to clean this floor. We've got someone shitting on the floor in here!" she screams the second she returns. On cue, two inmates arrive with a mop and a bucket.

I just stand there for a minute, then I hear Jayce's voice once again. "Come on. It's time to see the magistrate." I just follow him. My brain isn't working anymore. This is military basic training all over again where there is so much to process that you lose the ability to function.

We arrive at Magistrate Tibbet's desk, and within five seconds I think I'm talking to Mark Wahlberg's dad because this guy is such a larger-than-life Bostonian. "Wut happened? Tell me wut happened? Oh, she was nakid?

Down by the pahk? Did anyone see her? Oh, her son did? Figures. Oh, you got a victim? Who's ya victim? Ya gotta have a victim, right? Yuh chahgin' her but there's no victim? That ain't right. Did Sully hear 'bout this?"

Okay, he didn't say the Sully part, but the rest is pretty much exactly what he said. He stops and looks at me for a brief moment, and I see a gleam in his eye. He knows I'm broken. I don't care anymore. The lady didn't offend me. She's just batshit crazy. I don't care if she goes to jail. I just want to leave, dig a hole, and die in it.

He changes tactics. "Tell me what happened, young man."

I do. I tell him all of it. Every detail. The charge. The stripping. The grinding. The shitting. The assault with President Obama. The kicking. The additional shitting.

When I'm done, he looks at me with just a little smile on his face. "All right, heah's what we're gonna do. Go back and retype this, and I know there ain't much room, but if ya go to the bottom and open a new fahm, you'll have moah room to type. Once that's done, hustle back heah. Come back and we'll write some new chahges. We'll get this all sorted out."

This is the first kindness I have received all day and it refills me. Hope wells within me, and I remember that there were days like this in the military and it all turned out all right . . . well, maybe not quite like this. There was less assault, less shit, similar levels of nudity, but mostly male nudity . . . With a spring in my step, I head out to write my new chahges . . . I mean charges, damn it.

As I sit down and start happily typing away, Jayce adds his first words of wisdom to the mix: "Tibbet's an asshole, but he's the best kind of ass-hole. He just wants to make sure you did it right and you had probable cause. We hold people's lives in our hands. It matters." And with that, he walks away like some kind of bored Yoda.

———

As I close the car door, I tell myself that while that was a rough start to my first day, it cannot get any worse. *Maybe now I'll get that coffee-and-donut experience I have been desperately craving.*

I start the car and Jayce looks at me. Either by mere coincidence or divine intervention, he says, "Feel like a coffee?"

"Absolutely!" I respond, maybe a little too excitedly. And if I'm externally grinning, inside I'm doing the entire opening dance routine to the movie *Bring It On*. Yeah, the one about the cheerleaders.

"Okay, let's do it," he responds.

With a big smile on my face, I put the car into gear and head to Dunkin' Donuts, one of the few places in the area I know how to get to without assistance. Just as that glorious pink and orange logo comes into view, a crackle comes over the radio. "421 David, Raleigh."

That's us.

"Answer the radio," Jayce barks.

Crap. Even though I've learned all this stuff, I'm used to the military methodology on the radio, where you can talk a little. Cops want everything to be number codes and that's it. So if you forget the number code for something, you might think you're showing up for a domestic disturbance, but there's really a cat stuck in a tree or some shit. Naturally, when he told me to answer the radio, I forgot everything I knew and had ever learned.

"421 . . . David . . . Raleigh . . . uh . . . Go . . . ahead," I say in the slowest, saddest way possible.

"421 David, we've got a disturbance at 123 This Isn't The Real Address Lane."

Well . . . looks like I won't get my coffee . . .

———

As we arrive at my second-ever call, I see a young, attractive, professional-looking black female wearing a business suit and standing in the middle of the street. As we approach, she waves us down. It's hard to gauge the exact emotion on her face. There's definitely anger in there, with a good helping of disgust, and maybe just a soupçon of fear? It was the kind of look my mom would give me when I passed gas at church.

I exit the vehicle and approach her. "Ma'am, what's wrong?" While still maintaining eye contact with me, she points her finger ninety degrees to her right. "There is a naked man in my car."

We just stand there staring at each other. *What? How does one follow up on that bad boy? If I ask her if she knows him, it might be offensive. Do I ask what he looks like? No. That's stupid. I can just go look myself. Maybe just ask her if she's okay?*

As my rookie brain wrestles with this conundrum, she takes mercy on me and breaks the ice, whispering, almost like she owes this man some kindness. "I was backing out of my driveway on my way to work, and as I turned my head to look out the back window, I saw him in the back seat." She pauses, briefly covering her mouth, and I think she's about to vomit. *At least it's not shit . . .*

"Saw who?" I ask.

"A naked man in my back seat! Oh God! He smells so bad." She is waving her hands up and down rapidly, clearly on the verge of a meltdown.

"Ma'am, is he completely nude?" At this question she loses all her composure and walks away, practically hyperventilating. I can tell by the way she's dressed and by the manicured nature of the front of her home that this lady likes things "just so." She might very well burn this car to the ground when this is all over. Still, how bad can it be?

I look over to Jayce for some guidance. I don't know why. He's been such a bucketload of help so far today. Smirking, he gives me a simple thumbs-up and a slight wink. *Awesome. At least you're having fun. Huge fucking help, boss.*

I walk over and look through the cracked rear window of the victim's car, and sure enough, there he is—stark naked, all curled up in the fetal position with his twig and berries mashed out the back of two excessively hairy legs. To add a little spice to the whole image, there are flies buzzing all over his balls, which makes me think of those nature documentaries where there're always flies buzzing around animals. That in turn makes me think about rhinos, because of all the animals out there, rhinos seem to always position themselves so that their genitals are just right there in your face.

I sniff the air. *Yep, smells just like Bigfoot's jockstrap after a hard day of pickleball with the other forest creatures.* I get a little kick of gag reflex but hold it together. Jayce has a fist balled up in his mouth to keep from laughing.

No more waiting around like a bitch for guidance. Time to do what I'm paid for! I dramatically throw the car door open and announce, "Raleigh Police!" On TV shows, this shit always results in the criminal taking off at a sprint, resulting in a badass foot chase, or with them putting their hands up in an obvious show of respect for the power and authority of the job of peace officer.

This dude doesn't even move. He just lies there balled up (pun intended), snoring away.

I am bummed (pun intended).

That's when my eyes pick up on other things in the car besides testicles. Little things that only a trained officer would pick up on . . . like the fact that he is using wadded-up women's panties for a pillow . . . or the fact that he is covered in rose petals and that rose petals are covering the floorboards . . . I mean straight up, this dude is lying on like sixty dollars in rose petals.

I turn to the woman and ask, "Ma'am, are you missing any panties?"

"What!? No . . . I don't think so . . ."

"Do you normally keep rose petals in your car, by chance?"

"Eww, what? God no!" She shakes her head, offended and disgusted. *Yes, this car is being burned to the ground or sold by day's end.*

Summoning my strength, I turn my attention back to the car and announce myself even louder than before.

"RALEIGH POLICE! Hey, man, wake up!" I roar.

Slowly, like an olde-tyme cartoon character waking up to some classical music, he lifts his head from the wad of panties and looks up at me. Unimpressed, he casually stretches and yawns.

A little aggravated at the fact that he isn't giving me my due, I bark in my best not-a-rookie voice to get out of the car and to keep his hands where I can see them. Not that he can really hide them anywhere.

In the same slothlike manner in which he reacted to me, the man slides himself out of the car and stands next to the trunk. The proper, put-together car owner gasps and shields her eyes as he does, because this guy doesn't give a fuck. His dark skin makes the salt-and-pepper hair covering his whole body stand out, and because he's like 3 percent body fat and slight, he's basically a muscular skeleton, albeit one who's hung like a rhino. To make matters worse, as we start our conversation, he straight-up Peter Pans it, hands on hips. Out of the corner of my eye, I see Jayce shaking in quiet laughter.

"Hey, man, what are you doing in this lady's car . . . naked?" I ask.

"Maaaaan, I just got out of jail last night. I needed a place to sleep . . . her car was unlocked and it looked comfortable," he replies, as if I'm the asshole in this situation.

"Okay, sure, that makes sense . . . I guess . . . but what's up with the panties and flowers?" I ask, trying to rein this back in.

"I don't know about dat. Dey ain't mines," he says.

"What?" I respond, a little taken aback.

"Dem ain't mines!" he proclaims with gusto.

Standing there in front of me, he is so matter-of-fact, so confident, so shameless, and so very naked that I start to question myself. He doesn't appear to be drunk or high. *Am I missing something? Am I the bad guy? Wait, no!*

"You're under arrest, sir."

"Fo' what?!" he asks me.

"Well, for breaking and entering a motor vehicle," I reply.

"Oh damn," he answers.

"And for indecent exposure, man."

"Yeah, I can see dat . . ." He trails off.

As I am about to put him in the car, I remember the valuable lesson I learned thirty minutes ago. I look at the car owner and say, "Ma'am, I noticed a pair of Guess jeans in the back of the car. Are those his?"

"No, they are mine," she responds. As I start to form my next question, she blurts out, "Yes! He can have them."

"Would you like me to return them to you when we get him to jail?" I ask. She holds her hand over her mouth and shakes both her head and her other hand at me in the most forceful "no" gesture I have ever seen.

But the pièce de résistance is watching this dude put on women's jeans. I mean this guy puts on a performance. Hip swivels. Gyrations.

Jumping to clear his ass. And finally, a deep inhalation, coupled with a hand stuff to get the family jewels into jeans that make no such allowance up front. When he finally clasps that top button and pulls that zipper true, he crosses his arms and smiles like he has just won the WWF championship belt.

We never did find out where the panties and rose petals came from, or where his clothes went, but I'm sure it's a very romantic story.

———

I pull into my driveway and sit for a minute. After bringing him in, Jayce and I had twelve more calls. It's now 9 p.m.

I drove to work this morning at 4:30 a.m. I was supposed to report at 6:00 but I couldn't sleep last night worrying about my first day, so at 4:00 I just decided to drive in. Pulling in this morning, I was scared shitless. All you hear about SED—the legendary Southeast District—is that it's nuts. It's hard-core. If you're working there, you have to be good. You have to be on your shit. It's the military equivalent of choosing to be in Ranger Battalion or Special Forces. There are much easier paths. I knew all of that and I thought I wanted it, but the whole day made me question that.

From the moment I pulled into the precinct, which was nestled behind a bank and a seriously overgrown set of tree branches that made it feel like I was pulling into the Bat Cave, to being hazed for having too much gear when I walked in, to the shit, vomit, nudity, and assault I dealt with all day, my shift drove me to my knees. I had nothing left. It ended at 6 p.m., but that's when the paperwork started. After a quick dinner in solitude and a lot of slow typing, I finally left the station at 8:30 p.m., very confident that whatever I had typed was not going to be good enough.

I take a deep breath and exit the car door, dragging myself up the stairs and through my front door, where I am greeted with a hug and a kiss from my wife, Ashleigh.

"Tell me about your day! How was it?!" she musters, showing excitement for me and my new profession.

I want to meet her energy, but I can't. I don't have it in me to recap my day. I just lived it, then recapped it for the magistrate every time I had to bring someone in, then recapped it in reports for the last two hours.

"Babe, if it's okay with you, I just need to take a shower and go to sleep. I have to be at PT [physical training] at 4:30. Everyone in the squad goes to the gym together."

"Whatever you need," she offers, surprised by my attitude.

As I trudge to the shower, her voice follows me: "It'll get better."

Man, it needs to. It fucking needs to.

2

THE LORD'S WORK

L *ook at that glorious fucking thing.*
Officer Serious's mustache wraps around his chiseled features and gives additional gravitas to an already imposing 6'1," 185-pound panther of a man. I realize there are only four men who have ever existed who can pull off the lip rug that this dude is sporting. They are, in no particular order, Tom Selleck, Sam Elliott, Wyatt Earp, and Officer Serious.

Officer Serious is a legend, and let's face it, very few people are legends while still on the job. George Washington got dragged through the mud by Thomas Jefferson's people in his second term. Tom Brady was called a system quarterback until he retired. Vincent van Gogh wasn't appreciated until twenty years after he died. Officer Serious is the exception.

Serious never planned to be a cop.

He was running a successful landscaping business that covered most of the Greater Raleigh area when one of his employees, on his lunch break, was murdered during a bank robbery. Now, most employers, even really, really good ones, would perhaps have set up a fund for their deceased employee, maybe helped the employee's family in some way, and maybe given the rest of the employees some time off. But then, in short order, they would have gotten back to business.

Not Serious.

Although in his mid-thirties, he saw a real problem and decided he needed to be part of the solution. He decided to become a cop.

So he sold his business and went to the police academy. He embraced the training and transformed himself into Officer Serious, and unlike me, he immediately excelled on the police force. He listened and learned from anyone and everyone, and because he was older, he didn't look at the job quite the same way most young street cops did.

Serious never had any interest in rousting people for small crimes like simple drug possession. Instead he would identify frequent low-level criminals and pull them over for traffic violations and the like. Invariably he'd find drugs or guns or any number of offenses. Then, rather than charge them, he would offer to trade information for leniency. He was really interested in finding out "Who's the guy above you?" Moreover, as he gained more information and achieved greater success, he began working with the district attorney to cut deals with the people who provided really good information. Sometimes previous charges were dropped and in some cases records were completely cleared for repeat minor offenders, all the while opening up a trove of information about previously untouchable career criminals.

In a matter of months, Serious was delivering high-quality field-level intelligence and was responsible, time and time again, for the biggest drug and weapons busts in the history of Raleigh. With success came power, and if Spider-Man taught us anything, it's that with great power comes great responsibility.

In no time, Officer Serious and those who became his disciples became very busy police officers. So busy, in fact, that eventually the department would form a squad dedicated to that line of work. Officer Serious, of course, would unofficially occupy the helm. They would gather information on murder suspects, prostitution rings, gang meetings—anything and everything. The more dangerous the job, the more they embraced it. All these dudes wanted to do was hunt evil men, no matter the risk. Their success allowed them to evolve their own schedules and obtain whatever resources they needed. Due to their flexibility and creativity, they would eventually be dubbed the FLEX Team. But that sophistication was years away.

Right now, in my fourth week on the job, I am looking at the three scary meatheads who are the heart of that future team: Officer Serious, Ralph, and Spoon, all members of the Southeast District D squad. They are all glaring at me.

You see, Jayce, my training officer, is out on paternity leave, leaving Rookie Officer Tansey with no one to babysit him. Officer Serious is suddenly my new training officer.

He clearly does not want to be my training officer. He isn't trained as a training officer. When his name was called at roll call, the expression on his face said it all. This was as much of a surprise to him as it was to me.

Officer Serious and I currently hold different surprised looks. My surprised face is like a kid walking into a candy store. I was just given the gift of working with a legend. What incredible luck! His face, however, looks like he just ate some bad borscht. Full disclosure: I've never had borscht, but it seems like the kind of thing that would be really bad when it is bad, so I used it here for dramatic effect. My point is, he really doesn't look happy. Nor does he look lucky.

Unfazed, and sure that once they get to know me they will love me, I approach the threesome that at this point is dubbed "The Dream Team."

"Gentlemen, I'm Officer Tansey and I look forward to learning from you today," I say with a smile.

"Okay," replies Officer Serious. He then just walks away from me, with his consiglieri, Ralph and Spoon, in tow. As I follow them, I take in my new "partners."

Ralph is a 6'4", 220-pound muscle. Honest to God, I've never seen a dude who has less of a neck than this man. Even his jaw and forehead. *How do you work out your forehead? Maybe scrunch your eyebrows?* His nickname is Wreck-It Ralph, not just because he looks like a shredded Wreck-It Ralph, which he does, but because he acts like one too. Ralph's reputation is that he enjoys the hunt every bit as much as Serious does, but that he likes it even more when the altercations get physical. His joy ends when the suspect is in cuffs and in the car. Then he immediately gets bored and just wants to find another challenge. Whereas Serious and Spoon revel in the interview process and the flipping of a suspect, Ralph just wants the action. If this were a heist movie, Ralph would be referred to as the Muscle.

In the same heist movie, Officer Spoon would be the Brain. At 5'11" and 175 pounds, Spoon is a former college wrestler and a former Mormon missionary. He is very cultured. He lived in Ecuador during his missionary years and is fluent in Spanish. While he isn't quite at the Matt Damon in *Good Will Hunting* level, his superpower is memory. He knows every gang member's name, nicknames, and affiliations. He knows where they hang out, who their associates are, and what they are doing at any given moment. You could tell Spoon where you last saw a gang member, and he would tell you why they were there and who they were meeting. And 99 percent of the time, he'd be right. Spoon and Ralph are best friends and seem to have an ongoing competition for who gives off the best "I'm the coolest cop but I care the least about actually being a cop" vibe. If there was an explosion behind them, neither would look back, I can tell you that. They complete this vibe by sporting unruly hair and unshined brass, and dragging their feet as they walk cockily through the station. They remind me of my friends in Special Forces.

They are inseparable and have their routine on lock. Every day starts with picking a small area of the district at the beginning of the shift, and they laser-focus on that area all day. They are consummate professionals with a rigid code of what's fair play—they don't fabricate issues or anything like that, but if a car driving by has any minor violation, they stop it. Most of the time they'll simply give people warnings. They don't care at all about taillights or registrations. All they want is drugs and guns.

They look for certain indicators like needles, needle caps, Brillo wadding, odors of marijuana, or excessive nervous behavior from the occupants. No indicators? "Have a nice day, sir or madam! Here's your verbal warning." But if a car has indicators of more nefarious activity, that's when the real magic kicks in. The guy who stopped the car immediately calls the other two for backup. Then they'll have everyone get out of the car, and Spoon and Ralph use their humor to get the occupants to loosen up and give them consent to search the vehicle. If they hit on drugs or illegal guns, which they almost always do, then Serious steps in and wheels-and-deals for quality information. If they run, Spoon the Gazelle chases them down. If they try to fight, Ralph will . . . well . . . wreck them.

But we aren't doing that tonight. As I get in the car with Officer Serious, his phone rings.

"Yeah, I know the complex," Serious answers. I can't hear the other side of the conversation, but it goes on for a minute. "Got it. I'll be right there." With that he hangs up and we start to drive, us in our car with Spoon and Ralph following in theirs. "Where are we going?" I ask, a little scared to embarrass myself with the question. "We have to meet a contact of mine," Serious answers seriously.

We drive for a little while and I watch the buildings go by, wondering where the fuck we are going. This job has been fast-paced so far. Every day has been different; crazy, often scary, and unlike anything I expected. Nevertheless, I am hopeful each day, and on my way to work I offer a morning prayer, asking that if there is one person I can help and change for the better, then Lord please help me answer that call.

Every single day I mean this prayer, but I am quickly finding out that the hardest part of this job is that while I believe I am making people's lives better, it almost never feels that way. When someone's house is on fire, firefighters show up and spray suds and water all over the place, literally ruining the house and everything that the people who live there own, and they get hugs and thank-yous. Cops almost never get any kind of thanks or compliments. Even when we do everything perfectly, someone always has something to say about what we could have done differently, should have done better, or my favorite: that life would be better if we ceased to exist.

Maybe that's the way it's supposed to be? Maybe that's part of the bargain, society says. "We'll grant you extraordinary authority, the power to arrest, and the power to use force when necessary. But every time you use it, we'll be watching." Maybe that kind of scrutiny is a good thing. But I'll tell you the truth: it wears on us. It's worn on me already, and I am only a month into the job.

My thoughts and the occasional squelch of a radio are the only sounds I hear while driving to go meet a mysterious contact at a mysterious complex. Officer Serious says nothing to me. I think he is pretending I don't exist in the hopes that I will disappear.

"We're here," he says as we pull behind a shitty grocery store near a shittier apartment complex. There's a dude leaning against a car wearing a Hawaiian shirt. I can't tell if he is a criminal, a source, or what. I've gone from doing regular cop shit with Jayce to meeting a strange man who looks like he's a guest star on *Magnum, P.I.* waiting next to the dumpster of a third-rate grocery store. *This is awesome.*

As soon as the guy starts walking, though, I know he's a cop. There's a little confident swagger that cops and military guys have. Turns out this guy is a parole officer, also known as a PO. POs check up on criminals who are on probation to make sure they are living up to the terms of release. Magnum here had a bad feeling that the heroin dealer who just got out of prison was now—and this will come as a real shock—back to dealing heroin.

The terms of this guy's parole were that his home could be searched at any time, but everyone here knew from experience that when you show up to do a search, criminals are exceptionally good at getting rid of everything before letting the police into the premises. However, if you do what's called a "residence check," where the parole officer is simply going to ensure that the parolee is actually living where they say they are, they usually just hide the drugs and let the police in.

After some brief discussion, Serious announced the plan. "Magnum, you're going to call this guy and let him know you're coming by for a residence check. When we get there, Ralph and Spoon will cover the back exit in case they try to squirt out and get away. You'll knock on the door to do your check, and the second you do, I will stick my foot in that door and Tansey and I will pour in and stick guns in faces if we meet resistance."

Holy shit. I'm living a freakin' Michael Mann movie right now! Do I get my linen suit now, or does that come later?

These guys all nod like this is everyday life for them, when to me it's the coolest thing that's ever happened to me. That's when I realize that this is literally what they do all the time. I get hit with a sense of nervousness immediately. *Don't fuck up. Be cool.*

While I am wrestling with my emotions, the PO is already on the phone with the parolee. He's home and he agrees to the residence check.

We are a go.

The drive to the complex from the grocery store is short, and as we arrive I see that the target is a dilapidated town house connected to other town houses. Ralph and Spoon have parked a block away and are already working their way around the back. They text that they are in position and we move to the front door.

Serious and I take our positions to either side of the front door, out of sight of the peephole or the windows. *Am I Jason Bourne? Possibly.* The PO casually knocks on the door. The parolee opens it and Serious immediately sticks his foot in the door and he and I pull him outside in a friendly yet forceful manner. I'm new, but I've already learned that putting your hands on a drug dealer is tricky. Most of them carry guns, so you have to be a little aggressive in order to stay safe, but they also might not have a gun, so you have to be a little friendly too. It's a delicate balance. Dying is bad, but so is ending up on the news for police brutality.

Now that we surprised him with a full search, ensuring that he couldn't flee the scene or get rid of any drugs, we enter the house. We immediately detain a few more people who are inside. And speaking of the inside, it looks like it is inhabited by a dozen teenagers. The place stinks of body odor and rotting food. The dishes are stacked so high I wonder how often they have to buy more dishes to stack, instead of just cleaning the ones they own. Mold is on everything. Piles of dirty clothes seem to be everywhere. The adrenaline has my senses firing on hyperdrive and I sense movement out of the corner of my eye. My eyes chase it, only to find over and over again that the movement is from the roaches streaming across the floor and up and down the walls.

Serious moves to the back door to let Spoon and Ralph in and they begin their search, leaving Magnum and me with the detainees. Magnum immediately goes into professional mode and reads a court order informing them that we have the right to search the whole premises, ending with "I'm giving you guys an opportunity to confess to any known contraband right now, before we start this search. It will be worse for you all if we have to find it."

To a man, they all deny that there is anything in the house, and add that if we find anything, they didn't put it here. They look at him, then they look at me, then I look at me. Magnum has on jeans and his awesome red Hawaiian shirt with a bulletproof vest. I'm wearing my sharply pressed uniform with my bright shiny shoes. Everyone knows who the cherry is in this room, and that knowledge puts a little more pressure on me. *Be cool.*

Nevertheless, even a cherry like me can tell the jig is up. Their voices are trembling and they are adding too many words to overcompensate for their nervousness. Sweat is beading on their foreheads and dripping down their noses and, in the case of one extreme sweater, off his beard. I'm expecting one of them to run for it at any moment, and I loosen my muscles and lock into prepared mode. I don't get the sense that any of them is going to try to take me on, because they are obviously users and not dealers, but I've already learned you can't take any chances. I'm ready.

"Can you guys sit on the couch for me? It's going to be a little while, and I'd rather we all be comfortable," I say, very pleased with myself at the control tactic. They all sit.

As I watch over them, I hear a sound above my head. A light thud, followed by a subtle and slow creak. All three hooligans on the couch snap their necks at the ceiling, indicating that they had heard the noise too. "Sooo . . . are there any mice in the attic?" I ask. They answer all at once, stepping over each other in a bid to be first:

"No, there's no mice in the attic!"

"Yeah, man, we have mice . . ."

"We don't have an attic!"

Their contradictory statements raise the hairs on my neck as I watch them descend into panic. They're tapping their feet and fidgeting in their seats like a group of third graders sitting outside the principal's office waiting for the ax to fall. One of them is even rocking back and forth while biting his nails. The only way it could be more obvious that something is in the ceiling would be a neon sign and a brass band playing, "Hail to the Guys Hiding in the Ceiling!"

Ninety percent of me believes someone is in the attic, but there is that 10 percent that doesn't want to call everyone over and make a big deal about it, only to find out it was the wind or a tree branch or something. *Shit. Shit. Shit. Shit. Shit.* I take a deep breath. *Fuck it.*

I call out to Serious. He immediately stops his search and makes his way down the hallway to me in the living room. "Someone is in the ceiling," I whisper. He looks at me like I'm crazy, but only for a second, because one of my couch buddies can't control himself and tries to defuse the situation with this amazing string of verbal vomit.

"Guys, there isn't anything in the attic! We don't have a ceiling . . . attic . . . thing. I mean, I don't even think that if we did have an attic thing, anyone . . . What attic? Could an attic even fit in this kind of . . . you know?" (Public service announcement: Don't do drugs, kids.)

Serious and I stare at him, wide-eyed. Then we slowly look at each other, and let our gazes drift up toward the ceiling. As if on cue, we hear a horror-movie-like creak above us. "Stay put," he whispers and goes down the hallway to retrieve the other officers.

He returns with the guys and we huddle up in the living room. As I try to explain what I heard, Ralph seems unimpressed and maybe even pissed that we interrupted his search. Spoon is smiling like a Cheshire cat, obviously amused by my concern. "I heard the creak too," Serious explains. Immediately they're all paying attention. "We need to at least check it out," he continues. With Serious's verbal support, they slowly become believers in the possibility of a secret army of attic dwellers. Magnum looks over at the three on the couch and asks, "Who's in the attic?"

They begin jabbering all at once again. The staccato melody of chaotic speech, confused looks, and palpable panic fills the air. My new partners immediately change their expressions. Magnum looks at the rest of us and says, "We need to check that attic."

"Let's send Tansey!" Ralph and Spoon offer simultaneously. Serious agrees with them because he understands the need for "rookie hazing."

Even though he didn't really care about or participate in the games, he knew it was my role as a rookie to do exactly these types of things. And after all, I am the one who heard it.

But he wasn't going to let me go alone. "I'll go with him," he quickly adds.

Serious and I walk down the hallway until we find the entrance to the attic, and Magnum follows. He points down at the floor to a debris field of dust and ceiling particles. Someone has recently pulled down the attic door. Serious looks at me and his face gets deadly . . . well . . . more serious. In a very low tone, he says, "Someone is probably up there, and that means we have to go up there and get them. Are you good with that?"

"Yeah, I'm good," I respond.

"Look, going into an attic sucks and there's no real safe way to do it, okay? The trick is to go fast and keep moving upward so I can get up there right behind you. Pick the path of least resistance, and if you don't see anything in front of you then look behind you. But don't stop no matter what. Just keep moving up. You got it? The shitty thing is that once we open the door the secret is out that we're coming up there. That means there's no escape for him, so he's going to be like a cornered snake. You have to be committed and you have to be aggressive, okay?" Serious says, looking deep into my eyes to see if I have it in me.

"I understand," I say, drawing my pistol. Serious does the same.

On the count of three, Magnum pulls down the ceiling hatch and the ladder unfolds. I sprint up the ladder into the deep black void with one hand on the rail and the other hand pointing my gun into the abyss.

There is nothing "not scary" about going into an attic for me, even in my own house. Maybe it's from too many horror movies, but even when I go up there to get the Christmas ornaments every year, I always pause at the top for a quick peek—just to make sure there is nothing up there that's going to rip my head off. Add to that the many police stories about guys getting killed in situations just like this one, and my lived experience in the military, where stairways and ladders are basically the worst place to find yourself in close-quarters combat, and my pucker factor was at an all-time high.

Right now, I don't have the luxury of a quick peek. I have to get up these stairs and get out of the way of the entrance so my partner can get up here with me, for both of our security. This is not my attic. There is definitely going to be someone up here. The only question left is whether they want to rip my head off.

As my head gets closer to cresting the attic floor, the adrenaline lights my body on fire. Right before my head pops up, I let go of the railing, grab my flashlight from its holster, and balance myself. This is it. If the suspect has a gun, he will have an easy, clean shot at my skull and there is next to nothing I can do to stop him. The only thing I have left is what Serious had just told me: to go in fast and committed.

Go.

I launch myself up the final steps and drive into the darkness at the top with my gun and flashlight pointed out in front of me. "Show me your hands! Raleigh Police!" I shout. My flashlight cuts through the darkness with the high-powered beam of LED light. There was an odd beauty to it, amid my internal panic. I felt like I was waving the Bat Signal around. But wave as I might, there was nothing but darkness.

I hear Serious reach the top, and even though I know that doesn't make me safe, at least I know I'm not alone. But the vastness of this attic quickly elevates my heart rate once again.

This attic is not divided between the adjoining town homes, so to my front and rear is just a long corridor of shadows and pink insulation. *One, this is scary as fuck. Two, was I wrong? It's all just beams and insulation.*

I push forward and step deeper into the blackness, with Serious not far behind. *Rip!* The pink insulation in front of me explodes as a man bursts out of it and begins to run down the long beams deep into the darkness. Every muscle in my body tightens and somehow, some way, I don't shit myself or die on the spot from a heart attack. *This is why we keep the finger off the trigger.* Now it really is a horror movie. My light bounces around in the darkness as I try to give chase across the beams, creating a strobe effect on the suspect. *Is this guy a fucking gymnast?* The dude is sprinting down the beams like they are two feet wide instead of two inches. Meanwhile, I'm just trying to not fall through the ceiling underneath me. *How is he not falling?*

On cue, the suspect disappears from my vision and the light emanating from my flashlight, and I hear a crash. I stop and focus my light downward. Both of his legs have fallen through the ceiling, and he is now straddling a two-by-ten beam. This dickhead has fallen off the beam and through the floor, then landed on his dick. There's some poetry in there, but I don't have time to think about it now.

"Show me your fucking hands! Put your fucking hands up!" I scream. He is trying to get his bruised nuts off the beam but with his legs stuck in the ceiling, he is having a real hard time, pun intended. I'm having a hard time too. Do you know how hard it is to move quickly through an attic with both hands occupied? I didn't before, but now I do.

FYI, it sucks.

This guy is only partially complying as he keeps moving around, trying to take the pressure off his balls.

"Keep your fucking hands where I can see them, asshole!" I yell.

"My hands are up, don't shoot me!" he wails.

I flinch as another muffled, screaming voice pierces the darkness. "Man, what the fuck am I doing with some muthafucka's legs coming through my goddamn house?! Who gonna pay for this shit? Somebody gonna pay for this shit! Ya'll muthafuckas have gone too far!"

My brain catches up to my ears and I realize the sound is coming from the poor bastard who lives next door to these assholes. *Not a threat. Return to the moment.*

I close in on him with my gun aimed at his back and my flashlight aimed at the back of his head. As I get closer, I see that he has a duffel bag slung across his back. Then it hits me. I have no idea what to do next. *How do I safely get this guy into cuffs?*

Thinking I've won the fight now that he is literally stuck in the floor, my brain switches gears to the logistics of cuffing him and getting him out of the ceiling. In that mode, I shove my gun downward into its hard, plastic holster. The second I do it, I hate myself. *Never holster your gun before you cuff someone.* The suspect hears the metal clank into the heavy

Safariland holster and knows he has another shot at getting away. Both his hands immediately drop toward his stomach as he doubles over onto the beam. *Oh fuck!*

I instinctively jump down on top of him, having no idea what he is trying to do but knowing his hands are down beneath his body, and that's every cop's worst nightmare. A suspect's hands can disappear below the beltline for several different reasons, but none of those reasons are ever good.

I am now straddling him as he straddles the beam, and I know my life depends on getting his hands back into my sight. I punch him in the back of the head, my right fist making contact with the top of his ear. He bellows out in agony. I rear back and punch the same spot again, this time causing him to turn his head away from me and release his hands from under his body. He tosses up his hands and throws something out into the darkness, causing a muffled thud in the insulated abyss. He whimpers, "I'm done, don't hit me again, please."

I stop. I can see a little blood trickling down from the top of his ear, mixing into his sweaty hair and unshaved whiskers. "Put your fucking hands behind your back or I will hit you until I'm fucking tired!" I command, mustering my best sergeant voice from my time in the military. Thankfully, he surrenders, flopping his hand onto the small of his back. I reach behind me for my cuffs, but when adrenaline goes up, fine motor skills go down, and I am having a hard time getting my fingers to manipulate the clasp. I simply cannot wrap my head around how to unhook something.

As I fumble with this problem, another voice cuts through the darkness. "Tansey, here, take mine," Serious says. He stretches out his cuffs toward me. A field training officer would have made me work through the adrenaline to get my cuffs out on my own, but Serious isn't an FTO, and doesn't want to be. At this moment, I feel like I am part of the team.

As the adrenaline dump hits me, I realize this attic is hot as fuck and I no longer want to be here. As I finish cuffing his slimy arm, I feel my own sweat pouring down my forehead and off my nose onto his back. My thighs are cramping from the awkward bracing between the beams, and my lower back is screaming from being bent over. But I can't leave. We still need to get this guy out of here, and by the way, what did he throw when I was hitting him?

I slowly back away from him and adjust my weight onto another set of beams. Serious and I bump knuckles and make a quick plan to get him out of the attic, using an intricate system of pulleys and a welding torch. Just kidding. We decide to balance him between us as we slowly walk him across the beam. Just to add a little fun to the mix of intense heat, heavy body armor, and precarious balancing, the suspect keeps trying to throw himself to the ground in the hopes of landing a police brutality win in court, or a lawsuit for not ensuring he was safe after custody.

After a long, arduous, and excruciating team effort in the North Carolina heat, exacerbated by the itchiness crawling over my skin from the fiberglass insulation, we successfully get this asshole onto the couch with his asshole friends.

Serious and I regale Spoon, Ralph, and Magnum with the story of our adventure in the attic and about how the dude threw something.

"Man, that sucks. I really feel like I missed out," Ralph says.

"Yeah, I wish I was covered in sweat, fiberglass, and that guy's body odor," added Spoon.

"Since you've already gone through all the trouble of getting sweaty, maybe you two should go up there and find whatever he threw?" Ralph chimed in.

"I agree," smiled Spoon.

After chugging some water, Serious and I head back up. After digging around where I had heard the thud, I find something metal. Pulling it into the light, I come face-to-face with a large Dirty Harry–style .44 Magnum revolver. Upon inspection, I realize the gun is fully loaded, with one in the chamber.

The duffel bag has over ten bundles of heroin in it and a trafficking quantity of assorted pills.

For the rest of that shift, after I change out of my gross uniform, the guys treat me differently. I'm not necessarily one of them, but they now know I don't completely suck.

As I drive home that night, a lot of thoughts sit with me. In my mind, I had hit the guy two or three times when he went for his waistband. Serious had informed me that it was way more than that. I now understand how you see such overreactions from those cop videos where the internet plays judge, jury, and executioner. *It all happens so fast.*

But also, the man that I fought is a convicted felon with a trafficking quantity of heroin and opioids on him. He was, in fact, that cornered snake that Serious warned me about, and if it would have meant getting away, he would have happily put a bullet through me, Serious, and everyone else there.

He meant to kill me.

After I pull into my driveway and shut the car off, I sit for a moment.

Would I have lived today if I wasn't a combat veteran? Would a normal rookie have flipped the switch in time and engaged in the fight?

I don't have an answer.

The stink of the day weighs heavily on me, though. I need to wash it off.

I get out of my car, take a deep breath of air to settle my thoughts, and walk inside to greet my wife.

3

YOU ARE NOT A JEDI YET

"Faak that matherfaaker! I want a faaking davorce!" screams the five-foot-nothing attractive young lady in front of us in a thick New England accent. Naturally, she is wearing a long Patriots hoodie like a dress as so many classy girls do at 3 a.m.

"Okay, ma'am. Unfortunately, we do not deal in divorces but maybe we can mediate this situation? Can you tell me what happened tonight that makes you want a divorce so badly?" asks Officer Quiet, my fellow trainee with perfectly steepled hands in front of him.

"No! Faak that matherfaaker! I want a faaking davorce right gawdddamn now!" comes the shrill reply.

"Okay, I understand that you want a divorce, but can you first just tell me what happened?"

"No! Faak you, and faak that matherfaaker in there! Where's my faaking davorce!" She claps her hands and stomps her feet for an even more dramatic effect.

She is obviously wasted, and we are getting nowhere with her. Quiet looks over to me and says, "Hey, man, can you go make contact with anybody else in the house to see what's going on here?" *Oh, I absolutely can!* I can't wait to find out what this bullshit is all about. I've spent the last few weeks answering a paltry three calls a day, and hoping someone rolls through a Stop sign so I have something to do. This kind of shit is the only thing that keeps me going. The second half of my training time had seesawed between total boredom and having front-row seats on *Jerry Springer*.

In sharp contrast to my time with Jayce and Serious in the Southeast District, where we dealt with armed robberies, domestic violence, and drug dealers, I am now in the Northwest District, where we get calls about how the neighbors are too loud after the streetlights come on or about how someone's bushes are growing over their property line. You know—real cop shit. Halfway through training, they move you to another district with another training officer. My new training officer is really cool and a total nerd, so I call him Han Solo.

Officer Quiet and I actually go way back. We went to the Special Forces Qualification Course together. I kind of knew him there, but not really. Truth be told, I hated him for a while because he almost died at the course because he was too tough to quit, and as a result, my favorite instructor got relieved because of it. None of that was Quiet's fault, but when I first met him at the academy, I created this fictional beef between us. Unfortunately, he was actually awesome, so I had to grudgingly admit I was wrong and started liking him.

Quiet was often eerily quiet (by now I hope you're noticing how witty my nicknames are). He didn't say anything that didn't need to be said, and pretty much maintained a stoic expression. The only time he would break his stoic expression was if someone told a great joke, in which case he would muster a slight grin and shake his head. When it was time to talk to people on calls, however, he was masterful. Something about him came off as kind and disarming, and people usually warmed to him fast. But not this Masshole lady in front of us. She wasn't having any of his charm.

Time to find out why.

I saunter up to the front door and knock. A huge white Clay Matthews–looking dude, standing at about 6'7" and 270 pounds, opens the door and stares down at me.

Oh shit.

This man can rip my head off without breaking a sweat if he wants to. Time to steeple the fuck out of some fingers. "Good evening, sir. I am Officer Tansey with the Raleigh Police Department. Can I speak with you for a minute?" I say in the most respectful manner humanly possible.

The man sniffles and nods. His eyes are bloodred, swollen, and glassy. He has fresh pink scratch marks on his neck and cheeks. The scratches aren't still bleeding, but you can tell that someone with fingernails had gotten ahold of him. *I have a pretty good guess who that someone is.*

Quiet must have seen the size of the man and come over, because when I step back to give myself room, if this goes south, he is right behind me. It's comforting to know he is there, but it would be even more comforting if either this man was half the size, or we were twice the size, or both.

"Sir, what happened tonight that made your . . . wife . . . so angry that she is contemplating a divorce?"

"Honestly Afficers this whole thing staated over a faat," he replies in the same thick New England brogue as his smaller half.

"A what?" I ask, genuinely trying to understand.

"A faat!" he sobs. "A goddamn FAAT!"

Quiet and I both stand there confused. This guy looks like a Viking. He has blond hair, blue eyes, and a muscular structure that Schwarzenegger would be proud of. Yet here he stands, weeping before us.

"Sir, what are you saying? What is a 'faat'?" I ask.

"He faatted in my olives!" comes the shrill feminine voice from behind us.

"What?" I ask again.

"He faatted in my faaking olives!" she screams.

"I'm sorry, ma'am, I have no idea what you are saying," I repeat, desperately trying to understand the situation.

She bulldozes past the giant and into the house. I follow after her, more than a little concerned, and desperate for some answers.

Grabbing a jar of olives off the kitchen counter, she yells, "He faatted in my olives! He waalked over to my olives, he opened the lid, he staack

his asshole up to the jaar, and he faaking faatted into my gawddamn olives!" She holds the jar of olives up to her backside to illustrate her point.

Ah, farted.

I glance over at the Viking. "Sir, did you . . . did you *fart* in this young
lady's olives?"

He squints up his face and gives me a sobbing nod.

"What possessed you to . . . fart into a jar of olives at three in the
morning?" I ask, not even really caring what the answer is but so enjoying
the conversation. *This is fucking great.*

"I'll tell you why he faatted in my olives! Because he's a gawddamn
asshole, that's why! He's a sick faaking bastad! Who the faak faats in
someone else's faaking olives! You sick faaker! He needs some faaking
help, that's what the faak he needs! Gawddamn twisted faak!" The young
lady offers to help us understand the situation.

"Okay, okay, let's all calm down," I say, knowing saying that has never
calmed anyone down in the history of the world. I pull a large, 1.5-liter
bottle of Cavit pinot grigio out of the trash bin.

"I think this may be the problem, right here. Did you guys drink this
entire bottle tonight? You know, cheap bottles of white wine after midnight are never a good idea," I offer.

The man responds with a sniffle. "Well, actually, Afficer, she drank
that whole bottle. I drank all that beer." I look farther down into the
trash bin and realize it is absolutely stuffed full of Natty Light beer cans.

"Good grief! She drank that huge bottle of wine and you drank all
that beer . . . tonight?" I ask, horrified and impressed at the same time.

"Faak you, don't faaking judge us, matherfaaker. We didn't staat
drinking until our baby went to sleep, so we weren't drinking all night!"
the young lady once again offers, to help provide Quiet and me with
greater clarity.

"What? There's a baby here?" I ask, now truly horrified.

"Yeah, but she's upstairs, sleeping," she shrieks, as if that somehow
makes it better.

Wondering how the baby is sleeping through this, I take a deep breath.
"Okay, well, what can we do to help resolve the problem tonight?"

"Faak him, I'll tell you what you can do. You can get me a faaking davorce!"

"Sorry, ma'am, we can't issue a divorce. You'll need to call your lawyer to help you out with that. Maybe if y'all separate for the night and sober up a bit, that would solve this issue? Sir, is there anywhere you can go tonight? Maybe a hotel? Just to let things cool down a bit?" I offer.

"No! Faak him, he can stay here! I'm going to my parents' house!" our new favorite New Englander screams while pointing at the giant on the other side of me.

"Well, I don't want to have to wake up the baby and stuff. If he leaves, you can just stay here with the baby, and we won't have to disturb her," I say, figuring this young mother might want to be close to her child.

"Faak that. He can watch the baby. He doesn't do shit around here anyways!" she yells, almost poking him.

"I'll waatch the kid," he says, defeated, and heads back inside the house. She's apparently already called her folks and they apparently live just around the corner.

I'm not sure what I was expecting them to look like, but when her parents finally arrive, I am completely surprised. They roll up in a nice Buick LeSabre. The mother exits the passenger side of the car with her white hair set neatly in rollers. She's still wearing her crossword puzzle pajamas. It'd be hard to top the classic "sweet old lady" motif she's got going on right now. She looks like Happy Gilmore's grandma.

With shame in her eyes that her daughter is involved with the police, she speaks meekly. "I'm so sorry, Officer. What is going on? Is the baby all right?"

"Yes, ma'am. Everything seems to be fine now," I answer, in the most reassuring way I can.

"Then . . . what's going on?"

"Well, you see, um, well, ah, okay . . ." I don't want to say it. She is just too sweet of an old lady. How do you look her in the eyes and tell her she was roused from her sleep at 3 a.m. to deal with . . . olive farts? But the look on her face, eyes begging me for an explanation, steels my resolve.

"Ma'am, it appears your son-in-law may have . . . uh, well, he—I'm just going to say it. He passed gas into your daughter's jar of olives?" (Yes, I said that with a question mark like I was Ron Burgundy from *Anchorman*.)

Her expression transforms from curious fear to utter disgust right before my eyes. Covering her mouth before her gasp escapes it, possibly to prevent her soul from leaving her body, she averts her gaze and aggressively mumbles to her daughter to get in the car.

Angry Girl gets into the back seat of the car yelling, "Maaaam! He faatted in my olives! He faatted in my gawddamn . . ." *Slam!* The closing of the car door muffles her complaints, interrupting her midsentence and allowing her to fade from my present to my past. "I'm so sorry, Officer . . . I . . ." She doesn't know what to say either. "I'm so sorry," she finishes, and then climbs into the front seat. I take one look at the man driving. He shakes his head in disgust as they drive away.

Now alone, Quiet and I just look at each other for a moment in disbelief and then over at our training officers, who have not participated in any part of this fiasco. "Hashtag white girl problems!" laughs Han Solo.

God, I'm starting to love this job!

The rain beats against our windshield, making my eyes heavy. It's been like this for a few days, and the slow pace of things makes my time in the NWD pass by like watching a sloth run a marathon. Props to Han Solo, though—he tried like hell to give me a great experience. He volunteered to take nearly every call that went out, no matter how big or small. He wanted me to have experience and be prepared for when I was finally out on my own. Tonight, though, has been painfully quiet . . . until the radio buzzes.

"Raleigh to any units near Shady Tree Apartments for a security check. Complainant says she hasn't seen her neighbor in over a week, and she thinks her shower has been running the entire time." I look over at Han for permission. He just nods and points us in the direction of the call.

"213 David to Raleigh, we will take that call," he says into the radio.

As we drive, my mind goes full Hardy Boys. I'm thinking it's time to solve the mystery of the missing neighbor and figure out why she's left her shower running. When we arrive, the complainant is standing by the door with the apartment maintenance man.

"Hey, folks, I'm Officer Tansey. Can you tell me what's going on?" I ask.

"Officer, I live across the hall, and I've noticed that my neighbor's windows are foggy with condensation. If you listen carefully, you can hear water running. I'm worried about her," the woman says.

Han and I put our ears up to the door and listen closely. Sure enough, it sounds like a shower is running. Han points to her mail slot. It's full of mail. *Crap.*

We knock repeatedly and shout, "Raleigh Police!" Nothing. No response.

Han looks at me and says, "Well, because of the mail, the sound of the shower, the wet windows, and no answer at the door, we have enough to make entry and make sure there's no medical emergency." The maintenance man gives me the key and I walk over to the door. The second I unlock it and crack it open, we get hit with the foulest stench imaginable. A creepy sensation tingles down my spine. "Ma'am, this is Officer Tansey, Raleigh Police! Are you there?" I already know that no reply will come.

I fully open the door and the stench of decay almost knocks me to my knees. I shield my nose with my arm, choking on the foul air, but there is no hiding from it. The thick fog, created by the shower and blended with the rot, sticks to my skin and saturates my clothes.

We step back from the door, trying to escape the stench, but it follows us. The maintenance man and the complainant have already retreated from the door and are standing out in the rain, oblivious to the pelting droplets hitting them.

"There's going to be a body in there. We have to put eyes on and see what's going on. I'd like you to go in alone so that we don't disrupt the scene too much. Walk slowly and carefully, and take note of everything you see in the apartment. You good to do that?" Han asks. "I am," I respond.

I take a deep breath and enter the foggy living room. There's a couch to my right and a coffee table. The table is covered in used tissues and half-empty bottles of orange juice. There is a soggy newspaper plastered to the carpet, and a couple of medicine bottles strewn across the table. Taking mental notes for my report later, I inch farther into the apartment.

I see the body on the floor in the hallway. It's a woman's body, and she is naked. There's a black and orange substance petrified into the carpet near her face and a cordless phone along with an empty carton of milk lying within arm's reach of her body. *The poor woman died alone. I can't imagine going out that way. No family. No friends. Just staring at a milk carton emptying onto the floor hoping for help that will never come.*

I yell all this information back to Han and he tells me to back out using the same path I took to enter, which I do happily and quickly.

As I breathe in the clean, wet air outside, Han asks, "Does it look like a suicide, a homicide, or a natural death?"

"I don't know, man. All I saw was a dead, naked lady on the floor of the hallway."

He rolls his eyes and calls for detectives over the radio.

They arrive and question me about everything I saw in the house. As I relive every detail for them, they write it all down on their big detective notepads and then enter the apartment, shielding their faces in the crooks of their elbows and letting out a few muffled coughs and gags as they struggle to breathe in the air inside. Several minutes later we hear the shower turn off and the steam began to settle. The detectives emerge from the apartment. "She died from the flu," one says dispassionately.

"Last time she checked the mail was eighteen days ago, and the newspaper is from the first of the month. The medical examiner agrees, so we're gonna call the next of kin and go from there," the other adds.

What a way to go.

The next of kin is in Utah. I get her sister on the phone and she informs us that the woman was getting sick the last time they spoke, about twenty days before. We alert the funeral home, and within the hour, the body snatchers show up. This is my first "code blue" (dead body call) and

I expect the body snatchers to be overweight, creepy balding guys wearing all black. I am shocked when two pretty hot young women in their mid-twenties wearing tidy business suits exit the vehicle. *How are those two girls going to lift that body onto a gurney?*

The two women enter the apartment without even bothering to cover their faces, look at the body, look at us, and say, "Yep, we're gonna need some help with this one."

"A perfect job for the rookie!" Han offers up, smiling.

Damn it.

"Come on, rookie, it will be a cinch!" one of the body snatchers insists, smiling even bigger. I'm somehow more aggravated with her because she's cute.

I'm glad this is fun for everyone else.

Unwilling to let any of these motherfuckers see that I'm bothered by this, I go back into the apartment and look down at the body. The smell is atrocious. This poor woman's body is misshapen and bloated, and to add a little punctuation to my personal hell, it is glistening with slime from the two-week steam bath she has just endured. The deceased had been a pale white woman with very dark hair and a thick build.

"We have to get her rolled over first," the leader of the body snatchers says.

I hastily put on my gloves and give my arms a quick stretch.

"Rookie, you get the torso, I'll get her head, and Liz, you get her legs. On the count of three we'll roll her up and over," one woman says.

This sounds like an easy enough plan. She counts to three and I lift with all my strength. I feel the body shifting and hear what sounds like ripping Velcro as the body peels off the carpet. As we get her rolled over onto her side, gravity takes over and we let go. The body flops over, and I nearly faint. I've seen some shit, but I haven't seen this.

The blood has pooled in the lowest points of the body. Her face and breasts are as black as the keys I'm typing on. My bearing goes right the fuck out the window, and I cough and choke, rushing to the door to gasp for some much-needed fresh air. The snatchers snicker a bit and shout for me to come back.

"You're not done yet, rookie! We still have to get her onto the gurney."

Oh God, I hate this job.

I return to them, trying to reclaim my dignity. My eyes are watering and my nostrils are burning.

"On the count of three you're gonna lift the body by the arms as we lift it by the legs. Once it's off the ground, we'll kind of swing it up onto the gurney, gently. Does that make sense, rook?" she asks.

"Umm. So just to be clear . . . we're swinging her by the arms and legs onto the gurney?" I clarify, wanting to make sure I don't completely fuck this up and add reasons to laugh about me later in the stories I already know they're all going to share.

"Yeah, basically," they chuckle while throwing me two dish towels. I don't know what the towels are for, so I push them to the side, grab the woman's wrists, and wait for the countdown. The snatchers count to three and again I lift with all my strength.

As I lift, I feel something give way, causing me to lose my grip and fall backward onto my butt. I look down to see what happened. The skin from her wrists had peeled back like melted wax and was now all bunched up around the palms of her hands, exposing the wrist bones. I just stare in absolute disbelief.

"That's what the towels were for, dude! So that exact thing wouldn't happen! Wipe the goop off your hands and then wrap her wrists in the towels. They won't peel back as much if you do it that way."

As much? So they're still gonna peel back? What the fuck kind of job is this?

I wrap the towels around her and we try again. The towel trick works, and we put the body onto the gurney. Han and I walk with the body snatchers out to the meat wagon, and they load her up. They shut the doors and one snatcher bellows out the window to Han, "At least your rookie kinda kept it together!" They all laugh, jump in the meat wagon, and speed off.

"What did she mean by that?" I ask Han. Smirking, he replies, "Some guys vomit or faint when lending a hand to the body snatchers. You did all right. The look on your face when her wrists peeled back, though . . . Ha! Classic! That never gets old!"

Never. Gets. Old. If it's all the same to you freaks, I would like it to get very old, and preferably never happen again.

Later that night we pull into a dark cul-de-sac so I can type out the "dead lady report." It's about 3 a.m., and the rain has finally subsided. I can see the clouds have lifted as the moon illuminates our vehicle. I finish the report and look out the window, up to the stars. It's dead silent outside and Han is getting some shut-eye in the seat next to me.

I start to think about the poor dead woman on the floor and how she died all alone. I hate being sick and I can't imagine being sick and alone. I think about how she must have given every last bit of energy she had to walk to that bathroom, strip her clothes off, and turn on the shower; then she must have realized that she was too sick to continue. She made her way to the kitchen, grabbed the phone, but then collapsed and died before dialing 911. Then two weeks later she was stuck to the floor and I was peeling her wrists back, gagging over her stench. I feel so guilty that I couldn't give her more respect in that moment. "I'm sorry," I whisper to her, hoping she can hear me, wherever she is.

"You done with that report?" Han blurts out.

My head snaps toward him, remembering I'm not alone. "Oh yeah, sorry. I'm done. I thought you were napping."

"Ha! No. I was just resting my eyelids. Was that your first dead body?"

"No . . . no. I've seen a few," I answer.

"What was your first?"

"I saw a woman pushing what was left of a dead guy in a wheelbarrow on my first day in Afghanistan. And then I saw a few more after that," I tell him, doing a quick internal recap of my combat experience.

"Afghanistan, huh? Sounds like a pretty fucked-up place."

"It was . . . but I never had to touch any of the bodies over there. Not like the one tonight. That shit was awful," I tell him.

"Yeah, man, well, get used to it. You're going to be an SED guy. You'll deal with a lot more bodies down there. I promise." As he delivers the last line, he turns away from me and looks up at the moon and stars out of his window. I know he's reliving the bodies he's found and the sad moments from his own career.

I suddenly understand why everyone was so callous around the dead body. You can't let yourself feel. It cannot be personal. If there's a dead person in front of you, you have to treat it as a *body* and not a *somebody*; otherwise you will never survive the job.

As the night wears on and Han goes back to resting his eyes, I make a quiet vow that I will try to never think of the story behind a body again. I will just handle it as an inanimate object and bury the memory away in the back of my mind.

———

"It's time to let this little birdy fly!" Han shouts as I exit the vehicle.

It's my last night as a trainee, and with two hours to go on my final shift, we get a call about a house party that is too loud. I have a nice three-day weekend coming, and after that I am going to report to work as a real cop with my own car and no one to make me do stupid rookie shit.

This 4 a.m. call on a Friday interrupts my comfortable fantasizing about not being a recruit anymore and, full disclosure, I am a little aggravated when the call comes in, because I assume it's just a mildly loud stereo or some other bullshit. But when we arrive at the complex, it is apparently more than that. The parking lot looks like every high school party from every eighties movie you've ever seen. Cars are everywhere, and apparently not a single driver can fucking park. Confident in my ability to handle this situation, Han sends me solo.

As I crest the third floor, where the party is clearly happening, I realize that it feels good to stretch my legs after sitting in the car all day. *This will be over in a jiffy. I'll break this party up and call it a shift.* But as I turn the corner, I hear screams. And not "Haha, we're having so much fun!" screams, but screams of pain.

Time to go. I run to the door of the apartment and see that it's been kicked in and is now barely hanging on its hinges. The bloodcurdling screaming is so loud now that it shakes me to my core. The hair on my neck stands up straight. I know someone is in serious trouble. I radio to Han, "Yo, dude, GET UP HERE NOW!" I pull my gun and sprint inside.

I make my way into the apartment. Broken glass and splintered wood are everywhere. *What the fuck?* I urgently push my way through the living room in the direction of the screaming. I yell, "Raleigh Police!" but the screams are so loud and the thuds from whoever is being struck are so violent that no one hears me—or at least no one reacts.

I come to a T intersection in the hallway and make a hard left turn in the direction of the screaming. I know how to clear a room, having learned both from the Army and the academy, but the urgent need to save this person causes tunnel vision to set in, so I simply charge to the sound of the victim. Rookie mistake.

As I round the corner, I see that the bedroom door at the end of the hall has been kicked in and splintered to pieces. The horrific screaming is coming from that room along with other violent thuds and brutal noises of flesh hitting flesh.

As I open my mouth to once again announce myself, I'm struck in the back of the head by something hard. I stumble forward, my vision blurring as glass rains down all over me. Fighting through the fog threatening my vision, I turn around with my head down and arms up, ready to absorb another blow from a blurry human figure in front of me. I need to close the distance before I get struck again.

I lunge forward and wrap my arms around the person's waist with my shoulder buried in their abdomen in perfect rugby-tackle form. Driving with my legs, I lift my assailant off the ground and push forward, sending us both crashing through a glass table. As I get up and my vision returns, I look down and realize that the person I just WWE-smashed through a glass table is a very young and very skinny white girl, wearing panties, a wifebeater, and cowboy boots. My gun is still in my hand, but thank God, it is pointed in a safe direction, even after the crash.

I can still hear the screaming victim and the relentless brutalizing that is happening in the bedroom. *Shit, what the fuck is going on?* I try to quickly get the rest of the way to my feet and out of the shattered glass table frame, but motor function eludes me. Blood is running down the side of my ear and I can feel its warmth tickling my earhole as gravity pulls it away from the wound.

Suddenly a kick fires up between my legs, somehow missing my junk and glancing off my inner thigh. Due to that thankful miss, the kick doesn't hurt, but it lunges me forward awkwardly, forcing me to land back down on top of the now-unconscious female that I had launched through the glass table. Rolling over to my back to defend against whatever is coming next, I look up to see another young, tiny white female standing over me. For one-tenth of a second I consider my next move, when out of fucking nowhere Han sends her careening back into the wall with an epic running Spartan kick. It's the most glorious and unexpected move I have ever seen from him. Up to this moment, my Northwest training officer had not used one lick of force. I didn't think he had it in him, but oh boy, did he come through when it counted!

Reeling from the kick, she flies across the room, not unconscious, but definitely out of action. Seeing this, Han continues in the direction of the bedroom. The screaming is somehow worse than when I first arrived. Finally getting to my feet and getting clear from the table, I hear Han yell, "Fuck! Get off her! Get the fuck off her!"

I round the corner to see a girl being whipped in my direction. Han is throwing women around like rag dolls. It looks like a superhero-movie Han smashing the alien horde with his superstrength, except oddly, all the aliens are wearing wifebeaters, panties, and cowboy boots. I shelve that thought in order to dodge the flying females and run into the center of the room.

I see another girl stomping the victim's face in with cowboy boots. I'm at a full sprint now, and Han's beat-down gives me more fuel to push. I use my momentum to tackle the wild boot stomper. I hit her with so much force that we fly over the bed and onto the floor on the opposite side. I shove my elbow into the back of her head, forcing her face down into the carpet.

Finally taking stock of the room, I see a badly beaten victim lying on the ground in front of the bed. She has skin dangling from her chin and gaps of hair missing from her scalp, where it has literally been pulled out. Wide-eyed, she gasps for air as she struggles to recover from the multiple sets of boots that had been stomping down on her for God knows how long.

Seconds after we finally have some control, cops flood into the room, rounding up the boot-and-panty squad. Apparently my initial "Dude, get up here!" radio traffic caused quite the stir. I guess the urgency in my tone alerted the whole district that I needed help and I needed it now. And you know what? They showed up. Even though I'm in pain and bleeding, I smile a little at that.

Then I look around.

The apartment is now pure chaos. There are girls everywhere and all of them are strangely wearing the white "wifebeater" tank tops, underwear, and cowboy boots. It's clearly a uniform of some sort. Cops are holding some girls around the waist as they are kicking and screaming in full tantrum mode. Other cops are holding girls down by their hair. It is out of control. To their credit, none of these evil bitches are willing to surrender.

We have everyone in cuffs and an ambulance on the way for the victim. Then we start the questioning. Yes, we need to do so as part of doing our job, but maybe more important, we need to know what in the actual fuck had to happen to bring an attack from the Panty Cowboy Boot Gang.

After Han tapes my ear wound shut, he sends me over to speak with the victim to get her statement. This is the first time I really get to look at her, and it is hard. She has skin dangling off her chin from girls ripping at her face with fingernails. Tracks of skin starting from her forehead and going all the way to her chin hang in skin loops off her face. In some places, her lips seem like they will separate from her face. She has to be in massive pain, and that's not even considering where she has been partially scalped in fist-sized missing chunks of hair from her head, or the two black eyes she is now sporting.

It boggles my mind but the whole incident erupted over a drunk Facebook post. The victim got lit and talked shit to a group of lesbian cowgirls online, so the cowgirls showed up in their boots to take her down. *What the fuck!!!!!!!!*

I've seen a lot of violence on a much larger scale in my life, but this over-the-top reaction, abject cruelty, and lack of humanity throw me. I can't help but look at these six skinny white girls as animalistic. I wouldn't do what they did to my worst enemy.

I walk back over as the rest of the cops are about to load the hand-cuffed "ladies" into the cars to take them to jail, when their "gang leader" decides to get tough. "You can't arrest me!" she shouts in the whiniest, venom-filled, rich-girl voice you can imagine. "Ohhhh, you don't even know who I am . . . you are so fucked! My dad owns the biggest peanut butter factory in the US!"

Without hesitation, Han steps into her, inches from her face, and says, "Crunchy or smooth?"

She looked at him quizzically. "What?"

He yells loudly, "CRUNCHY OR SMOOTH?!"

When no answer comes as she looks incredulously at Han, he does, in fact, arrest her.

With that arrest, my shift ends. I am now a full-fledged cop.

And maybe more important, that peanut butter heiress is now in a real jam.

4

THE LONE WOLF RIDES . . . ALONE

Raleigh, I'm behind a stolen vehicle. We're at a red light, about to cross New Bern Avenue onto Pettigrew Street."

Where the fuck is Pettigrew Street?

My first Friday night as a solo real cop started spicy—Friday nights are almost always crazy, especially in the Southeast District—but when the rain started pouring down, it went from busy to boring really fast. I know this sounds weird, but it's tough being a cop when there's nothing to do.

The rush of having my own car had been huge at first. It felt like the first time I had my own place outside my parents' house. "I get to make my own decisions? Woo-hoo! So exciting!" But then it got less exciting. On my own I came to realize my parents had better food and snacks, and paid for everything. Likewise, I realize now that in this job I have to remember everything, do all the paperwork, and watch my own back. In both cases, reality was a little different than I had imagined. And more stressful.

But a bigger stress plagues me right now: I've only been a real cop for a few days, and I really want to make sure everyone knows I am the real deal. The worst thing you can be as a cop, especially one in SED, is the guy or gal who doesn't get in the mix—the one who always has a reason why another cop answers the call first. My reputation is important to me, and I haven't been tested yet. Tonight could have been the night, but the damn rain is ruining it all. Let's face it, even drug dealers don't want to be out in the rain.

But now I have a chance to get on the map with my brothers and sisters in blue! *I just need to find fucking Pettigrew Street.* I crane my neck and squint my eyes at the upcoming intersection. My heart skips a beat. *You're on Pettigrew Street, dipshit! And the sign says the next intersection is New Bern Avenue.*

I grab the radio with the untamed, uninhibited zeal of Tom Cruise jumping on Oprah's couch, and with my voice full of adrenaline, blurt out, "I'm coming to ya! I'm less than a block out!" *Game time. This is my moment.* I can see the red traffic light as well as the headlights of the stolen vehicle. The light turns green and both cars pass through the intersection in my direction.

Suddenly the radio chirps up: "Tansey, when we pass you, just turn around and get behind us. Then I'll light him up." As he calmly gives me instructions, the stolen car passes by me. Like the noob that I am, I stare right into the suspect's eyes. This motherfucker smiles at me and nods at me like a celebrity on Rodeo Drive. He knows I know. I know he knows I know. With us both in the know, he drops a smirk and a salute, and floors it. The chase is on! The patrol car behind him hits his lights and off they go. I just need to hit a quick three-point U-turn and I'm right in the mix!

The excitement has me undershoot the first part of the turn, and my three-point turn ends up being a five-point turn and a scuffed tire on the curb, but *now* it's go time!

The radio lights up just as I hit the accelerator: "Tansey, we just made a left and now we're making another left heading back towards New Bern Avenue."

Oh shit.

The series of turns leads them to do a complete 180-degree directional shift, and now they are heading back the way I just was. I need to make another U-turn! This U-turn goes smoother than the last, and just as I'm finishing it, the radio blazes through the car once again: "Now we're making a left onto Bart Street, back towards Pettigrew Street."

Looking up, I realize that I am doing circles in that very intersection. Right on cue, the headlights of the stolen car crest the hill, barreling down the narrow street right toward me. I steel my resolve as I commit to blocking the road with my vehicle. As the car nears without any loss of speed, I know he isn't stopping. I leap into the passenger seat so I don't take the full impact of the hit with my body, squint my eyes, and turtle my head into my vest as I brace for impact.

But the hit doesn't come.

Opening my eyes fully, I realize that right before the car was to turn my blue chariot into a scrap heap, it swerved violently, cutting through the ditch and across someone's side lawn, back out onto the street. The officer in pursuit continues the chase with some top-notch driving, matching the suspect turn for turn. They make a left turn back onto Pettigrew, completing a full circle around the block.

No!

I'm back where I had started, facing the wrong direction on Pettigrew and not being helpful at all. *I have to make my third goddamn U-turn.* I knock out my fastest one yet, but by the time I complete my hopefully final U-turn maneuver in this godforsaken Bermuda Triangle of intersections, both cars are out of sight. To make matters worse, all this turning around coupled with my lack of street knowledge has left me with no idea which direction they have gone.

The radio is buzzing, of course. "I'm taking a left on Fleegenflaganfloopin Drive, and now a right on Nerfherdershiresmithsonian Street. No, wait! Now we're taking a left of BoogettyBlippettyBloorghetty Avenue." Now, that's not what he is saying, mind you, but that's sure what it sounds like to me. I don't know what to do, but I know I have to do something, so I just put my car into drive and start making turns onto random streets following what I think are the basic directions he is giving me.

Though I have no reason to believe so, I somehow think I'm getting closer. Then the radio buzzes once again. "The suspect has crashed. I'm giving chase on foot!"

I didn't hear a crash. How come I didn't hear a crash? Or sirens?

The radio is absolute mayhem. Tons of cops are arriving on the scene and giving chase. It seems like there are six or seven cars involved now. *Why don't I see any cop cars or hear any sirens?*

The radio breaks the total silence of my night once again: "Get back, everyone! I'm releasing the dog!"

What, they're releasing a dog and I'm missing it!?

Come on!!!!

Finally, after a long pause I hear, "Raleigh, I have one in custody. We got 'em. All other officers can back it down. Raleigh, we're gonna need a rollback tow truck and EMS."

In the time that it took this officer to chase down a suspect both via car chase and foot chase, send a dog after him, cuff him, and put him in the car, I had successfully accomplished four three-point turns. No, that's actually not fair. I accomplished one five-point turn, and three three-point turns.

Fuck me. I pull over to the side of the road and take stock of what just happened. I forgot everything I was supposed to do. I didn't do my combat breathing like I was trained. I didn't stay calm. I didn't focus. I open up the map to see where I am, compared to where the incident ended. After some quick plotting, I realize I'm a mile in the wrong fucking direction. I went "Full Rookie," and if Robert Downey Jr. taught us anything, it's that you never go Full Rookie.

I pull into an abandoned lot behind an old gas station and get out of my car. My heart is still pumping as if I had just sprinted away from a hungry tiger and somehow lived. My hands and legs are shaking, and as the adrenaline wears off and my thinking brain returns, disappointment covers me like a lead blanket.

If I had caught him, would I have been effective? What if there had been a gunfight? Could I even hit anything the way I am right now? What if he had gotten hurt while chasing him? Why did I just lose all composure and literally do everything wrong?! I know better than this! As I'm trying to deal with my failure and recover some composure, a car thunders down the wet road, skipping puddles at Mach 3.

At first I assume it's a police car, heading to the scene I just missed, and desperately want to avoid so I don't have to relay the story of my repeated failures. But it isn't a police car. It's a BMW and it's coming right at me, going way faster than the 35-mph speed limit.

The car covers the distance to me in seconds. As it races by, the driver makes eye contact with me and sees my police car, then instantly pushes the accelerator even harder, whizzing past me in the night air. He's easily going over 60, and maybe even over 70.

Snapping out of my pity party, I think I've just found myself another stolen car. Time for redemption.

I sprint to my car and slide into the driver's seat, hitting the gas before the door is even closed behind me, peeling out of the lot in hot pursuit of this speed demon. *Breathe, Tansey. What street are you on? What direction are you going? What crime is being committed? Can you pull someone over just because they looked like they were speeding? Of course you can. Right? Breathe. Don't fuck this up. Not again.*

After a short burst of speed, I see his taillights in the distance. I don't hit my blue lights, hoping he won't see me and will think he's safely away and will slow down. As I get closer to him, I look down to check my speed in order to pace him. When I look back up a half second later, the driver is halfway through slamming on his brakes and hitting a hairpin hard right turn down a side street. *Damn it, he knows I'm on to him. No U-turns this time. This is me.*

I look up to ensure I catch the street name as I replicate his hard-right turn, but by the time I come out of it, the driver is already making another quick left onto another street. I miss that street name. *Fuck. Stay with him.* I make the next left turn and miss that street sign too. I'm trying like hell not to lose sight of him.

It occurs to me that the gig is up, so I turn on my blue lights and sirens, hoping he will just pull over. He does not. I haven't jumped on the radio yet because my brain is trying to figure out what I'm doing. The only violation I'm sure I've got right now with my garbled brain is speeding and maybe the fact that I think he's trying to run from me, but I couldn't really make that claim if I hadn't turned on my blue lights and sirens to stop him. The second the siren bellows out, the car whips into a driveway and parks. *Oh shit. Maybe he didn't know I was a cop! This might be easier than I thought.*

The driver jumps out of the vehicle aggressively. *Well, forget that. Looks like he is going to run!* I slam my car into park in front of the driveway, blocking his car's exit, and jump out. "Get back in your car right now, sir!" I shout as I grab my radio.

"Raleigh, I need a check-in," I say, depressing the push-to-talk button.

"Get the fuck off my property!" the man yells just as I key the mic.

"Okay, 424, where are you?" comes the response. *Oh shit. Where am I?*

"Raleigh, I'm on a side street off Poole Road behind the mini-mart somewhere" is the best I can muster.

I instantly regret my answer, but I have no choice. This situation is escalating and I may need help. But this is not the kind of radio traffic you want to give out on the city net. Not knowing where you are is a big no-no, plus I'm out with an unknown car with no tag numbers given, no mention of a suspect description, and no stated reason for the stop. So basically, if this guy shoots me there will be literally no useful information available for them to ever find him.

No time to feel sorry for myself again. Back to the present situation.

"Sir! Get back in the car!" I shout again.

"Fuck you! You can't pull me over in my own driveway!" he responds, very sure of his legal position.

I pause, voice wavering at his confidence. "Yes, I can?"

"No the fuck you can't!" he says, even more sure.

"Sir! Get back in the car!" I shout for the third time.

"Fuck you!"

"Sir! This is a traffic stop! Get back in the car!" I say for the fourth embarrassing time.

"This ain't no traffic stop! This is my house ! You at my fucking house, bruh!"

This guy has me going. Despite objectively knowing that that has nothing to do with anything, I'm really starting to doubt myself. *Can I stop him at his house?*

The radio buzzes: "Tansey, I'm coming to ya but I need at least a street name."

"Sir, what street are we on?" I ask the subject, for some reason thinking the guy who told me to go fuck myself is going to suddenly prove an invaluable asset in my time of crisis.

"None of yo business, that's what street we on. None of yo fuckin' business."

Well, that was less helpful than I hoped.

"Um, Raleigh, I'm not sure, I made a right turn and then a left turn off Poole Road just past the mini-mart," I say into the radio, wincing with every word. I know every cop in the city is now undoubtedly laughing at me and the shitstorm I am in, as I proceed to give virtually no useful information over the net.

"Get off my lawn, bitch!" he adds for good measure.

"Get back into your car, sir!" I shout for the fifth time.

"No, you get back into your car, bitch!"

"Sir! Please get back into your car!"

Damn it, Tansey, try to at least sound like you're in charge!

I'm trapped in what we call repetitive repetition. It's when a cop doesn't know what he is doing, so he just repeats himself over and over again, trying to elicit a different response from the suspect. It's not a good place to be in, and I know it.

"Why you fuckin' pull me?" he asks, seemingly genuinely curious.

"You were speeding," I answer, just happy to have a different conversation.

"Nah, you pulled me for being black! You racist-ass white bitch!" he shouts, even angrier. *So much for improvement.*

"Sir, get back into your car." *Maybe the seventh time is the charm?* Just when it doesn't seem like it can get much worse, his girlfriend exits the car. I'm pretty sure like a great white shark in an ocean full of seal blood, she can smell that I'm a wounded little rookie, so she decides to join in for good measure.

"Get off our yard, you bitch-ass cracker. You fuckin' pig!" she snarls at me.

"Ma'am, please get back in the car!" I almost beg.

Just then I hear the wail of sirens followed by the roar of a Crown Vic engine. *Oh thank God. Help is on the way.*

Officer Banks, who looks like Banks from the *Mighty Ducks* movies, jumps out of his car and casually walks up, listening as the two suspects scream profanities at me.

"What do you got, man?" he asks, cooler than the other side of the pillow. *How is he so relaxed?*

"Um, they came speeding by me, and then they went even faster after they saw me pull out on them, like they were trying to run from me," I sheepishly answer.

"So, they were speeding?" he asks, nonplussed.

"Well, they were going really fast. And then when I tried to catch up to them, they just started making turns, trying to lose me, and then they pulled into this driveway and now they're yelling at me." My recap is somehow making what was a very dangerous situation sound silly.

Banks strolls down the driveway, "Ma'am. Sir. Please get back into your car."

"Fuck you! You know you can't touch me on my home base!"

Oh, you fucked with the wrong guy, my dude. I anxiously await whatever Banks is going to do now.

To my surprise, he turns around and walks back toward me. As he gets to my shoulder, he leans in real close and says, "I tried. They didn't listen. Go arrest them for Resist and Delay."

I desperately attempt to stare at him as coolly as he is staring back at me. He is completely unfazed and seems almost bored with my mishap, making me now wonder if I should even have called for help.

"Well, get to it," he says, when I don't immediately begin moving.

I glance at the male suspect. He is on his phone. "911? Yes, there are two cops that are trespassing on my property! I need help."

This pisses me off.

"Sir! Are you on the phone with dispatch?! Sir! Get off the phone, you are under arrest!" I shout.

He peeks over at me but keeps talking. "Ma'am, now they're going to

arrest me for calling you for help. Can you please talk to these officers?"
His voice is calm and humble now. He has a completely different tone
with dispatch. All innocence. It was quite the transformation. This dude
could win an Oscar with this performance.

"Sir, get off the phone! You are under arrest!" I repeat myself again.

"Excuse me, Officer, I am on the phone with 911," he says, respectful
for the first time.

Oh for fuck's sake, what the fuck?! What do I do now?

I look over at Banks, who is staring at me with his arms crossed, not
saying a word. He's still very calm, but now he seems annoyed . . . not
with them. He's seen this shit before. He's annoyed with me.

"Sir! Get off the phone!" I insist loudly.

"Okay, now he's yelling at me again, ma'am. Can you send a black
officer out here, ma'am? Please. I'm frightened," he continues. I would
learn over time that this is a common request, and to be honest, I wish
there were more black officers in our unit. People want to see people
that look like them—it's human nature. However, because the SED is so
dangerous, it is the only area in the city that is volunteer-only, and not a
lot of black officers prefer to work here, for a host of reasons.

"Banks, what do I do?" I ask.

"What do you wanna do?" he retorts.

"I want to take him to jail for RDO," I say, confident.

"Well then, there's your answer. Take him to jail for RDO."

I stare at him blankly again. *I mean, can't you just help me a little bit?*
But that is not the Southeast District way. I am not a trainee anymore.
I'm now a full-fledged officer and am expected to act like one. I failed all
night. I can't do it again.

Enough is enough. I have let this get out of control and pretty soon
there will be more cops here watching the new rookie make an ass out
of himself. I march up to the suspect. "Sir, this is the last time I'm going
to ask. Put your phone down and turn and face the car." After I'm sure
he's heard me, I reach out and grab his arm and place him under arrest.

Immediately he reels back, trying to create distance from me. I grab a
handful of his shirt and pull him toward me. He pulls back harder, rip-

ping his shirt in the process. He screams into the phone like he's dying, "Help! He's gone crazy! Send me a black cop! Please! Hurry!"

Slapping the phone out of his hand, I move forward to make the arrest, but as I do, he lurches back, tearing the bottom half of his shirt off. When the shirt clears his body, he makes the decision I was hoping he wouldn't make: he takes off into the night. In a weird way, I need him to run. Finally, there is something I know how to do. Bad guy runs. Cop chases him. *Let's go!*

I take off after him. There's still a light drizzle and the chilly air is making me taste a little bit of blood as I hunt for air in my full sprint. I can barely see the dark figure out in front of me, but floodlights randomly spotlight him, refocusing me as we run through neighboring backyards, shooting across properties and jumping fences along the way. Jumping chain-link fences on the run is not as easy as it looks in the movies. They have sharp points at the top and they're usually unstable, but we are leaping them like deer in the wild.

Adrenaline is pumping, but this time I'm not letting it take over. *Breathe. Watch his hands. Pace yourself. You train for this. He doesn't. He will give out soon.*

As we round the side of a house, he cuts through a hedge and runs up some stairs onto a front porch, slamming himself into the front door. He yanks on it, desperately trying to open it, but I am not going to let that happen. Bad things happen in houses at night.

I slam into him with all my weight, pick him up around the waist like a high school wrestler, and dump him onto the floor of the porch. *Hell yeah, Tansey! You got this!* He throws his legs up and locks me into the "guard position" from jiujitsu. *Shit, this dude has had training. Let's hope the couple of stripes on my white belt are better than whatever he has!* I push up to my knees and jam both my elbows into the inner meat of his knees and thighs. He releases, separating his legs from around my waist. This frees up my gun belt. I take advantage of the moment and unholster my pepper spray. *You're mine now, dude!*

I draw my can and spray a short burst, just like I've been trained. Unfortunately for me, the can is facing in the wrong direction, and I spray myself directly in my own face. *Fuck me!* Through burning, squinty eyes, I re-aim the canister, emptying the whole thing and painting the side of the suspect's face and head a bright orange hue.

Now, I imagine most of you law-abiding, model citizens reading this have probably never been on the receiving end of a blast of professional-grade capsicum. Just know this: it's a potent, four-inch-tall vial of pure agony. Imagine being hungover and your eyes are as dry as the Sahara Desert. Now imagine a bunch of angry ground wasps caught in a pillowcase. Take the pillowcase and put it over your head. *That* is what pepper spray feels like. The whole experience will humble any man quickly.

Sitting on the wet porch, still choking on my own pepper spray, with eyes that had already sealed shut and refused to open, I am feeling pretty humble. I'm trying to blink like we are trained, but that's easier said than done. The homeowner, reacting to the commotion, arrives at his own door (not that I can see them) and starts to scream, but immediately begins coughing because pepper spray is everywhere and slams the door shut.

The suspect begins to panic due to the effects of the spray. Rolling onto his belly, he attempts to crawl out from under me. Driven by need, he somehow rises to his feet. I wrap my arms around his waist and attempt to slam him back down onto the porch, but he doesn't easily give in and as I drag him down, he drags me forward. We both miss the floor and go tumbling down the wet stairs into the grass, coughing, grunting, and blinking the whole time.

Between blinks, I see the suspect trying to get back to his feet, so I spear-tackle him into the muddy yard. Once on the ground, I immediately gain a side-mount position (they don't just give these stripes away) with both of my elbows dug into his hip and armpit. Now I am completely in control. I have a dominant position and he's panicking from the pepper spray effects. "Stop fighting!" I tell him, but he refuses to comply. Still coughing and gagging, I give him a series of knee spears to the side of his leg and ribs.

"Stop, you're breaking my leg! Ahhhh! Stop, I'm done! Please! Please!" That's all I need to hear. I ask him to flip over, which he does, and I put him into cuffs, blinking the entire time. The burn is really setting in and the mud all over my face isn't helping. It has seemingly created a seal whereby the capsicum oils that coat my face can't dissipate into the night air, and instead decide to go inward into my pores.

As I struggle to my feet, I catch motion out of the corner of my eye. I spin to meet the threat. All I see is neon. I blink some more. In front of me stands a cop. I keep blinking. It's Banks. He was so worried about me that he took the time to take a neon rain jacket out of his car and saunter over in my general direction.

"Good job, rookie. I knew you could do it," he says casually.

This motherfucker really went back to his car to get his jacket while I was fighting this guy?

Just like in every cop movie, just as all the action ended, a blue wave of officers comes barreling onto the scene. A sergeant, who had just arrived, approaches me. "You okay?" he asks. "Yes" is all I could muster.

"You sprayed him, that means he's yours. Drive him to the fire department and hose him down before you take him in."

Drive him? I can't fucking drive, I can barely breathe! That's what I say internally, anyway. Externally I say, "Roger, Sergeant. Will do." As I do, an officer walks over with a bottle of water. "Bend over, man." I do, and he pours water over my face to take the edge off the burn. It gives me little respite. I can hear the suspect moaning near me on the ground.

We immediately go to the fire station, him wailing in my car's back seat, and me squinting and blinking. A cop car drives in front of me, guiding the way. My suspect and I get hosed off by the boys in red. Soaked, we get back in my car. It's a weird thing being in a car with someone who just tried to kick your ass and has been insulting you all night.

"Damn, man. How'd you catch me? I was a semipro baseball player, and no one can catch me," he says to me like we're old drinking buddies.

"I train really hard for this job, man," I muster back.

"Well, you're lucky," he replies.

"How's that?"

"If you hadn't sprayed me, I would have fucked you up, man."

"Maybe, man," I answer, smiling through my bloodshot eyes.

"Ain't no maybe about it," he answers, matter-of-factly.

At the jail, I process my new friend, and lo and behold, his blood alcohol level is way over the legal limit, adding DWI and Resisting an Officer to his litany of charges.

I head back to the station to shower and put on a uniform bereft of orange pepper spray, but as I walk in I am greeted by Banks and the Sergeant.

Like an intervention for a drunk, they sit me down and run through the night with me.

"You didn't know where you were and couldn't report it, leaving you in danger."

"You engaged in repeated repetitive repetition, making the situation worse."

"You sprayed yourself in the fucking face with pepper spray, bro. You know you're supposed to point that shit at the bad guy, right?"

After those two had taken what was left of my dignity, I shower, put my spare uniform on, and get back in my car. My shift isn't over.

I put the car in drive and head back out into the lonely night. For a brief moment after I finally subdued that guy, I had thought that I had done good work. That talk took all that away from me. But they added something else too.

At the beginning of the night, I was still looking for other cops to help me. But now I realize that no one is coming. This is a big-boy world and cops ride alone.

I can only depend on myself. Others may help but it is dangerous to depend on that help. I need to make smarter decisions going forward.

I need this lesson more than I know.

5

CALM THE FUCK DOWN

I n jiujitsu, white belts are notorious for being absolute spazzes. Even
though they are less skilled, they have a tendency to hurt their partners way more than upper belts do, because they overreact to any threat.
Where a black belt, brown belt, purple belt, or even a blue belt will
calmly address a problem, even if they are losing, white belts will pour
every iota of strength, athleticism, and breath into every movement,
leading to black eyes, hyperextended joints, twisted knees, and all kinds
of other injuries. Their unexpected movements and spasms leave a trail
of tears and injuries in their wake.

Until they calm the fuck down, white belts are essentially worthless.
Unfortunately, they don't know that they're worthless. And that's what
makes them dangerous. All their focus is on getting their blue belts so
they aren't at the bottom of the barrel. What they don't understand now,
but will much later, is that earning a blue belt actually has less to do with
knowing moves and improving skills, and more with finding tranquility
and control in moments of stress. Blue belts may not know a ton, and
they might not be able to do anything against a black belt, but they stay
calm when everything is going wrong. This leads to making better decisions and improves the probability of survival.

When it comes to being a cop, I am still a white belt looking for my blue belt. I sincerely and naively believe that if I keep throwing myself into the big cases, I will magically elevate myself and become one of the guys that I look up to. I really want it bad, and I don't understand why it isn't being given to me.

The supervisors are tired of the paperwork I generate, and I'm getting the vibe that the only fans I have left are Serious and Jayce. If not for them, I probably would be given the boot. They both openly seem entertained by my efforts, and the word on the street is that they have stopped the Sergeant from kicking me off the squad more than a few times.

My adolescent need to win everyone over is spilling into all elements of my job. In the last month, I've started ignoring any call that doesn't seem like it's going to have serious challenges or drama or involve serving felony warrants. It's not that I won't answer them . . . I'll just wait for the second or third call in the hopes that someone else grabs it first, which they normally do. Please don't get the impression that I don't care about small things. I absolutely do . . . but I am chasing Spoon and Ralph. I want them to let me into the fold and to see me as one of them. I want it so badly that I'm starting to miss the whole concept of "serve and protect."

While I think I'm craftily hiding my plans, they are obvious to the Sergeant. Despite Serious and Jayce's protests, he wants me gone. Luckily for me, he just got reassigned to a different part of the city and the squad has a new sergeant as of yesterday! The new sergeant, Tom, is coming over after being a detective for fifteen years. He doesn't want to be back on the line at all and has a reputation for being extremely ornery. His speech last night, when introduced to the squad, was hardly movie-worthy: "Stay safe, and don't do anything stupid." The only thing that made it a special moment was the look on the lieutenant's face after that brief but punchy dialogue.

Today's Sunday day shift is Sergeant Tom's first official shift, which is cool because even criminals generally take a breather on Sunday. Sunday mornings are for relaxing after the rough nights of Friday and Saturday, and it is our tradition to always take a squad breakfast (that the department frowns upon) to kick off our shift. Deciding that I will only have one chance at a first impression with Tom, I skip the breakfast. Instead I've found a juicy felony warrant to serve. The suspect has warrants for felony possession of firearms by a convicted felon and felony flee to elude law enforcement (speeding off and blasting through red lights).

My plan is not to serve this warrant myself, but rather to spend the morning doing research and tracking down our suspect. Once I have his whereabouts, I'll call Jayce and Serious to help me serve it. I start by looking up the suspect's Facebook page. Bingo! I see several recent pictures of him around Raleigh, so I know he's in the city. Step one complete.

He has an address in the southeast, but there are several notes in the system that indicate the southeast address is his mother's house. Officers have visited her twice in the last few days, and she claims she hasn't seen him in weeks. Since it's Sunday, I decide to just drive by his mother's house to see if maybe I'll get lucky and catch him picking her up for church or something. Even warrant jumpers love their mamas. Again, my goal isn't to actually serve this warrant, but to show the other guys currently eating breakfast that I can build a complete intelligence package so that we, as a team, can take this guy down.

I pull up to the mom's residence and I do not see the suspect's car out front. No surprise there. I didn't really think he would be here, but since I am here, I might as well go talk with her. I knock on the door. To my surprise, a young lady in her late twenties or early thirties answers the door.

"Hello, I'm Officer Tansey. Are you Rashid's mom, by chance?" I ask, smiling. I know she's way too young to be Rashid's mom, but I figure this will be a funny little icebreaker.

"Yes. I'm his mother, what's going on?" she answers.

Uh-oh.

Her lie triggers my heart to accelerate a little and I feel the adrenaline start to flow down my arms and legs, making my fingers tingle. I'm not a mathematician, but I know this young woman is not Rashid's mom, and that moreover, even if somehow she was his mom, she'd have known about the two previous visits to her home. I am now in a pickle.

My plan was to narrow the search and bring the team. Now I'm pretty damn sure that he is here. If I leave, he will leave, so I can't really do that. I also can't just go into the house. Warrantless cops are kind of like vampires when it comes to home searches. You have to be invited in.

Well, there is no way she's going to invite me in. So I'll just ask her if I can come in, then when she says, "No," I'll report back to the team that I think he's here. Yeah, that's what I will do!

"Well, Mrs. Rashid, your son has a simple warrant he needs to take care of," I say to her in a kind voice, as if this warrant is no big deal.

"A warrant? For what? What my baby boy do?" she asks, with a perfect replica of genuine concern. Her acting is on point.

"Um, he has an order for arrest for some silly traffic violation," I reply.

"Oh, I told him to take care of that ticket. But no, he ain't here. I haven't seen him," she says matter-of-factly.

Well, crap. Now I know she is completely full of shit and I am pretty damn sure he is in the house, but there is a huge lump in my throat. The two big rules of serving warrants is to never serve a warrant alone, and to never serve a warrant without letting dispatch know that you're doing it. Well, here I am in a strange doorway, having told no one where I am or what I am doing, very sure a violent felon is inside, when I hear myself say, "Do you mind if I just come inside to make sure he's not in here, and then I can do a change-of-address form so you don't have any more cops stopping by to check for him?"

That was dumb, Tansey. No worries, though. She's not going to let you in. You'll get back to the car and call for backup.

"Yes, come on in and look around, but he isn't here."

Well, fuck.

I nearly choke on my tongue. I really don't want to go inside this house alone. I stare at her for a moment, and then stammer, forcing a smile on my face, "Okey dokey, I'll just be in and out." I walk in casually, without my gun drawn, to look for a violent felon. What could possibly go wrong? The second this is over, I am going to slap my own face and give myself a hard wedgie.

I walk slowly through the kitchen and living room until I come to a long, dark hallway with two or three closed doors on each side. The woman who let me in follows close behind, completely silent, which makes the situation somehow more tense. There are four doors in the hallway. I give the first door a quick knock and open it. In front of me is a skinny, black male with long dreads trying to get a window open. It's Rashid. Seeing me, he quickly gives up on the window, grabs his Xbox, and smashes the window with it. It cracks, but does not break.

I run into the room and grab his arm, catching a handful of his dreadlocks as I try to pull him away from the window. "You are under arrest! Stop resisting! Put your hands behind your back!" I shout. Rashid is not having it. He might be skinny, but he is shockingly strong for his size and commences to vigorously fight back. Using his dreads as a handle, I sling him into the wall. Bouncing off the wall, he uses his own momentum to dive onto the bottom bunk of a bunk bed in the room and try to crawl out the other side. I have the sudden sensation that I'm playing chase with my three-year-old at bedtime.

I scoot around to the other side of the bed to intercept him, but the female is now slapping me in the back of the head with open palms like I am a bongo drum. I turn around and hit her with pepper spray, then shove her back into the hallway. Whipping back around, I see that Rashid is again trying to get through the window. I grab him again, once again gaining a fistful of dreads, which causes him to scream out just as I send a burst of pepper spray his way, accidentally filling his mouth with the substance. Now the room is full of spray and again my eyes are watering and squinting as I hear Rashid coughing and gagging as he collapses to the floor.

I key up the radio and shout, "Raleigh, I need some units to the Wayfield Apartments, Apartment F!"

"422 David, what is the nature of this call?"

I'm now on the floor trying to cuff Rashid while basically blind and choking on spray. Rashid is trying to crawl up under the bunk beds. I'm not sure what he thought that was going to accomplish, but in this moment he is doing it passionately. I follow the sounds of his coughing as I try to find his arms to cuff him. Grabbing the radio, I shout to the entire city, "Stop resisting!"

Letting go of the radio, I stand up, still trying to blink my way through the effects of pepper spray. Rashid is stuck halfway under the bed. I grab his ankles and rip him back out, jumping down on his back the second his body is clear, and push his face into the carpet with my elbow, wrenching his arm behind his back. He shrieks and finally submits. I cuff both of his arms as all three of us continue to cough and gag. I try to stand Rashid up so we can escape the lingering spray, but he insists on staying down on the floor, which drives me nuts. The spray is burning all of us. I resort to pleading.

"If you stand up we can get out of here and away from the spray!" I say.

This registers with him, and he finally stands up and we exit. As we hit the hallway, I stop and cuff the lady who hit me from behind and is now in the fetal position clawing at her burning eyes in the hallway. Just as I get both of them to the front door, Ralph comes smashing in.

"What the fuck, Tansey! What are you doing!"

"I just got Rashid, the guy with the drugs and firearm-by-convicted-felon warrants!" I say excitedly through squinty pepper spray–filled eyes.

"You are a fucking idiot. What is wrong with you? This is it, rookie. We're all tired of this shit!" he says as he pauses, looking at the whole situation, then back at me. "We're fucking tired of it. You are not a one-man army. We do this stuff as a team or not at all!"

I don't know what to say. This isn't the situation I wanted. Ralph and I just stand there staring at each other, my inflamed eyes looking at his seething ones, until Serious and Jayce come running in. Serious doesn't say a word. He just grabs Rashid and the female from me and walks them out of the house.

Jayce, on the other hand, looks at me, at Ralph, and then back at me with a smirk on his face. He starts laughing, and then just shouts, "LE-ROOOOY JENKINS!" after the viral *World of Warcraft* video where the guy hauls off and starts a fight on a well-planned mission early, ruining all the planning for the group, from I don't know how many years ago.

Ralph laughs too, and if Serious was capable of laughter, he'd probably be laughing outside.

And just like that, I have the nickname that will stick with me for the rest of my career.

———

The weeks since I was dubbed "Jenkins" have been rough for me. I had tried to impress Tom on his first day, but instead I became the crazy rookie who just does whatever the fuck he wants without worrying about the repercussions. I didn't want that to be my reputation, and I knew I was one fuckup from getting kicked out of the squad, or maybe off the force entirely, so I tried like hell to keep my nose clean.

No more Rambo shit. No more first on the scene. I had decided I would be the "gray man." In the military, when you went to a school, whether it was Airborne School, Ranger School, Special Forces Selection, or whatever, there were the spotlighters, who always tried to showboat for the instructors, and the fuckups, who always got negative attention from the instructors. You didn't want to be either of them. Spotlighters were hated by their cohort, and the instructors didn't really love them that much either. Fuckups . . . well, no one wants to be a fuckup. The goal was always to be the infamous Gray Man. Good enough that you aren't a fuckup. Subtle enough in your successes that you aren't memorable to the instructors. That's who I was going to be, and I committed to it.

I stopped being proactive and became reactive. I just sat around until a crime was committed and then showed up to take the report after the fact. I wrote a few tickets here and there, mostly in the mornings to make it look like I cared, but I hated writing tickets and it just made me hate my job even more. Eleven months of life in the SED had defeated me. I didn't even know what I wanted anymore. Day shifts came and passed. At least I wasn't getting into trouble.

But tonight, I'm on night shift. I now dread the night shifts. It's easy to lie low during the day, but you really can't hide at night. There's too much going on.

Not that I didn't try. After roll call, I slink off to my police car and log into the one million computer systems in it. I drive to my secret hiding spot, behind an old gas station, and start watching Gary V wine videos. I'm pathetic, really. I'm hiding from the world and dreading whatever the future has in store for me, because I'm pretty sure that whatever it is, I'm going to fuck it up. As I ponder my recent failures, and my future as a failure, my phone rings.

It's Serious.

"Hey, man," I answer. "What's going on?"

"I thought you might like to come to dinner," he answers.

"Of course," I answer, because what else am I going to say to Serious?

"The hibachi place. See you there in thirty."

Serious has never invited me to dinner. Is this gonna be some sort of intervention about my laziness? Are Spoon and Ralph gonna be there to make fun of me? I steel myself for whatever is about to happen and drive over to get some hibachi. When I arrive, I notice a K9 Chevy Tahoe parked outside next to Serious's car. *Oh great, a K9 is here. There's definitely a roast coming.*

When I walk in, I see that the K9 officer is Bruno, the ex–Marine Corps dog handler. He's wearing his navy-blue military-style BDU handler's uniform with his long blond hair curling just under the edges of his baseball cap. Not unlike Ralph, he's built like a defensive end at 6'3" and 250 pounds, and boy, is he ever a character. He's a stereotypical Boston Irish Catholic hooligan if one ever existed. Everywhere he goes, he is the party. He can walk into any bar or any conference room, and the first thing out of his mouth can be "What's up, you motherfuckerrrrs!" and everyone else would be like "Heyyyyyy!" and it would all work out. If anyone else did the same thing, people would be wondering who the asshole was. Dude's an absolute legend, of an entirely different variety than Serious.

This is gonna suck.

Menu in hand, Serious looks up. "Hey, Leroy! What's up, man?"

"What's up, man?" adds Officer Bruno.

Sheepishly, I reply, "I'm good, man. Thanks for asking?" I sit down, observing both of them. I'm waiting for the barrage of insults. I can't think of any other reason why they would invite me here.

"How are you doing, man?" Serious asks.

"I'm okay," I answer.

"How's the family?" Serious asks.

"They're good. No complaints," I answer, eyes flickering between the two of them, trying to figure out the angle.

"Well . . . we haven't heard you on the radio much lately," Bruno adds.

"I'm . . . uhhh . . . just trying to keep my head down, man," I answer, a little shaken from the last comment.

"Why? That's not you at all," Serious asks in a tone I have never seen from him. Something about the way he asks the question makes me drop my guard and lay it all out there.

"Look, man, I am just trying to be a part of the team. Every day I show up to earn my place and to fit in with you guys. And I know . . . I know from day one my inclusion has been forced and I get that. I know I'm not your first pick, or maybe even your pick at all. I never wanted to come to this squad just to be a constant liability, you know? But it seems that's what happened. I have given my all and I've tried like hell to live up to your standards. But I have come to realize that no matter how hard I try, the truth is that my best just isn't that good. I'm sorry."

My verbal diarrhea complete, I finally look up, making eye contact with both of them.

"What do you mean it ain't that good? You're good; you are just untamed and wild and people are worried that you're gonna get hurt. Look, Bruno and I have been talking and we think it might help if we team up and just roll with you for a few weeks and see what kinda shit we can stir up. But let's be a little more safety-conscious, okay?" Serious says.

"Yeah. Leroy, you got that golden-horseshoe black cloud following you! Either you are really good at finding the shit or the shit is really good about finding you!" Bruno laughs. "Either way I want to get into some shit!"

I can't believe what I'm hearing!

Then I realize what they are really doing and I don't want to be their charity case.

"I mean, yeah, that sounds rad but you really don't have to . . . I can figure it out," I say sheepishly.

"Look, you are at the gym every shift. I see you doing dry-fire drills, even when you're smoked. I see you studying and staying current on laws. And I know you actually give a fuck about this community. That's all good stuff, man," Serious says. The earnestness in his voice makes me think this isn't charity. He really does see something in me. He continues: "You are serious about this and we can tell. You just need a little massaging. You keep trying to hammer a square block into a triangle-shaped hole. You need to relax and let us help you."

I look at both of them and suddenly realize how badly I need this moment.

"Okay," I answer.

"Okay!" Serious responds.

"Eat up, Leroy. After chow, we are gonna go fuck some shit up!"

With that we put our heads down and eat. I didn't understand at the time, but Serious and Bruno had just adopted me. For the first time on the police force since I stopped being a trainee, I no longer felt alone.

6

HE WHO ENDURES . . . WINS

You know how in the television cartoon series *Voltron* there are five lions that form into one mega-robot? Every time the lions form into Voltron, they kick absolute ass, which always makes me wonder why they don't just stay as Voltron all the time. Without fail, at the beginning of every episode they are always separated into the individual lions and they always end up getting their asses kicked. Then they're like, "Hey, I have an idea! Maybe we should form Voltron!" And when they do, they win.

Hanging out with Serious and Bruno is like rolling around as Voltron 24/7. Only a few weeks in, I see now that I spent my rookie year as the green lion: small like the red lion, but not as fast or as cool . . . Actually, though, the green lion does get to hold the sword, and that *is* cool, so I'm probably more like the yellow lion. I don't know. Maybe I should have compared us to a wolf pack instead of Voltron to get my point across.

Back to the point I was trying to make: Life is so much better now. We're taking down criminals and my name is regularly getting mentioned in major reports that are going all the way to the top. Moreover, because Bruno is a K9 guy, I get to see him launch his fur missile (his dog) on the regular, which is awesome.

I'm also growing as a cop significantly! I'm learning the streets, learning the players, and learning how to multitask without sounding like a train wreck on the radio.

And it isn't just me. The whole squad is on fire, and each little group of partners in the squad is making a name for itself. I finally feel like I'm part of a winning team and it feels good. Every night some part of the squad makes waves in the district, and like clockwork, the rest of the squad is there to back them up. This is what I wanted.

Every night starts the same way: Serious, Ralph, and Spoon create a plan, and unless there is something specific or big going on, that plan looks very similar. We send two or three units to one of the higher-crime areas in our already high-crime district, and they patrol that particular area until they get into some shit. Now, I realize that probably sounds nefarious, like we're trying to make problems happen. Not true! Quite the contrary, I wish it was harder to find those problems, because that would mean there was a whole lot less crime.

Unfortunately, finding trouble is really easy. All we need to do is run plates. Every other car has a bad tag, expired tag, stolen tag, no insurance, or the driver has outstanding warrants. We literally can do fifty to seventy stops a night just by checking cars. Now, as I mentioned earlier, Serious doesn't care about any of the minor infractions and neither does anyone in the squad. But when you stop fifty cars in SED, I promise you will find guns and drugs. We call this technique of policing "lemon law."

If we stop a car for a tag violation or registration issue or any of that ticky-tacky shit, we label that stop a "lemon" and send it on its way with a verbal warning. That shit is between you, God, and the DMV, and God is probably not siding with the DMV. We are only looking for the real bad guys.

As I write this, I know some of you are rolling your eyes and thinking this amounts to some kind of harassment, some sort of "stop and frisk" on wheels. But the communities actually love it. Believe it or not, people don't actually like stray bullets hitting their houses from drive-by shootings, or people dying in their driveway from stab wounds, or any of the other bullshit.

Think about it: If you live in a community with high crime, you're always worried about gangs and violence and drugs being peddled to your kids. And if the police do show up, act professional, and let anyone that isn't a piece of shit off with a warning, you're pretty happy. You realize the police do, in fact, care about you and your community. Once you trust the cops you see every day, you want to see blue lights. In a way, that sort of trust-building is the heart of what people call "community policing."

Our rapport with the communities we patrol is superb. They know who we are and who we're trying to get and it's not the law-abiding citizens grinding it out.

Tonight our plan is a little more specific. There is a maze of side streets and buildings controlled by the Bloods gang. Interestingly, the Bloods in this particular area have adopted a "don't shit where you eat" policy and they only sell drugs to folks outside their area. Because the side streets are small, old, and complex, kind of like downtown Boston, it's easy for multiple cars to enter an area block from multiple side roads, do God-knows-what inside, and exit from a different side street. In other words, it's extremely hard to track people using traditional surveillance methods. So we've decided to use the lemon-law method and run tags on anyone exiting any of the side streets in this particular maze.

Although we know that a ton of illicit activity happens on these blocks, the night has been pretty boring by SED standards. As I pull over a car, I inform Serious of the make and model, tag, and my location. I approach the vehicle and see a young-looking black male with short dreads twisted up into colorful rubber bands. I dig his style. I explain why I stopped him. I then notice the gang beads around his neck.

Understanding gang beads is like understanding wine. Most people have no idea what they're looking at when they look at a bottle of wine. They can only judge the wine by the label, by the broad color, and by the price. Even information on the label means nothing. Only through knowledge, experience, and taste can they appreciate the characteristics of the wine.

The same holds true for gang beads. Individual beads can identify the sect of the gang, their street location, and even the rank of that specific gang member. They are simple, color-coded strands of small beads on a necklace, but their placement, color, and color separation tell a story. For example, 9 red beads followed by 3 black beads may indicate the subsect of 9tre Bloods. If those beads are then followed up by a string of red beads, with no color break, this indicates a low-ranking individual. Different breaks and different colors point to more rank and status. They don't give those stripes away either.

After only a month or so with Serious, I've become a sommelier of the streets. I know right away that this guy is a low-level Blood from this neighborhood. But even if I had no idea what the beads meant, I can tell that by the fact that he is shaking so hard that I know he is up to no good and hasn't been in the game long enough to be cool about it.

"Hello, sir. Officer Tansey from the Raleigh Police Department. The reason I stopped you is because your tags are expired by more than five months. Is there any reason why you haven't updated your tags?" His eyes widen and I can see the veins pulsing in his neck, as his hands clench and unclench on the steering wheel.

"Um, this ain't my car, Officer. It's my sister's car. Can I just let her know that her shit's expired?" he asks, eyes pleading.

"Sure, man. Would you do that for me?" His arms are shaking even more now. "Do you have your license on you?"

"Yes, sir," he answers, attempting to reach into his wallet to pull out his identification, but having massive trouble fighting through his trembling limbs.

As I've mentioned before, when adrenaline goes up, fine-motor skills go down, and a simple task like getting your wallet out becomes more difficult due to the loss of dexterity in your fingers. Getting an ID card out is even more difficult. Just as adrenaline consumed me as a rookie cop, it is consuming this rookie criminal. He finally gets his ID out and holds it toward me with a shaking hand. Officer Serious pulls up behind him in his vehicle.

His demeanor changes. Before, he was hoping he was going to get away. Now he knows the jig is up and he is not getting away. I'm holding his ID, so I now know who he is, but he seems to forget that at this moment. He looks to me, then to the side mirror, where he sees Serious approaching, and then without warning he slams his foot on the gas, peels out, and nearly runs me over.

Game on!

I dramatically slide across the hood of my cruiser (well, I will in the movie version of this book) and jump in the passenger seat, while Serious gets in the driver's seat and floors it. I get on the radio (calmly) and let Raleigh know we are in pursuit. *Here we go! Hell yeah!*

But by the time I finish my excited thought, the young man we are chasing loses control of the car on the next curve and careens into a wrought-iron fence and then an electrical pole . . . and snaps the post in half, leaving debris and live power lines in his wake. As I take in the scene, blown away by how much damage was done in an instant, I notice the pole falling, right on top of his car. *Bam!* It completely crushes the driver's side of the cab. *Holy shit. If he isn't dead from the crash, he sure as shit is now. And if he isn't now, he sure as hell will be when his sister sees what he did to her car.*

But then I see the faintest of movement through the back window, followed by a boot kicking through what is left of it. Most people would have died in that crash. If they didn't die, they'd be in such shock that they would stay put and wait for help, regardless of what was hanging over them from the law.

This guy isn't most people.

He emerges from the crushed car like the Terminator, oblivious to the damage he just created. Hopped up on adrenaline, this young jacked dude takes a half second to make eye contact and then takes off at a sprint. Serious immediately takes off after him on foot, while I take the driver's seat and follow them from the road, radioing to other units to keep everyone informed of the situation. Serious is a fast dude, but it doesn't take long to realize this dude is faster. He's younger and isn't carrying thirty pounds of gear, so that helps, but he's also a physical stud.

The suspect cuts through a fenced-in, open lot and I know I am going to lose him if I don't get into this right now. I speed past them both to the other side of the lot and jump out, hoping my fresh legs can pick up the second half of this chase and run this guy down.

I cut through the opening at a full sprint, just as they reach the mid-point of the lot. I beeline it toward the spot I know he's going to hit in order to jump the fence. Passing Serious, who has been running far longer than I have, my plan is to catch him as he tries to climb the fence. My timing is impeccable. I'm closing on him. My lungs burn, but my adrenaline gives me power. As my hand reaches out, I almost grab him. Here comes the fence. Almost . . . there!

But then it happens. As "Ave Maria" begins to play from some mysterious orchestra in heaven, everything goes into slow motion and the suspect swan-dives over the fence without slowing. His head reaches the apex of the jump and he tucks his legs underneath him, doing a perfect flip in the air, landing on his feet on the other side of the fence and taking off in a full sprint. If this were the Olympics, even the Russian judge would hold up a perfect 10.

I leap into the air behind him in my own swan dive.

Now, I want to be really clear. Under any other circumstances, and in any other moment, and with even one half second of thought, I would not try to replicate his feat of athleticism, but there's nothing more competitive than the chase. About halfway through my aerial leap, I remember that my ancestors were not sprinters and jumpers; they were stodgy white guys prone to premature dad bods.

My head and chest clear the fence, but my gams do not.

My quads bounce off the fence, leaving a nice red mark across them that I will find later, sending me into my own backflip, but mine is completely against my will. Unlike him, who landed in perfect stride, I overrotate and stumble forward, before landing on my knees and then my face. The Russian judge gives me a 1.3.

I can't see him. I can't hear him. But I know Serious is laughing at me. Undeterred, without really losing any time, I pop up to my feet and continue the pursuit. I'm only fifty feet away from him now as he pushes toward another chain-link fence.

He clears it his way. This time I do it the old-fashioned way, throwing my feet to the side. Sure, I lose a second on him, but I don't almost die either.

The yard I land in after clearing the second fence is much bigger and filled with obstacles. There's a chained-up pit bull, barking his ass off, a clothesline full of clothes, and various toys, chairs, and pots covering the full breadth of the yard. At this point I am very much hoping he trips or gasses out before he gets to the tall wooden fence at the end of the yard.

Of course he doesn't.

I know I'm not going to catch him before he gets to the fence, but if I angle myself toward the corner, I might pick up a second on him. You see, one of the things you realize if you've been on enough foot chases is that tall fences are best cleared at the corners. You have two surfaces to kick off, and two surfaces to pull on, and tall fences tend to be unstable, so climbing at an anchor point is a huge help.

So instead of going right at him like my adrenaline is telling me to, I angle away from him and to the corner, using my thinking brain instead of my lizard brain. I get to the corner of the fence just as he's getting to the top of the middle of it. He's already having trouble with how wobbly it is, but me hitting the corner makes it worse for him, whereas I fly right over.

It occurs to me as I watch him that he thinks he's blown past me. He's not even looking back to see where I am. He just assumes I couldn't be enough of an athlete to keep up with him. *Damn, that hurts.*

My ego doesn't have time to feel the pain, though, because the bonus of him thinking I'm a sack of potatoes is that he cuts right toward where I am about to land. He's running full force toward the exit to the fence— you know, the one situated right near the corner of the fence—when I emerge from the freaking sky like Batman.

I'm as surprised to see him there as he is to see me, but I instinctively swing as he runs at me, catching him right under the eye. My adrenaline, coupled with his speed, results in a punch I could never pull off in a normal setting. He drops cold and continues to slide in the direction of the fence door, completely unconscious. I scamper over to where he is and grab his wrist. It's limp. I cuff him and reach for my radio to call for help.

Well, fuckbeans.

I lost my radio somewhere on the magical mystery tour of backyards this guy just took me on. *What do I have?* I reach down and pull out my whistle and blow it as hard as I can, over and over again, signaling for Serious, who hopefully is still in pursuit.

"Ohhh my Lordy! What is going on, Officer?" comes the shocked voice of an elderly woman who is very much surprised to see a police officer with a cuffed unconscious man in her backyard.

"Ma'am! Call 911 and give them this address!" I tell her.

"Oh Lordy! Okay, okay . . . is that man dead? Did you shoot that boy?" she asks, part concerned and part scolding.

"No, ma'am, but he does need medical attention and I don't have a radio. Please call 911!" I ask again.

"You white folk are always shooting our po' children . . . it's just sad!" The judgment is now on full display, and I feel bad about it even though that isn't remotely the situation here.

"Ma'am! I didn't shoot him! Just please call 911 and get us some help!" I beg.

With a bit of attitude, she casually walks back inside and I am left unsure if she is going to call 911 or not, so I just keep blowing my whistle until the blue wave comes barreling through her backyard fence to where I'm sitting.

The suspect begins slowly regaining consciousness as I talk to him and try to coax him back to the light. *Thank God.* Serious, now on the scene, runs straight up to me and pulls me to my feet.

"That's how you chase 'em down, Leroy! Nice job!" he says, patting me on the back.

Ralph and Sarge are next through the fence. "Nice job, Leroy! I even kinda knew where you were this time, so that's a plus."

"Thanks, Ralph," I say, accepting him being a dick, and the compliment, such as it was.

Then comes my sergeant. "You all right, Leroy?" Yup, even Sarge is calling me Leroy now.

"Yeah, Sarge, we hopped that fence and he ran right at me so I blasted him in the face with my fist and knocked him the fuck out!" If that sounds like a weird thing for a person to say, especially when it wasn't what I was feeling at that moment, I'd like to once again introduce you to an adrenaline dump.

Everybody who experiences an adrenaline rush has an adrenaline dump once the rush wears off. Every situation is different, and every dump is different. Sometimes you just get really tired; sometimes the dump comes in the form of vomit or diarrhea. My current adrenaline dump consists of me shaking uncontrollably and spewing verbal diarrhea, which, I have to admit, is superior to if I was actually shitting myself.

Luckily, Sarge has been around the block a few times and realizes where I'm at. "Ralph, bring this suspect over the ambulance," he says, which Ralph immediately does. Once Ralph is walking the guy away, he looks at me and says, "Okay, Leroy. I want you to head back to the station for the day and get a little breather." But before I can say, "Okay," the suspect has an adrenaline dump of his own and starts vomiting ramen noodles all over the place.

In the end, we find out that the suspect, who did not have a valid license and had a small amount of drugs on him, had stolen the vehicle moments before we stopped him, which is why the car didn't show up as stolen when we checked the tags. Now, I know it's not like I just took down a major drug syndicate, but it felt good to win that chase, and it felt especially good to be back in the good graces of the squad.

7

THE SHOE OF DESTINY

W hat a difference a year makes!
Now, I know that's cliched as hell, but this time last year, I was desperately trying to get a very large mentally disturbed lady not to poop on me, and I thought there was no chance I was ever going to succeed at this job. Now things are finally starting to work out for me at SED.

I'm being more assertive, both with suspects and my colleagues.

I'm also more proactive.

I am finally able to anticipate potential problems before they become real problems, and of course, I'm doing this solo instead of needing a babysitter like I did during the training days.

Daily successes have given me more confidence, and with that gift there is less drama and I'm getting more respect from my colleagues. Whether in the military, in police stations, and, hell, even on sports teams, if the people around you sense even one iota of weakness, they exploit it. If they know something bothers you, they pick at it. If they can shame you, make you blush, cry, or get angry, they're going to do it. That's just the culture of high-performing units. I'm sure there is some talking head who will explain to you why that's bad, but I've never seen a winning group that didn't absolutely beat the shit out of each other emotionally.

But it can't just be bravado. You can't fake it in the police world. Confidence comes from knowledge and experience, whether we're talking about physical strength and conditioning, knowledge of the law, or the emotional intelligence to read a situation and prevent it from getting out of control.

So on this fine, sunny day, I walk into the station at about 4 p.m. to get a good workout in before my shift starts. Serious and Bruno are already there. Bruno immediately starts lifting heavy things a few times like he's a football coach from the eighties. Serious and I start doing CrossFitty things.

Bruno looks at us in disgust as we do some handstand push-ups, burpees, and air squats. "I don't even know why you come in here every day, Tansey. I mean, there's a whole world of actual weights here, and you choose to do ballet with yourself." He chuckles. "Why not just pull out a yoga mat and commit to it?"

"Wow, you moved that weight two whole times, Bruno! If you ever have to push a rhino or your mom off your chest, that will come in real handy!" I say in response.

Even though Serious is doing the exact same thing I am, Bruno says nothing to him . . . because he's, well, Serious. As he is about to smash me with some verbal judo over my insult to his mom, Sergeant Tom walks in.

"Leroy, I need you in my office for a second. It won't take long."

Oh shit, what did I do? I walk into his office breathing hard and dripping sweat all over the floor.

"Here, take these keys and sign here. After you get done goofing off in the weight room, go inspect your new car and make sure there are no dents or scratches."

"Wow, a new car? Thanks, Sarge."

"Don't thank me just yet. It's an LPR car," he says solemnly.

"What's an LPR car?" I ask, knowing I should probably know the answer.

From his expression, I should, in fact, know the answer. "License Plate Reader car."

"Sounds cool. How does it work?"

"I don't know. Do I look like I'm an IT nerd? Call someone and ask them. Get out of my office, you're dripping sweat all over my floor."

I walk back into the gym, strutting just a little. "I just got a new car, guys," I say.

"Hell yeah, man!" Bruno says, genuinely excited for me.

"It's an LPR car," I say with confidence as if I knew what that was five minutes ago.

"Lerrrrooooy Jenkinnns!" comes the simultaneous retort from Serious and Bruno.

Why are they so excited about this?

"You guys seem more fired up about my car than I am?" I say and half ask.

"Leroy, it's a License Plate Reader! It scans plates as you pass by and alerts you if a car is stolen or the owner has warrants. It's awesome, and now that we have one on the squad we can really fuck shit up," Serious chirps, as excited as I have ever seen him.

"I am *so* surprised they gave that shit to you, Leroy," Bruno snickers, taking away 7 percent of my joy.

Nevertheless, the question is a valid one. "Yeah, I wonder why they gave it to me?"

"Sarge must want to see you stir the pot some more," Serious muses, while doing pull-ups nonstop the way most people breathe. "You have really been doing a great job lately."

For one second, I am rattled by the kindness of Serious's remark, before Bruno brings me back down.

"Well, fuckers! Let's give 'em something to talk about! Leeerrrooooy Jennnnkinnnns!" Bruno yells as he lies down under an overloaded bench press. "Come over here and spot me, bitch."

We finish the workout and head to the locker room; by the time I have my towel around my waist to take a shower, I have been asked 127 times about my new fancy car. You think middle school rumor mills are bad? You think the ladies in your suburban HOA like to spread the hot goss? Let me tell you about cops. If there is something new and spicy, everyone knows about it inside of five minutes. Today my new LPR car is the talk of the department.

I think Sergeant Tom senses I am getting overwhelmed by it all and starts answering questions like I'm Taylor Swift and he's my bodyguard/publicist. "Yes, we have a new addition to the squad. Yes, we got an LPR car, and yes, Leroy has the keys, so listen out for him on the radio. Anyone have anything else? Good, go to work." Sarge is a man of very few words. That's why the squad loves him, and also why he is probably not the favorite of other sergeants and lieutenants.

I walk out to the lot and see my new ride sitting out front. She's gorgeous. And by gorgeous, I mean she's a standard blue and white Crown Victoria, but new and shiny. Probably more important, though, she has red lights protruding out of the four corners of her roof and a string of antennas popping out everywhere. *That stuff looks important.*

With no time to waste, I load all my gear into my new ride and turn on the computer. On the screen pops up directions on how to log in and get the system running, and then a phone number to call for further instructions. Not wanting to fuck this up, I call the number.

The IT guy introduces himself and briefly explains what the car is for, how it works, and then goes on a thought-provoking diatribe about how because this is fairly new technology, no one is yet sure how the courts are going to see the use of this information. "The real questions they're gonna ask are about the Fourth Amendment. Is there an invasion of privacy? Can you rely on a computer to make the decision about who to pull over?" he muses. They are good questions and all, but right now I just want to operate this thing without embarrassing myself, so I try to get the guy to talk about that, and not how the Supreme Court will see things in five years.

"Cool, man. That's super interesting. So how do I turn it on and get it to look up license plates?"

After going back and forth for a while, I see that the system is kind of simple—not how the tech works or anything, just how it affects me. The little red lights are actually cameras and lasers. They scan license plates and take pictures of them, as well as the car on which they are affixed. The pictures of the tags are then stored in a database for thirty days unless they are tagged. If they're important and you want to keep them long term, you need to tag the photos and save them, in which case they stick around for ninety days.

Left to its own devices, the LPR will only audibly alert you if a car is stolen or the owner has open warrants, but that is as far as it goes. For the most part, it just documents plates and cars at specific time periods when asked to do so. It also isn't being used for ticky-tacky shit. It doesn't tell you if a car has expired registration or insurance violations or anything like that. It is only looking for stolen vehicles and owners with outstanding warrants—real crimes and criminals.

There's more cool stuff that the IT guy wants to tell me about, but my brain is already overflowing with information, and perhaps more important, it's dinnertime. I'm starving.

Police shift changes happen at either breakfast time (6 a.m.) or at dinnertime (6 p.m.). I love working the night shift and I love dinnertime. However, although my shift starts at 6 p.m., my workday actually starts at 3:30, when I leave my house, followed by a 4:00 gym workout. By the time my shift actually starts, I am famished. Today is no different. So the IT guy and I mutually agree to take the LPR out for a spin and then connect again later that night to work out any kinks and learn more about it.

On to dinner! Bruno has chosen a Mexican restaurant for us and is already on his way there. I don't always agree with Bruno's food choices, but Mexican sounds perfect today and my stomach is rumbling, telling me it is time for some enchiladas. Serious must feel the same as he speeds out in his souped-up Caprice.

Hungry as I am, I take the time to adjust the mirrors, check the lights and sirens, and place my shotgun on the rack. I then practice taking it off the rack several times. The placement of the rack in this car is a little different than my old one, and I need to be able to grab it without thinking, if it comes to that. I then check the back seat to make sure there isn't anything back there that shouldn't be—drugs, weapons, or contraband from a previous arrest. Although this is a new car and no arrests have taken place, I know that sometimes internal affairs will plant something in the back seat to test you, because you're supposed to clear it out every time. I don't want to be the guy who gets the fancy new car and then gets dinged on night one for not doing his job.

Everything is perfect, and I am satisfied, so I gently pull into traffic. The second I do, the car goes nuts. Lights and noises and everything are blaring at me. It's like someone decided to combine a quinceañera with a rave in here, except instead of some cool Spanish lyrics, I get "Stolen car ahead BEEP BOOP BEEP BOOP! Stolen car ahead! Approach with caution! BEEP BOOP BEEP BOOP!"

A massive wave of adrenaline washes over my body. Suddenly I'm a day-one rookie all over again. *There's no fucking way this is real. Either I fucked something up or someone is fucking with me.* As I'm already out into the traffic lane, I continue moving forward until the alleged stolen car is right next to me in the adjacent lane. *This is crazy! There is no way someone stole a car, decided it was a good idea to drive right past the police station, and that car is literally the first car I see in my LPR car. The odds of that are millions to one. This cannot be right.*

I can't blow this off, though. I reach for my radio.

"424D Raleigh, can I get someone to run a tag for me?" I say, calmly.

"424, you have DCI for running tags," a snarky voice replied.

That pisses me off. Once I figure out this whole stolen-car thing, I'm going to find whoever the fuck that is and punch him square in the face.

"424, this is Serious, what's the tag?"

Looking down at my computer, which is now vibrating at me, yelling at me, and throwing little pickles at me, I read the tag off the computer. Just as I finish, the traffic light turns green and the car in question lurches forward and starts passing everyone while aggressively changing lanes. Blasting across two lanes of traffic and cutting a car off in the process, he makes the next available turn.

This isn't my first rodeo. I remain calm and trail him from a distance, hoping he doesn't realize that I now know he's rolling in a stolen vehicle. I casually take the same turn he did, and the second I do, he knows. He immediately transitions from driving fast to hauling ass, making every turn he can, with the express purpose of losing me. Now I close the distance and stay with him. I do everything right, except, just like in my rookie days, I forget to check the road signs. It's not a huge deal because although I may not know all the road names, I do know where I am, and I know he's heading toward a dead end.

Sure enough, he hits the back of a small apartment complex and has nowhere to go. At this point I'm fairly certain this car is stolen, but I don't *know* it is, so I'm at a bit of a loss on how to proceed. Regardless, it's go time. We both jump out of our cars at the same time. The driver, a well-muscled black male, looks at me and shouts, "Why you following me?"

I don't want to just come right out with a stolen-car accusation, so I lie to him.

"Sir, I just wanted to let you know that your tags are expired and it looks like your left rear tire is going flat."

"It is? Okay, I'll fix it," he curtly responds.

For a moment we just stand there awkwardly gazing into each other's eyes like we're on a bad reality television dating show and we're about to cut to commercial break. He knows the car is stolen and he desperately wants to get away, but on the off chance that I don't know it is stolen, he doesn't want to create an additional problem for himself.

I think the car is stolen but I need to buy more time to find real proof, because if I jump the gun, this could all go terribly wrong.

The pause continues for too long. Nature hates a vacuum. He looks over his shoulder and then through me. This is an indicator that someone is about to run. They always first look around for where they are going to run to. I really don't want him to run, and I interrupt his scan.

"Hey, man, you want me to have a look at the tire for you and help you change it?" I ask him.

Now he's confused, and for one glorious instant, I have the upper hand. In a weird way, he reminds me of me as a rookie: adrenaline is coursing through his veins and fight-or-flight is firing through every synapse in his body. My calm question knocked him back a little. Now, it's not like he trusts me or anything, but I've moved him to the point where he thinks I don't know it's stolen.

I set the hook a little more by taking my eyes off him and strolling over to the back of his vehicle. My plan is that I hope he follows me to the back of the car and then when I bend down to look at the tire, I can jump up and detain him until we figure this all out, one way or the other. Is it a perfect plan? Maybe not, but it seems to be working.

Here he comes. His guard is down. I can grab him in three . . . two . . .

Just as he is two steps away from grabbing distance, my radio chirps up.

"424, um . . . yeah, that car comes back stolen. Where are you?"

Fuck. Me.

The same snarky voice that was fucking with me before just threw fucking protocol out the window. Normally you'd talk about a stolen car on the radio using a 10 code so the suspect can't understand what is going on. This keeps people from . . . I don't know . . . *running.* In this case, to make sure the suspect would have no clue what was going on, he should have said, "424, that car is 10-99, what's your 20?" Instead he took a dump in my punch bowl and made my night a hell of a lot harder.

The suspect is about 5'10" and 220 pounds. He has shoulder-length braided dreads with beads dangling from them. He's wearing all black clothes with bright red sneakers, a clear indicator that he is a Bloods gang member. The small apartment complex we are in is predominantly Bloods gang territory, so I've got that going for me . . . which is nice.

As his face registers the words "that car is stolen," I know the fight-or-flight switch in his head landed on FIGHT because his next move is a quick right hook to the side of my face. The shot hurts but doesn't drop me, but now he sure as shit has a head start. The chase is on! I take off after him and yell into my radio, "Raleigh foot chase, Vardaman Apartments towards Rock Quarry Road."

The suspect cuts behind the apartments, with me right on his tail. As he feels me come closer, he leaves the sidewalk and heads toward the woods, losing his footing in the process and starting to fall down the hill. The only way to keep up with him is to dive myself, but I am apparently the Greg Louganis of hill diving, because my forward momentum sends me right over the top of him, whacking my head on a tree branch. Like a cat he rolls away in the opposite direction and springs to his feet. Immediately he sprints back the way we had just come and toward the road. Somehow I am still right on his heels.

"Run, Tyrone! Runnnn!" a woman shouts from her balcony. A man standing on the stairs launches a can of beer at me as I pass by. *It's nice to have fans.* Ahead is a ten-foot-tall iron fence. *Another fuckin' fence!* I really need to get him before he gets over that fence. The suspect launches himself up and over, with incredible athleticism driven by adrenaline. I reach up and grab his foot and then feel the resistance fall out of it. It takes my brain a second to realize that I am now holding one of his red shoes.

I hear him fall to the other side, but now I've lost my momentum. I try to jump up, but it's too high. I back up a few steps and get a running start, this time clearing it, but by the time I land he has already crossed the street and is running into the woods on the other side. As if on cue, Bruno comes squealing to a halt in the road.

"Tansey, get in! I know where he's headed!" he shouts.

I jump into the front seat. My adrenaline has turned to rage.

"Fuck that guy! I don't even care about him! I want to go find that snarky fuck on the radio that just decided to say 'fuck 10 codes' and tell the whole world the car was stolen. I swear, I don't care if I get fired, I'm punching that fuck right in the face!" I scream in uncontrollable rage.

"Tansey, caaalm down."

"No, fuck that! That dumb fuck could have gotten me killed! I got punched in my fucking face because of his smart-ass attitude, so now I'm gonna return the favor."

"Tansey!" Bruno shouts.

"WHAT! WHAT, BRUNO!"

"Dude, I'm so sorry . . . That asshole on the radio was me."

"WHAAAT? ARE YOU FUCKIN' WITH ME . . . NOW?"

"Sorry!"

I can tell he really is sorry because he has an endearing tone in his voice for the first time ever—literally ever. Even though he doesn't deserve it, his confession takes the wind out of my sails.

"Fuck you, Bruno, I'm punching you in the face later."

"Much deserved, bud, but let's go find this asshole first."

Police cars are now flooding the area and spectators are everywhere. It is now impossible for a K9 to track and that much harder to find our guy. After an hour of work, we come up empty-handed. I'm beyond frustrated.

You see, I had worked so hard over the past few months to restore my reputation and to escape the "Leroy Jenkins" nickname. And now, just like that, I've all but reclaimed my spot at the bottom of the long rope I had just finished climbing.

Bruno drives me back to my car—back to where it all started. I get out of his Tahoe and slam the door. Bruno knows I'm pissed, but it's not just about the asshole radio chatter. Nor is it about this one incident. It's the totality of all the events of this past year. Once again I had started a shitstorm, at mealtime, alone, with a felon, and to make it even worse, I lost a foot chase. It all feels like nothing has changed and I'm still that green trainee.

I get in my car, which, by the way, is still yelling at me. I fight myself not to yank out the shit-ass computer's plug, realizing I would lose any unsaved camera footage and be in a real world of trouble. I take a deep breath and as I close the obnoxious LPR screen I see Sergeant Tom in my rearview mirror approaching. *I finally got his respect and I ruined it. Fuck this car! I didn't really want it anyway. And while we're at it, fuck this district!*

"Leroy," Sarge says with a half grin on his face. I look up at him in utter defeat and cut him off before he can make fun of me. If I'm gonna be scorned, I'm gonna be scorned on my own terms.

"Sarge! I'm done. Seriously, this shit isn't for me. Take the fucking car! I don't want it. Move me out of the district. I'm fine with it. I just don't want to hear any more bullshit. Just let me leave like a man with a little bit of fucking dignity." There's a long pause, and then I add sheepishly, "It's not like I didn't show up every fucking day trying to be a good cop!"

Tom just stares at me. I know he isn't going to say much, and whatever he does say probably won't be very nice. I start to get pissed that he is just staring at me, ignoring my blatant insubordination. I look down at my steering wheel, breaking eye contact.

"Call the victim and tell them you found their car. I'm sure they'll be happy to know it's rather clean and in decent shape and hasn't been wrecked. Call Serious and Spoon and tell them to look at your dashcam footage to see if they know who that guy was." And then just like that . . . the motherfucker walks away. I'm dumbfounded. *Didn't he hear what I just said?*

I sit for a minute thinking about what he said and why he said it and I can't come up with anything, so I just go right back to work. For some reason, the insecurities are gone.

I immediately call the female victim, and upon hearing that her car has been found and is generally okay, she breaks into tears. "Yes, ma'am," I say. "It's in good shape. I'll wait for you here so you can take it back home."

"I'll be right there!" she blubbers through the tears.

When she arrives and I hand her the keys, she hugs me tightly, then catches herself. "I'm sorry about the hug, Officer. I'm just so happy!" She beams.

"Not an issue, ma'am. I could do with more hugs. See that guy on the porch over there? He threw a beer can at me! I'll take the hug!" She smiles.

"Now do me a favor and go through your car to see if anything is missing."

She quickly checks everything—the trunk, the glove compartment, all the various pockets and whatnot.

"Is there anything missing, ma'am?" I ask.

"Just a pack of Newports," she replies, still beaming. "Do you think insurance will cover them?"

"I doubt that, ma'am," I reply, smiling myself.

She puts the key in the ignition and squeals with excitement.

"What is it, ma'am?" I ask.

"When it was stolen, the car was empty. Whoever stole it must have filled it up. I needed that! I don't get paid for another two days."

The Lord works in mysterious ways.

"Did you catch the person who stole my car?" she asks.

"No, ma'am. He got away."

"Awww shit! That motherfucka faster than you? You get outran, babe? These motherfuckas is fast out here, Twelve," she chirps, suddenly changing her tune.

"Twelve" is what they call the police in the SED.

I look up to see Serious getting into my vehicle. While I am getting punked by this young lady for not being fast enough, he's going through the footage in my car. Spoon is with him, holding the red shoe.

"Thanks for grabbing that. I'm guessing it will need to go into evidence?" I ask.

"This? Ha, nope. This is definitely *not* going into evidence. This is the new Shoe of Shame. It's getting mounted, and you're going to be the first to sign it," Spoon replies with a Cheshire cat grin on his face.

I groan, knowing my unsuccessful chase will be memorialized and displayed in the station for all to see.

The Shoe of Shame isn't a new thing. In fact, there is already a shoe mounted in the roll-call room, covered with signatures. Later that night the shoe I managed to snag is mounted on a nice wood-stained plaque with SHOE OF SHAME stenciled across the top. The squad circles around as they present me with a Sharpie so I can sign it. That plaque, with my signature, is still hanging on the wall in the SED, now covered in ink because, believe it or not, I am not the only cop to lose a foot chase over the years.

I should've gone for his waist, damn it.

8

A NEW SET OF ROOKIES

Remember your first day as a sophomore in high school?

There was no anxiety. There was no worrying. It was just fun. And why was it fun?

Because you were no longer the bottom of the fucking totem pole. There was this whole group of new assholes running around called "freshmen," and they were so screwed-up, so nervous, and so weird that you had no choice but to feel good about yourself.

Today is that day! I am no longer a rookie, and I have to tell you, my friends, it's pretty damn glorious!

I'm staring at the two rookies who were assigned to SED, and they are about as different as you can imagine, but they both came with sterling reputations. Truth be told, I was hoping for either another military veteran I could take under my wing, or a total fuckup so "Leroy Jenkins" could fade into the annals of cop history. Instead I got Red and Rabbit.

Red, so named for her fiery red hair, is 6'2", 150 pounds, and heavily into CrossFit. If every police PR person in the world got into a room and imagined the perfect policewoman, it would be Red. She's smart, well spoken, and good-looking. She was also captain of a major university's basketball team and held several school records. She was so good, in fact, that her jersey and number were retired when she graduated and are still hanging from the rafters at that university.

Yeah, well, I have a shoe, with my name on it, nailed to the wall of the station, and I'm not a rookie, so there.

Red is dating a detective. So, this, in addition to her good looks, her personal gravitas, athletic ability, and background, makes her cybernetically designed to be the perfect cop. Even before she arrived this morning, everyone was talking about her because it's really clear to virtually everyone that with her resume, she is going places. Moreover, she probably has the right connections to succeed. All the cops know this and so they all want to endear themselves to her. Everyone, that is, except me. My priorities and daily focus are: live through my next shift and not be a fucking rookie anymore. I don't care at all about playing games or making political alliances.

The second rookie, Rabbit, is also a college grad. He's a swarthy lad from the middle of nowhere, North Carolina. He played soccer at a smaller college and isn't so much a record-breaking athlete as he is an academic. He's about 5'9", 200 pounds, but I will find out soon enough that he is exceptionally fast for his size. He is classy, a bit of an introvert, smart, and chooses his words carefully before he speaks. I kind of want to give him a wedgie. In other words, he is my polar opposite.

Their training officers, including Jayce, my old TO, swoop them up and lead them away and that is the end of it. Underwhelming, actually.

For the first few weeks, I barely see either of them. Their training officers keep them busy. But on this fateful morning, Red meanders into the gym at the same time I am there with Serious and Spoon. She is wearing a sports bra and some micro-spandex shorts. This is well before the current era of men and women showing up in the gym wearing nothing, and it makes things instantly awkward inside what had been our Man Sanctuary.

In this gym world we created, there is always loud, aggressive music blaring on the radio, tons of profanity bantered about, and loud grunting with every dropped bumper weight . . . and frankly, 87 percent of the time, there is a penis drawn on the dry-erase board. It's filthy, sweaty, and gross, and this is just the way we like it. So when Red walks in, it's part weird that there is something feminine here, and part embarrassing that we live like this. The whole moment is awkward and we just stare at each other. Then something snaps inside me. She's the rookie, not me. If I had pulled something like this, they would have fileted me for weeks! *I'm not letting this stand!*

"Nice shorts, rookie! Where did you get them, THE SHORTS STORE? HAHAHAHAHAHA!" I yell obnoxiously over the loud music, making what I think is a phenomenal reference to *Anchorman: The Legend of Ron Burgundy.*

Spoon and Serious glance at each other, and then at me, in abject horror and shock.

"Um, thanks, I guess?" Red shrugs.

Them not laughing instantly makes me the weird and creepy guy. Serious covers his eyes in secondhand embarrassment.

"What? Guys? Get it? From that movie?" I plead.

"You're an idiot, Leroy," Serious offers.

"Come on, that was funny," I insist, not even considering that it may have been a C minus joke at best, in lieu of believing this is an enormous anti-me conspiracy. They both ignore me, which pisses me off. Serious goes back to lifting weights and Spoon walks over to turn down the music.

I am appalled!

Men have asked in the past to turn the music down and the response has always been to turn it up. Here this rookie didn't even say anything, and Spoon is going out of his way for her?! And to make it even worse, they're ignoring my amazing humor?

"Seriously, guys, we're turning the music down for her? And we can't even make jokes at a rookie's expense?" I yell.

"Leroy, shut the fuck up," Serious warns.

I will not shut up. I need to stand up for all us sophomores out there in all the world! It is my right to make fun of the freshman. So it is written. So it shall always be. "Man, this is bullshit! You guys would never have turned music down for me!"

Red is still just standing in the doorway, her gym bag in hand.

"I'm sorry, Red. Leroy is an idiot. Welcome to D squad," Serious says. *She does not get to call me Leroy!*

Oblivious to the idea of inclusivity, not dropping misogyny like Eminem drops rhymes, and the very obvious signals that everyone in the room is giving me, I go full Sisqo and decide to unleash the dragon.

"Oh, come on! So a good-looking female shows up half naked and now all of a sudden you're all nice, modern gentlemen?! Look, Red, nothing against you, but they are the ones crapping on women's equality. They're not treating you the same. If they were treating you the same, they would've shamed you into putting some decent clothes on," I tell her in the most genuine manner possible.

"Leroy! Enough!" Serious shouts as his eyes almost explode out of his head.

"No! The first time I walked in here you grabbed the radio and reported a 'larceny of sleeves' at the Southeast District Station, and I have to tell you, that was pretty fucking funny and extremely embarrassing. It took me months to wear a sleeveless shirt again. She walks in here with only panties and a bra on, and nothing? No fucking comments from you two? Sorry, Red, you should report them both for misogyny. This is bullshit."

Serious and Spoon are just staring at me. Red is the only one smirking.

"Leroy, you really are an idiot. We're so sorry for this moron's behavior, Red," Serious offers again.

"Hahaha, it's fine, I've already been told all about Tansey. I hear him on the radio all the time, so I'd expect nothing less. I can't wait to get into a foot chase with you. I haven't got into one yet and my training officer said that when it's time for me to get into one, we're just gonna follow you around until one happens. How do you get into so many foot chases anyway?" she asks me, in the same kind of devil-may-care way that I tend to employ.

Spoon and Serious burst into laughter. I turn slightly red. *I get into foot chases all the time because I am a train wreck and continue to be an absolute shit magnet.* But she doesn't know I'm a train wreck yet and I want to keep that a secret. Plus it's kind of cool that she wants to learn something from me. Up until this point, while I no longer screw up on the daily, no one is exactly coming to me for advice either. I could get used to this. "Well, when your training officer thinks you're ready, I'll teach you," I fumble out.

Clang! Clang! Clang! I snap my head just in time to see Serious's weights rolling around on the ground as his head drops back in time with his snorting laughter. *Fuck you guys.*

Red walks over to the music and turns it back up—a small sign of respect. Then she ignores us buffoons, sets her time, and goes to work. And when I say she goes to work, I mean she does some athlete shit. Not phone playing. No selfies. No wasting time. She gets after it. Respect.

Finally, we all finish up and head back to the locker room. I feel good about myself . . . until the door closes.

"Holy shit! You guys should have heard Leroy when the new rookie came into the gym! Who wants to go over/under on how fast he gets a hostile-work-environment case against him?" Spoon sneers.

I'm still pissed that she is getting off so easy, and this sets me off more. *I mean, isn't that what women are fighting for? Workplace equality? I'd be disrespectful to her and her ability if I wasn't a complete prick.* I'm trying not to treat her differently because she's a woman! Meanwhile, these guys are all perfectly comfortable changing literally everything about how they act because of her gender.

"Whatever, guys, you should have seen Spoon and Serious sucking up to her! 'Yes, ma'am.' 'Pardon us, ma'am!' 'Here are the weights for you to lift, your highness.' They even changed the radio station to Taylor Swift's greatest hits," I snap, smiling wide.

"Oh, Leroy, we love you, even if you are an idiot," Spoon fires back, grinning.

Later that night, I'm cruising around the district. Everything is copacetic. Nice weather. Quiet night. No LPR mission to keep me busy. My major challenge tonight? Stay awake. *It's nice to have a chill night every once in a while.*

The second that thought enters my mind, the silence of my perfect evening is ruined by the squelch of Serious's radio. "Got one running! Gun! Gun! Gun!" Silence, then . . . *Oh shit!*

I hit my lights and siren and speed toward his location.

A suspect darts across the intersection just as I arrive, my car still not at a complete stop. Milliseconds later, Ralph appears, close behind and in pursuit.

I speed up and get ahead of them, turning sharply to jump the curb and block his path on the sidewalk. Without missing a beat, the suspect leaps up and butt-slides over my hood. *Here we go.* I jump out and give chase, but he jumps over a brick wall, leaping into the Veterans' Memorial Cemetery. As you all know by now, I love a good wall-jumping as much as anyone, so I sprint toward it and hit the wall at about the same time as Ralph.

Like synchronized swimmers, Ralph and I clear the wall and land on the other side in a perfect mirror of each other. I honestly wish someone had captured it on camera. Truly a gorgeous display of athleticism.

Our raw, unbridled gymnastic routine is too much for the suspect to handle, because he is so startled by our quick scaling of the wall that he turns to run without looking where he is going, slamming his knee into a gravestone. Now hobbling, he is no match for Wreck-It Ralph, who plows into him at full speed, driving him face-first into the ground.

Immediately the suspect starts clawing at his waist, trying to get his gun out. Ralph counters with three hard punches to the back of the head, while he tries to control the suspect's hand with the other. After the third punch connects, the suspect throws his hands wide to each side and begs him to stop, which Ralph does, just as I get there with my cuffs.

"I got him, Leroy!" Ralph tells me. "Go back to Serious—he's outnumbered!" *Oh shit, once again!* I run back toward the intersection, again clearing the wall like a combination of an Olympic gymnast and a cheetah—just beautiful, raw athleticism, wrapped in a beautiful bow.

When I hit the ground, I catch Serious's car in my peripheral vision and sprint to it. Serious has his foot on a suspect's head, pinning him to the ground, and his gun pointed into the back of the car at another suspect. It looks like a Tarantino film standoff.

"Leroy, there's a gun on the seat, so get the guy in the back seat first," he says to me before redirecting his voice to the guy in the car, never taking his eyes off him. "Sir, if you reach for that gun while he is detaining you, I'm gonna put one in your face. Are we clear?" I had already run to the other side of the car before the man could answer. I immediately rip him from his seat and cuff him, clearing him of his weapons. Then I get the front passenger out and cuff him as well. That threat averted, Serious bends down and cuffs his suspect, just as Ralph arrives back with the first guy.

Just as Jayce and Red show up, Ralph's guy starts vomiting profusely and his adrenaline dumps all over the concrete.

"Damn! Looks like we missed the fun, how can we help?" Red asks excitedly.

I used to be just like that.

"Well, Red, you can take this guy and put him in your car," Ralph offers. Classic Ralph—pawning off the guy who is covered in puke. Still, at least he isn't catering to the rookie.

"You got it! Right away, sir!" Red says as she excitedly takes Pukey McPukerson and loads him in her car.

Serious, Ralph, and I round up the other three and transport them to the station. The sergeant hasn't made it back yet when Serious downloads his video and mine. We start watching them and they are awesome.

In the video, Serious is like a real-life Wyatt Earp—you can't write this shit. As he's pulling the car over and approaching it, he notices the rear passenger acting squirrelly, so he opens the back door instead of the driver's door. Just as he does that, Ralph's car comes into view and Serious can be seen ordering the man to show his hands. When the man doesn't comply, Serious grabs him by his dreads and rips him from the car, delivering a quick series of uppercuts to the face. The man falls face-first onto the pavement as Serious instantly steps on his face, pulling his gun and pointing it at the rear passenger, who is armed. Then the driver opens the door and takes off as Ralph follows. You can hear Serious's audio as he yells, "Gun! Gun! Gun!" When he releases the mic, he is still yelling: "Don't you fucking move!"

Next, the video switches to my in-car camera as the man is seen running past the intersection. I speed past the two men and then the man flops onto my hood. It almost looks like I hit him because the camera is not wide-angle. We laugh at the chaos and then show the footage to Tom.

Tom doesn't share our excitement. "Looks good. Take them to jail, then come back and do your Use of Force reports. They're due end of shift."

Foolishly, I laugh, because this one isn't on me. "Ha! Yes! Well, boys, this isn't my shit show so I get to sit back and watch y'all type for once."

Tom looks at me. *Oh fuck.* "Leroy, you write a report about hitting that man with your car."

"Wait, what? Sarge, he ran into my car! I didn't hit him," I whine.

"That's not what it looked like from my angle. I look forward to reading your report about it later," Tom says dryly.

I leave the station to the raucous laugh of Ralph and Serious, who are happy that I got sucked into it even though I had nothing to do with it. Flipping them off, I walk out of the station and drive over to where Red and Jayce are—it's always better to type in groups so you can't get ambushed by some criminal walking up on you while you're not paying attention. I lower my window and Red chirps up instantly.

"Hey, so what happened out there? We heard the radio traffic but like . . . what actually happened? Were you in the foot chase?" She is so fascinated with police work and you can tell she is champing at the bit to get in the mix. I realize she is the very opposite of what the rumors make her out to be. She isn't out for a free ride to the top. She's here to do work.

"Yeah, I was kinda in the chase. I was pretty far behind them, because

I had to get out of my car first, but I caught up with athleticism and speed probably not seen by anyone in this lifetime."

She ignores my sarcasm. "How did you catch him? Did you tackle him or did he just give up?" *Was I this exuberant?*

"No, a fallen veteran sniped him from the underworld," I reply.

"What?" she asks, genuinely confused.

"He tripped on a gravestone in the veterans cemetery."

Red erupts into laughter. She seems genuinely entertained by my description of the event. For the first time, watching her be enthralled with the everyday life of a cop, I realize I'm not going to be the rookie forever. I now have some real experience under my belt. It feels good.

Jayce snaps us all back to reality when he breaks up our little moment. "That report isn't going to type itself."

"Yes, boss!" she says, giving me a little side-eye before going back to typing. I make small talk with Jayce, procrastinating the writing of my own ridiculous account of the gun-wielding suspect who ran into my car.

Driving back that night, I realize that I like Red. *She's going to be a good cop.* She's proactive, pushes herself, and is genuinely trying to learn. I know this sounds terrible, but it is a weird thing to think. I have never really worked with women. The special operations unit I was with didn't really have women, and I had only ever worked with one other female cop—Barbie—and it was sparingly.

Now, the whole squad doesn't exactly share my feelings—at least not at first. Perhaps in the beginning there is some resentment as she is seen by the higher echelon as the poster girl and is most certainly being groomed for bigger things. And of course there is the perception that her detective boyfriend will give her leads that the other cops wouldn't get. Lastly, she did get breaks simply because she is a woman. (Or in any event she was treated differently because she is a woman.)

But to be fair, she didn't ask for any of that shit. To me, she does her job and gives as good as she gets in the banter department. She keeps her ego in check and asks tons of questions—always trying to learn. She doesn't demand or want any special treatment. If some of the guys resent how she is treated, they should resent the higher-ups for treating her differently—not her.

But fair or unfair, the overwhelming majority of the guys think that although she will do great in training because she has a good attitude, she will probably fail when the training wheels come off and she has to run her own car.

Only time will tell.

9

A TOUGH BREAK

As I rack my weights, Red storms into the gym. I can tell something is wrong, but I don't want to ask. She starts to set up her workout, looks over at me, opens her mouth, and then goes back to moving bars, weights, and mats so her CrossFit workout can be as efficient as possible.

She grabs her timer and stares at it, then looks back at me. We are the only two in the gym.

"I just want you to know, I'm putting in for a transfer. I'm not cut out for SED," she says matter-of-factly, keeping her eyes low to the ground.

"Why?" I ask immediately.

"Why? I can't do anything right around here! I haven't had a single good night since I left training. Serious doesn't respect me. Ralph and Spoon are relentless. I actually think they want me to fail!" she blurts out.

I smile reassuringly. "They don't want you to fail. It's just part of being a rookie! You're going to figure it out. Trust me."

"Well, I'm not going to figure it out here. I know they all want me out," she says, a resigned, resolute sadness in her voice.

I know that voice. I had that voice. When everything is going wrong, you can't help but feel like the whole world is against you. I spent the better part of a year speaking exclusively in that voice.

Now, to be fair, Red has screwed up a lot. She reminds me of someone—an earnest, good-looking rapscallion of a man who tried to bite off way more than he could chew too fast, and got himself in a host of trouble.

To make matters worse for her, the cases her boyfriend has thrown her way have done more to hurt her than help her. And, of course, the guys have been brutal. To be fair, most of them are no more brutal than they are to any rookie, but there are a few who may be cheering on her struggles a little too much.

"Hey, do me a favor. Come to dinner with me tonight and let's talk about this?" I ask her, remembering all too well how much I needed this very dinner a year ago.

"You don't have to do that," she answers.

"I know. Now finish your workout so we can go eat," comes my quick response.

Red smiles and hits her timer. I finish my last set and grab a shower.

We meet at the same restaurant I visited a year ago. We have the same conversation. She considers my offer and grudgingly agrees to give working with me a shot. And I now have my first cop to mentor. *I can't let her down.*

On patrol that night, I teach her the same "lemon law" method that had been handed down to me and after a while, we get a golden egg! Not only does the driver have warrants, but there's a plethora of cocaine in the car as well. Red takes the arrest and writes the report. By the end of shift, she has her first winning night, ever. She is absolutely thrilled. I smile for her, because I know that rare feeling. Unfortunately, I also know that most nights won't be this way—they will be far from perfect. She is going to need to learn to find her own contentment in the job, even when it gets ugly. I'm hoping I can help.

———

Day shifts on Mondays suck. Let me rephrase that. Day shifts on Mondays really, truly suuuuuuuck.

As one might imagine, most crime happens at night, between 12 a.m. and 4 a.m., so the start of any day shift requires filling out paperwork from whatever chaos happened the night before. You're dealing with angry citizens who had their cars broken into, or their stores broken into, or something vandalized. Many of them also believe their misfortunes are your fault for not doing your job, while at the same time bemoaning that there are too many police around. Good times.

But Monday day shift is a double whammy.

If you're the victim, your weekend is over and you're starting your week off with your car stolen, your house broken into, or some other terrible thing, so you're pissed. You're pissed at the world and maybe even God. But most of all you're probably pissed at the police for not "protecting you, your property, and your well-being."

One guess as to who has to deal with the irate victim!

And of course for the cop, Monday is also when shift changes happen. If, by chance, you were on night shift the preceding week, your body is in "fuck you, why am I awake during the day?" mode, and you still have to deal with the victims who just had their world turned upside down. On these Mondays, it really sucks all around.

On this Monday morning, though, the gods decide that the normal Monday pains are not enough. They decide to grace me with another challenge. As I walk into the roll-call room, I notice it is empty except for a young black man sitting in the back, wearing a smart, collared shirt and a pair of perfectly pressed slacks. He's got close-cropped hair like he is in the military and is sitting with his back as straight as a board.

"Good morning, sir!" he almost shouts at me, grinning from ear to ear.

"Good morning," I answer as cheerily as Monday will let me muster. Just then Sergeant Tom walks in.

"Morning, Sarge," I offer.

He responds with his own greeting: "Yeah, go get the ride-along vest and get him to fill out the ride-along form. Gary, is it?"

"Yes, sir!" he shouts. Gary is very enthusiastic. His enthusiasm hurts my ears. It injures my soul.

"Welcome to the Southeast District. You'll be riding with Officer Tansey. If you need anything or have any questions, he will be happy to answer them for you." And with that, Sarge exits stage left, leaving me with . . . well . . . Gary.

I have never been assigned a ride-along before, so this is all a bit of a shock. I don't even know what ride-along paperwork looks like or what I'm supposed to do, but I know that I have to fake it for Gary. I gesture for him to follow me, grab him a coffee, and sit him in the report room.

"I'll be right back, Gary. I need to grab the paperwork."

Twenty minutes later, after checking every damn file cabinet in the room, I find a folder that says "ride-along" in the next-to-last drawer. This instantly annoys me. If I had found it right away, I would have looked like I know what I'm doing. If it had been in the last drawer, it would be a funny story. Instead, it's just annoying.

Anyway, after filling out the paperwork, I grab a bulletproof vest and strap it on him. He seems very excited about this new gear.

"So, why are you doing a ride-along?" I ask.

"Well, I'm moving to New Jersey this summer," Gary says. "I applied to be a New Jersey state trooper, got selected, and so I leave for the academy in June. I just wanted to ride along with some officers here to see what it's like, so I'll have a little knowledge of the job before showing up to the academy."

I'm actually really impressed. I wish I had done something like this before the academy. It might have been eye-opening. Still, his timing couldn't be worse.

"That's awesome! Great initiative and I applaud your proactive approach. I have to warn you, though: the first day of day shift is the absolute worst time to do a ride-along."

"Why is that?" he asks, his face growing a small frown.

"Because it's boring as fuck and there isn't much crime happening. Everyone's going to work or sleeping off a hard weekend bender. Even the criminals! We're just going to be taking some reports and then getting coffee. What time are you riding till?"

"I'm riding until noon," he says, his eyes widening a little, clearly hoping that noon is late enough for some crime to take place.

"Yeah, well, sorry in advance, but it's probably gonna be very slow and not very exciting," I say, feeling a little bad for him. *Seems a little fucked-up, doesn't it? Apologizing for there not being any crime!* Gary is just earnest as hell.

Unfortunately for Gary, the day is going exactly as I expected. We start off by taking a few reports, and I get to know him a little. His story is the same story that 95 percent of all cops have: he wants to help people and serve his community. If not him, then who, right? I tell him about my experiences and he's amazed at all the happenings and adventures I have had in my first year-plus on the force.

"It's been a hell of a ride," I tell him, "just not on Mondays . . ."

After an hour and change, we stop in to a coffee shop to grab an early morning caffeine pop with the rest of the squad. Red is missing, which bums me out. She and I have been doing a lot of great work together: she's getting more confident and really coming into her own, and we've built a really effective rapport. Unfortunately, she hasn't gotten there with the rest of the guys, which might explain her absence. After all, she still sees them as trying to "take her out." While it's definitely not true for Serious, Spoon, and Ralph, there are still some who would like to see her fail. And believe me, I understand how it is to be on the receiving end.

The guys are enjoying having Gary there and he is sitting wide-eyed as they regale him with tales from the past few nights. Noticeably, he is not drinking coffee like the rest of us, instead choosing to sit down with some tea and an egg muffin. Gary is lucky. If he was a rookie, this would be enough to mock him for the rest of the year, but the hazing only applies to the rookie who has completed the academy.

The storytelling is broken up abruptly as our radios come alive.

"Attention, Raleigh units. Strong-arm in progress, Poole and New Hope."

"Is that in this area?!" Gary perks up, hoping.

"No, it's pretty far away, but if you want to head that way for a little excitement, we can," I tell him, knowing that by the time we arrive, this will likely be all over.

"Oh, yes, sir! Can we please go?" he almost begs.

Spoon and Ralph laugh at his enthusiasm. Serious stands up and stretches.

I raise my eyebrow at him. "You going with us?"

"Yeah, I'll head that way. I have to pee first so I'll meet you there. I'm sure we'll get T-22'd [stood down and sent home] when Rabbit and Jayce get there."

"See you there," I say as I grab Gary and we hurry out to my car.

"Buckle up, bud! We're at least going to drive fast. We aren't that close to this call but for some excitement, I'll pretend like we are."

"Awesome, thank you. Do you think it's serious?"

"Ha, no! Typically, a strong-arm on a Monday morning means someone's boyfriend or girlfriend snatched their cell phone to see who they were sleeping with over the weekend. It's probably a bullshit call. Besides, there are two other units that will get there about eight minutes before us, so they'll most likely have it under control by the time we get there. Sorry, man," I say when I see him slump in sadness.

The radio buzzes again. "Units heading to the strong-arm: we are getting additional callers stating that a large black male is clubbing a black female in the head with a bedpost."

Well, shit.

"Oh, maybe this isn't bullshit," I say, realizing the seriousness of the situation. Despite his head being pinned to his seat by my sudden acceleration, Gary's excitement is oozing from him as he realizes this is real. As my sirens wail, he scoots up a bit and grabs the armrest tightly with one hand while bracing his other against the ceiling. Out of the corner of my eye, I watch his initial excitement turn into nervousness.

Trying to console him, I offer up, "Don't worry, man, I'm not gonna wreck us, and the only reason we are going hot is because they may need help if this guy flees the scene."

Gary does not want to show weakness and hands me some young-man bravado. "Yeah, no, this is awesome. Drive as fast as you want."

"You think he'll run?"

"Do you think she is bleeding? I mean, he is clubbing her, right?"

I know these questions sound horrible, but ask any cop, soldier, or firefighter about these moments and they will tell you that it's completely normal. His adrenaline faucet is wide open and the only thing he has control over right now is his one thousand questions. For me, this is nothing. I'm not even driving fast enough to tingle my own adrenaline. But to him we're in a combination of NASCAR and *Mad Max*.

"Units heading to the strong-arm: the 911 caller is now advising that the suspect is dragging the female to a white F-150 truck. The caller is advising that the police are not yet on scene, and he is going to attempt to stop the suspect from leaving with her."

"Oh shit, that's not going to bode well for the caller," I mutter.

"What? Why? Is he gonna try to stop that guy?" doe-eyed Gary asks.

"Sounds like it."

"That's good, right? Why is that bad?"

"Everyone wants to be a lion until it's time to do lion shit. If that guy doesn't know what he's doing, we are going to have two victims on our hands," I say, having seen this more than a few times.

On the one hand, I respect a man who intervenes to help another person. That is the righteous thing to do and takes character and bravery. On the other hand, if you don't know how to fight, very rarely do you figure it out on your first try. Remember how terrible I was as a rookie trying to control my adrenaline and the situation? And I was a combat veteran!

The radio pops off once again. "Units en route, we are getting an additional call that the previous 911 caller is now being bludgeoned by the suspect. The female is bleeding from the skull and is unconscious and unresponsive. Break. Break. Break. The suspect is now fleeing in the truck, making a right onto Poole Road."

Jayce immediately responds. "Raleigh, we are getting on scene from the opposite direction the suspect is fleeing. Do we have any units responding from the west?"

Serious chirps up, right on his heels. "Tansey is heading that way from the west. I'll try to intercept him but I'm still about six minutes out. Tansey, I'm about two minutes behind you. Let me know if you see him."

Jayce acknowledges, "T-4, Raleigh, the units from the west will go after the suspect. We are getting on scene. Send us EMS quickly. I have two victims." A moment goes by before he repeats again, in a much more serious tone, "Raleigh, send EMS T-18. We have two severe head injuries, and the female is not responding. Suspect vehicle is a white or gray Ford F-150 with lots of furniture in the back. Last seen heading west on Poole Road."

Gary was black when this ride started, but his face is now white as snow, and his eyes are glued to the road. He is experiencing full-on fight-or-flight and his body is choosing flight, but there is nowhere to flee. It's so easy to judge cops or soldiers watching videos from your home, but unless you've been in it, you can never know what it feels like to be in the moment of truth—where your life is on the line. The best cops and soldiers develop a muscle memory that allows them to function in that zone and still make good decisions. But no one, and I don't care how cool they are, no one starts there. Gary is getting his first full dose of this reality.

As we get close to where I think we'll meet him, I turn off my lights and sirens and slow down. We are on Poole Road, about four minutes from the crime scene. Poole Road has four lanes, two in each direction, with no median or barrier. It's mostly a residential road, with just a few businesses and neighborhoods branching off from it. I position my car to the inside lane.

"Why are we slowing down and turning off the sirens?" Gary asks uneasily, probably hoping the answer is that someone else got the suspect.

"Because we're getting close to the suspect vehicle. We don't want to spook him. If he hears our siren or sees our lights he can shoot down into one of these neighborhoods over there. We don't want that." On cue and approaching from the opposite direction is a white Dodge Ram pickup truck with a lot of furniture in the back. It slowly approaches the four-way intersection.

Let's play this cool before he has a chance to know what hits him.

"That's it! That's it!" Gary points and yells. I snarl at him to put his hand down, but it's too fucking late. The bad guy sees us and guns it.

Game on. I whip a Vin Diesel–style U-turn in the intersection, tires smoking.

"Hold on, bud, it's fucking on!" I say to ol' Gar-Dog, then grab the radio. "Raleigh, I'm behind the suspect, west on Poole Road, approaching Donald Ross." Out of the corner of my eye, I see Serious blow past us in the opposite direction and then do a sliding U-turn to get into the chase. *Damn it, I think his U-turn was cooler than mine.*

Just as we catch up to him, the suspect slams on his brakes and turns down a neighborhood street, but then realizes it's a dead end and whips around back onto Poole Road, just as another police car arrives on the scene, heading right toward the white truck.

He's got nowhere to go now.

The very second that thought touches my mind, I regret it. I see the man turn his wheel and the tires on the truck start spinning. Gary puts words to my thoughts: "Oh God! He's gonna—"

Before Gary can finish his thought, the white truck careens violently into the approaching cop car, head-on, driving up and over the hood and into the windshield. My heart sinks. The officer, someone I likely know very well, is either in serious shape or dead from that collision. *It's time to work.*

"Get out and find cover!" I scream at Gary. "We are about to get into a gunfight." Gary's eyes go wide and he doesn't immediately react, but I don't have time for him. I slam my car into park and jump out, gun in hand. I yell back at Gary one more time. "Open the door! Get out of the car! RUN NOW!"

Finally, the wheels in Gary's mind start turning. He throws the door open and starts running away from us. Seeing that, I sprint toward the truck. Seconds before I arrive, the door opens and a large black male emerges from the wreckage and leaps off the hood of the smashed patrol car.

This guy just murdered one of my coworkers and friends and I am in no mood to be trifled with. "Turn around and face away from me!" I shout. He stares right at me, glaring his ass off, and keeps walking toward me with his hands up. "Sir!" I yell. "Turn the fuck around and get on the ground!" But he does not comply, still walking purposefully in my direction with his hands up. I know this is going to get ugly. Suddenly his walk becomes a sprint, and I am determining if I need to shoot or fight. Out of nowhere, Serious runs up from behind me and meets him halfway. *If I had pulled the trigger I would have shot Serious in the back.*

Their collision is basic physics. This asshole and Serious are going about the same speed, but Serious is about one hundred pounds lighter. The end result is that they are barreling right toward me while locked in the beginning of a fight. Gun still in hand, I reach out and wrap my arms around this mass of man, trying to stop them. Instead we all fly back toward the curb.

I am going to fall and they are going to land on top of me with this asshole in dominant position. *My gun is still in my hand. He could get it.* Even though I have no wrestling background, the first thing that enters my mind is that maybe I can kind of bridge and twist and suplex these two so that the criminal lands on the bottom and then Serious and then me, so that I will be on top with the gun. I step back, about to execute a perfect Dan Gable wrestling maneuver.

POW POW POW!!!

Oh shit! Oh shit! Oh shit! I just sent rounds down Poole Road. Oh my God, I hope I didn't hit anyone! How did that happen? I didn't feel any recoil. I don't think I moved my finger. Oh fuck.

I will have to deal with the aftermath of that later. I need to get back into the fight. I push myself up to my feet . . . and immediately fall back down again, pain coursing through my butt, leg, and back. The pain is so great that it radiates back up my body and seems to fixate on my groin. *Oh shit, I shot myself in the dick.*

I take a deep breath and look down to see if my wife needs to trade me in for a newer model, and am thrilled to see that there is no blood coming from my penis or groin area. That joy dissipates quickly, however, when I notice that my leg is facing to the left, but my body is facing to the right. I didn't just break my leg, I snapped it clean off.

Okay, the bad news is that my leg is completely fucked and I am prob-

ably bleeding internally. The good news is that the POW POW POW was
just my leg breaking in three places and not me firing a gun randomly into
the city!

If you've never had a traumatic injury like I am currently experiencing, you don't know that adrenaline will let you ignore pain and function, even when you're completely screwed. That's what we have going on right now.

So instead of being filled with horrific pain from my shattered leg, I'm filled with a weird, oddly happy feeling, and my vision refocuses to the present. I watch the suspect's head bounce off the ground again and again as he fights with Serious and the latter lands shots on his face. As Serious lands the punch that takes the fight out of him, a *snap* reverberates through the air, and Serious jumps up screaming. "Goddamn it! Fuck!" he shouts as I see his arm flapping wildly about a quarter way up his forearm, where, last time I checked, there is no joint.

I'm on the ground with a shattered leg, Serious is jumping up and down with a broken arm, and the suspect is lying on his back immobile with a bloody face from Serious's punches. He looks at me and I look at him. Our eyes meet in a psychedelic haze of a moment.

"I'm sorry for all of this. I'm sorry for everything, man," he says to me, as if beating a woman with a club, then beating a man with a club when he tried to stop that beating, then murdering a cop with a car, then attacking me and Serious, resulting in both of us shattering bones, could be remedied with a "Golly gosh, gee whiz, my bad."

"Eat a dick, asshole," I reply.

Seconds later, a blue blur is by my side. I look up to see Red. She's bleeding from her face and head, and her hand is on her neck. Taking in the image of me, she says, "Hey, your leg is broken."

"Thanks, Red, I hadn't noticed. That's very helpful."

"What's up with him?" she asks, pointing to Serious.

"Oh, he broke his arm, I think," I say more matter-of-factly than the moment probably requires.

"Is that guy in handcuffs?" she asks of the asshole who caused all this.

"Not yet," I answer.

"I got it," she replies, letting go of her neck and reaching for her handcuffs. Blood squirts everywhere. In an instant, her shirt is drenched and everything around her is bright red. She places her palm against her neck, instantly feeling woozy. "That's not good," she mutters, plopping down next to me, realizing cuffs are off the menu for now.

The blue wave comes roaring in, sirens blazing. In an instant, the man is in handcuffs and Sergeant Tom comes meandering over, taking in the scene as he approaches.

"I bet that hurts," he offers, pointing to my leg. "Did anyone call for an ambulance yet?"

Red chimes in: "Not yet, Sarge."

"What's wrong with you?" he asks her.

"I cut my neck," she says, as if the severed artery in her neck is a skinned knee.

"I see that. Was that from the car wreck or after?" He gestures at the pickup truck sitting on the hood of the police car. It's only then that I realize that the cop I thought had been killed is Red. She had somehow taken a full-on hit from a pickup truck and lived. Five minutes ago, I would have bet big money that whoever was in that car had died, and even though I am in massive pain, and this situation couldn't be more fucked if I made it up, I am filled with profound happiness that we didn't lose anyone today.

"It's from the accident, Sarge," she tells him. Sergeant Tom nods and shouts, "We need two ambulances right away!" As he is getting acknowledgment from the other officers that they are handling that task, Red leans over to me. "Hey, Tans, I'm sorry I missed the fight. His truck pushed my front seat all the way back and up toward the roof of the car. His front bumper was in my windshield so I had a really hard time getting out and over here to help."

This crazy-ass rookie is apologizing for not getting in the fight faster!

I smile through the pain and muster a laugh. "Ha! Shit! I'm just glad you're alive. I thought for sure whoever was in that car was dead. How did your neck get cut?"

"I think it's from the shotgun mount. He hit me so hard that it pushed me and my seat into the ceiling. I'm pretty sure the corner of the shotgun rack is what cut my neck."

The ambulance and fire trucks arrive and split off. The EMS guys go to the suspect and we cops get the firefighters. There is nothing a cop enjoys more than messing with firefighters, and vice versa, and while I'm not in a playful mood, sometimes you can't help yourself.

"Hey, man, I think your leg is broken," the firefighter says, completely serious.

"Oh shit, man? You think so? Is that why it's facing the opposite way it usually is? That makes total sense! I'm really glad you're here to solve this mystery. You know, there are some detective spots open if you ever want to jump over to the blue!" I deliver, possibly fueled by pain, but I think mostly because I'm an asshole.

"We need to take your boot off," he answers, clearly not being a guy who enjoys banter. With no warning, he reaches down and grabs the boot, turning it.

"What the fuck are you doing?!" I screech in pain.

Looking at me like I don't understand English, he repeats, "I told you. We need to get this boot off. Your leg is swelling really fast."

"Okay, *doctor*," I retort sarcastically. "How about you go find a fire to fuck with or something and let the medical professionals handle medical shit . . . like my leg!"

"Are you sure? I have a nice ax I could use to get that boot off," he says, finally showcasing that dickhead-firefighter personality I knew had to be in there somewhere.

"Fuck you and the truck you rode in on," I fire back.

The approaching medic hears our banter and thinks we are really fighting. "Sergeant, please take away his gun and his belt before we proceed," he tells Tom.

"Whoaaa, what? Hey, man, me and Dr. Fireman—is Fireman medical school as long as real medical school or is it like one PowerPoint deck on a Tuesday—anyway, Dr. Fireman and I are just debating holistic approaches to curing a broken leg. We weren't really fighting. You don't need to take my gun."

Not completely believing me, the medic tries another approach. "Well, I'm about to give you a whole lot of drugs to make that leg hurt not even a little bit, so it's best we take that gun first."

Despite my protests, Sergeant Tom sees the validity in this request and calls Jayce over. "Jayce, they're about to dope up Tansey and he can't have a gun while they do it. Secure his gun, then ride with him in the ambulance. You are now his gun. Don't leave his side until you are relieved."

I hope someone tells me I'm a gun someday.

Jayce nods and then looks at me with a huge, shit-eating grin on his face. "Oh, I'll take care of him, Sarge." He leers at me and winks like a creeper.

"Officer, can you secure his gun?" the medic demands again.

"Yeah, let me get his belt off." He reaches down and begins taking off my belt and keepers. I wince in pain. Seeing this, the EMT hands Jayce a pair of shears. "Just cut the belt off to make it easier."

Jayce's eyes light up at the sight of the shears. He flourishes them like he's some kind of samurai or at least one of those hibachi chefs, and then dramatically cuts off my belt. "I am done!" Jayce proclaims loudly. Ignoring him, the medic secures my leg to a board so my injury doesn't get worse in movement.

Unhappy with no one appreciating his artful cutting and rhythmic gymnastics, Jayce starts cutting my shirt.

"Jayce! What the fuck are you doing? Why are you cutting my shirt?" I immediately screech.

"Shhhhh, just let this happen, we are fixing you, bro," he whispers.

"What? You aren't fixing shit. Stop cutting my shirt. Ohhhhh shit this hurts. What is he doing to my leg!" I ask.

"Tansey, stop being a little bitch and hold still while I cut this!" Jayce yells as the medic is doing actual work on my leg.

Jayce grabs a handful of my clip-on tie and looks me right in the eyes. Before I can say another word, he cuts the clip-on in half.

"What in the fuck, Jayce! What is wrong with you!" I shriek.

"Tansey! We are saving your life right now and you are being extremely ungrateful."

"You are acting like a child, and you aren't saving shit! Hey, Doc, get this asshole off me and please, whatever you're doing to my leg, just fucking stop!" I beg.

"Okay, all done, let's load him up," the medic says. Apparently during my duel with Jayce, the firefighters had transferred me from the concrete to a gurney.

"Tansey, what is your first name?" the medic asks.

"It's Eric, why?" I ask.

"Okay, Eric, are you allergic to morphine?"

Jayce interrupts with his hands on his hips like a superhero. "No, Doc. He is not! And I will be taking care of all his medical decisions from here on out. Sarge put me in charge, so I say when to pull the plug. And I say give him as much morphine as you can without killing him!"

Unimpressed with us cops, the firefighter medic ignores Jayce's antics. "Okay, yeah, that's not how this works. I need you to just sit over there and be quiet. Eric? Are you allergic to morphine?"

"No, I'm not," I reply.

Suddenly a commotion breaks out. I look up from my gurney to see that two cops are forcibly detaining a young black man. Apparently he emerged out of nowhere and started sprinting through the crowd of police toward the ambulance. I can't quite make out who it is at first, but then in a shrill, familiar voice, I hear "WAIT! It's me, Gary, I'm a ride-along!"

The two officers, holding him by each arm, look up at me. Realization hits me in the mouth. "Oh shit, I forgot about the ride-along. Hey, man, how's it going? Where did you go?"

They release Gary.

"Man, this is crazy. You said 'run' so I opened the door and I just ran! But then I got really lost and I had no idea what to do. I was just standing in the middle of a neighborhood with a bulletproof vest on feeling like a jackass. I came back when I heard all the sirens. Did he shoot you?" Gary spurts out, delivering four hundred words in about three seconds.

"No, man. He just broke my leg," I answer as they slide me into the ambulance. "Hey, we're leaving. If you want to go with us, then get on the truck."

Gary looks absolutely petrified. I feel for him, but not much, because the morphine is making me tingle. "Hey, bud, I have to go to the hospital now. You don't have to go, but if you want to, we are leaving now. If you don't want to go, that officer beside you can take you back to the station and get you squared away," I say as forcefully as a man with a cut clip-on tie and loaded up on morphine can muster.

"Is it okay if I leave? I mean, are you sure you don't need me to go with you?" Gary asks. *Very thoughtful, Gary.*

"Unless you're a surgeon, no, I'm fine."

With Gary bowing out, the doc shuts the doors and we head off to the hospital. The ride is a blur of morphine. I know they stuck me with an IV, because the medic missed the first time and I gave him shit about it, but the rest is lost in the annals of history as far as my memory goes.

When we arrive at the hospital, there's a wave of blue on each side of me. I realize they are cops. *Wow, why are they all here? It's not like I'm dying or something. Wait, am I dying?* They take me to the emergency room and Jayce follows. A small, Asian doctor cuts my boot off and assesses the leg.

"Looks like we need to amputate it, right?" Jayce bellows.

"No, but we do need to set this leg before it swells anymore," he says as he motions to other doctors. "Doctors, I'll need your help with this."

As they enter the room, closing the glass doors behind them, Asian Doc jumps on top of me and looks me square in the eyes. "Look at me. This is going to hurt really bad, and I'm sorry, but we have to do it right now, because of the swelling from the boot. I'm gonna count to three, okay? One . . ."

"Wait, Doc, what are—"

"Two . . ."

"—we about to—"

"Three!"

"Fuck!" I scream as I hear a series of pops and massive pain shoots through my groin and stomach. I pass out from the pain, only to wake up seconds later—and pass out again. The second time I wake up, I am screaming in agony, but the doctors are climbing off me and appear calm.

"What the fuck just happened?" I scream.

"We had to set your leg. It was really twisted the wrong way around. When the swelling subsides we may have to do it again, but I think we got it," Asian Doc says as if he were describing frosting a goddamn cake.

"Holy shit, Tans, that was the most fucked-up thing I've seen in a long time! I almost passed out watching it. Did that shit hurt or what?" Jayce asks with a smile on his face.

"Hell yeah it hurt! What did you think it felt like?" I scream at him.

"I think it felt like I need to cut these pants off." He pulls out the scissors and begins trying to cut my pants off.

"Ahhh, stop it! Get off me, you demented fuck. Stop cutting my shit off!" I yell at the man I once respected as my training officer, who now is acting like an asshole toddler.

Sergeant Tom walks in just as Jayce gets the shears all the way to my underwear. He is not impressed with our shenanigans.

"Hey, you two lovebirds. I need Tansey's gear so I can give it back to Property. Looks like he will be out of commission for a while."

Hearing that gives me immediate anxiety. "Sarge? Are you taking my gun too?" I know that sounds like a weird question to ask in this moment, but a cop's gun is like his baby. It goes everywhere with him at all times.

"Yes, we have to take it, but Jayce will make sure you get a loaner, right, Jayce?" Sergeant Tom emotionlessly responds.

"Yeah, I got him squared away," Jayce says as he grins and slaps my thigh, just above where my leg is broken.

"OH FUCK!" I yell at the top of my lungs, just as the door opens. It's the Raleigh chief of police.

"Well, that's not usually how I'm greeted, but how are you holding up?" she asks.

"I'm so sorry, ma'am. That was directed at him because *he won't leave me alone*, but I'm good, ma'am. Sorry I broke my leg and all, but I won't be out long, I promise." The drugs are really kicking in now, because I think I'm Batman and the city fucking needs me.

"Oh, please don't apologize, and please don't rush back. Just get better and take care of that thing so it heals properly. And you"—she frowns at Jayce—"stop messing with him."

"Yeah, stop messing with me!" I sneer at Jayce before returning my gaze to her. "Thank you, ma'am."

With that she jokingly points sternly at us, as if she were our grandmother chastising us for being bad, and leaves. It's nice to be greeted by the chief, even though that is literally her job, but for a young, patchless officer, it feels good to have someone at that level recognize you.

Moments after she exits, the door opens up again, and I look up expecting to see the chief. Instead Red walks in wearing her booty-showing workout shorts and a black tank top that reads I'M HIS BITCH in bright pink letters. She has a big patch of gauze on her neck.

I smile. "Real classy, Red. You are really the kind of woman a man could take home to meet his grandma."

She grimaces. "Ugh, I was wearing this under my gear, and because my gear was all covered in blood and stuff, they stripped me down to what I had on underneath. I'm not gonna lie, I'm a bit embarrassed."

"No, don't be. You look classy as fuck, Red!" I say as the morphine hits its peak, and her detective boyfriend enters the room, making her shirt that much funnier to me.

"Well, I was just checking up on you. Do you need anything before I go? They put ten staples in my head and a bunch of stitches in my neck, so I'm ready to go home and have a glass of wine."

"Don't have a glass of wine," the remaining doctor offers, but everyone in the room knows she's blowing that off.

I carry on. "Thanks for coming by, and yeah, there's one thing you can do for me: take Jayce with you." She laughs and waves goodbye. As they leave, I close my eyes and start to fall asleep when I hear Bruno's horrifically loud voice.

"What's up, fuckerrrr! Brought you a gift!" he shouts. The gift in question is my wife, Ashleigh. I can tell she's doing her best to hold back all the feelings.

"Oh, heyyyy, babe," I slur, feeling high as a kite. "Good news is that you only have to rub one of my feet now." Ash laughs and rolls her eyes as she walks over to me, gently placing her hand on my arm. She's always had a bewitching peace about her, and her touch calms me into a state of euphoria . . . or maybe it's just the morphine having its effect again. No, let's make this romantic: her steadfast love of me bewitched me and made me realize that as long as she is here, nothing can harm me.

"He's heading into surgery soon," Asian Doctor tells my wife. "Could you answer a few questions for us first?"

I watch Ash exit the room, leaving me with Bruno and Jayce, but before they can cut anything else off my body or say any more dumb shit, I pass out.

———

My eyes open. The last thing I remember is Ash leaving the room, but I notice I now have twelve screws, two pins, a rod, and a plate in my leg. There is a cast on my leg over all that. Oddly, there is also a stray piece of duct tape. I reach down and remove it, only to see that underneath it is a drawing of a penis. I replace the tape. I will find out later that Bruno immediately drew the penis, and my wife immediately covered it up with the tape.

I already know recovery is going to be torture. I'm going to need to do something. I've never been on the bench before. I can't just sit around and wait or watch television or whatever. I'm already going nuts and I've only been awake for a little while.

"Look at this as an opportunity," Ash says later that night. "You can learn a new language, read all the books you've wanted to read, maybe take up puzzles?"

She means well. These are things that she would enjoy. But I know they will kill me. I need a new challenge. I have to find a new way to push myself . . .

10

START WINING

’ve got it!” I exclaim to my startled wife in the other room.

It’s week two of my recovery and I am bored. No, bored isn’t a good enough description of how I feel. I’m yearning for a meteor to hit my bedroom so that the sweet release of death can end this misery.

I tinkered with my wife’s recommendations for easing this boredom. I read a little. I even messed around with learning some Spanish. I did not try the puzzle thing, however, because I knew that would end in tears. But now, I finally know what I am going to do.

Ashleigh walks into the bedroom with the face that she has on 99 percent of the time when I call her. It’s a calm face, bereft of emotion, but there’s always something in her eyes that belies the question “What now?” No matter. *She’s going to love this.*

“I’m going to study for the Certified Specialist of Wine Exam!” I excitedly blurt out.

When you tell your wife that you’re going to be a sommelier, you don’t exactly know how she is going to react, but you don’t expect her to laugh. Yet laughter is Ash’s reaction.

To her credit, the laughter is polite, and when she realizes that it cut me a little, she quickly stifles it, comes over, and sits on the edge of the bed to talk through it.

"Oh, honey, that's very ambitious of you, but that test takes a lot longer than a couple of months to study for. Remember when Dave was studying for that test? It took him a lot of time and he was already in the wine industry with a fundamental knowledge of wines. I know three months feels like forever, but it's really not. You just need to find something to do for three months until you recover."

I do remember. Dave, a good friend of ours, had dedicated two years of his life to studying for this exam. I remember hanging out with Dave for wine nights with our wives, and listening to him lecture us on flights of wines. The amount of knowledge he had gained from studying so rigorously for that test was impressive. I now have the time and desire to make that knowledge my own.

"Nope, I want to do this. I've been obsessed with wine forever and I already know a lot about it. We got married in a vineyard, for goodness' sake. We love wine! Think about how awesome it would be to study wine together; we could even blog about it. Team Tansey, babe! What do you think?" I ask, with the biggest smile I can muster.

"I think you have glossed over the fact that you'll need to taste [drink] a lot of wine while you are studying, and clearly you can't drink with the pain meds you are taking," said Ashleigh, offering yet another reason why I shouldn't do this.

"Good point, throw that shit away and go get some wine!" I respond.

Laughing, she kisses me on the forehead. "I'll go get you a wine book, how about that?" True to her word, she leaves the room, blowing me a kiss on the way out, and heads to Barnes & Noble. By the time I hear my wife pull into the driveway, I have already paid the $500 registration fee. My exam date is in exactly eighteen months. I've also signed up for the online Gallo Wine Academy.

I hear the main door open up and her soft footsteps head my way. I know what's coming next. Ever since I've been injured, Ashleigh has this weird habit of opening the door and sticking her head into the room slowly, so as not to wake me. She thinks she's being a stealthy ninja, but the effect is more like creepy Peeping Tom.

As the door cracks open and Peeping Ash sticks her head halfway in the door, I shout, "I'm awake! Just come on in!"

"Okay, honey. I just didn't want to wake you if you were asleep," she says sweetly.

"Oh, I've never been more awake," I say like I'm freakin' Morpheus from *The Matrix*.

"Ooookay, I don't know what that means, but I do have a surprise for you!" she says as she reaches into a black grocery bag. I have no idea what is going to come out of this bag, but I'm hoping for a new gun or some chocolate, or maybe a ventriloquist dummy. *No, the dummy won't fit in that bag. Also, why would she get me one?*

"Look what I found!" she says excitedly while pulling out a used book. *Not a dummy. That checks.* "It's called *Wine and War*. I found it at Pauper's. Looks like it's right up your alley. It's about how the French hid their wine from Hitler, and how POWs would make wine and stuff, under incredible adversity. It looks interesting, doesn't it?" she asks, her eyes hoping for me to enjoy my gift.

I'm thrilled! "Yeah, it actually really does! I'll add it to my reading list I've created as I study the Wine History portion of the CSW exam."

She looks at me sideways, with a little smirk. "Ha, you're still thinking about that, are ya, babe? You know me, I'll always encourage further education, but maybe you should just start small and join a wine club or something, and then build up to that if you're still interested."

Ashleigh has two college degrees. She graduated summa cum laude (whatever that means) from Florida State University at age twenty, then lived in France for a year. After she returned to the States, she took a year to chill (when she met me), then moved to Raleigh in pursuit of her master's in French language and literature. She even taught French at North Carolina State for a while. The point is: my wife is very smart. She fully understands the magnitude of the test, and until this moment has never seen me want to undertake anything remotely academic. She's trying to carefully protect me from my impulses without hurting my ego or insulting me.

Choosing to ignore her subtle message, I instead nod confidently. "I'm glad you're in support of the mission! I need some help with some supplies. I will need some note cards, a binder, some paper, and a sharpened pencil with a good eraser . . . please. Oh, and by the way, I signed up for the exam. I have two years to take it. It was eight hundred dollars total for the test and study material."

Her eyes go wide. "*Eight hundred dollars!* Babe, we really don't have that kind of money! You're on workers' comp and you're not bringing in any extra money from off-duty. This test isn't something you just study here and there over the course of two years! You'd have to really dedicate yourself! I wish you would have talked to me before just signing up and paying all that money!"

She's right. I know she's right. But Robin Hood didn't beat the Sheriff of Nottingham by considering the odds. Or by heeding Maid Marian. I'm going to do this. "I'm sorry, love. The pain meds made me do it."

Rolling her eyes, she can't help but smile. "You don't even take your pain meds, because you're a stubborn ass who enjoys suffering. What did I marry?!"

"Babe, really, I'll make it up to you by passing that test and becoming a Wine Jedi." I choose the word *Jedi* carefully, appealing to Ashleigh's nerd side, hoping to find a crack in her judgment of me and my decision-making process. It yields no results, so I continue. "All of your friends will melt in my presence, consumed with wine lust and dirty thoughts of me."

That is a fail.

"Eww. I don't know what that means. I just hope that you didn't just spend eight hundred dollars on a whim! Do you not understand that?"

"I understand your concern. But in the same way that I left the Army to chase you because I knew you were the woman for me, I know that I must pass this exam and become a master of wine unlike any the universe has ever seen." Staring at her nonplussed reaction, I realize I invoke our love story too much to have any effect on her, so I continue, hoping more words will improve the situation. "I promise if you get me some note cards and shut the door, I will get cranking! Now I've got something more to do than just sit here and watch YouTube all day!"

Expressionless, Ash leaves. She does eventually come back with all the requested study materials, though, and I am now off to the races.

———

It feels good to have a purpose again! I can't tell you how many wine videos I've watched at this point. I've been watching Gary Vaynerchuk's wine-tasting videos since before he was the godlike influencer he is today, so I started there and picked up his first book, *Wine 101*. Rather than take a focused approach to different aspects of wine, I try to absorb all of it: viticulture, viniculture, winemaking, red wine, white wine, sweet wine, fortified wine, wine history and theory . . . if it is wine-related, I am into it.

Even Ash is surprised at my intensity. I've drawn maps of all the wine regions of the world. I have stacks upon stacks of flash cards. And my approach is all-encompassing. I don't have a study area. I've built an intense multipronged study guide that includes all facets of my life. I've replaced the art in any area I frequent with wine maps and facts. Our coffee table is littered with wine literature. There are note cards in every room of the house—especially near the toilet. Don't you judge me.

But more than that, over the last three months of effort, my wine test has grown from a little mission that I created to what is now a family affair. Anytime we get into the car, Ashleigh reads aloud from my notes while I drive. When we sit down for dinner, she quizzes me on wine and food pairings. I don't fully appreciate how much it has taken over our lives until the day we are driving to physical therapy with our oldest son, who is only a toddler. Ashleigh, quizzing me as always from the passenger seat, asks, "What is the leading white-wine grape of Austria and Hungary?"

Before I can answer, Duke blurts out from his car seat, "Gruner Vetliner!" We sit in shock, realizing that he's right. Our one-year-old had not only said the Austrian words *Gruner Vetliner* correctly, but he said them in perfect context. When the Tanseys commit to a goal, we commit all the way!

Three months ago, I was a cop focused on being the best I could be, when my whole life fell apart with the breaking of my leg. But here I am now, and so much has changed. First, my son went from crawling to walking and I got to experience it. In fact, we kinda learned how to walk together. Second, the guy who did this to me has taken his own life in prison, which leaves me with a very weird and uneasy feeling. Third, I have developed a robust passion for and knowledge of wine.

And, as if all my wine work wasn't enough to make me happy, I just got the go-ahead to return to work! I admit that though recovering from my injury took a while, I actually enjoyed physical therapy. The therapist had set rehabilitation goals and the respective timelines for reaching them. That structure was something that set me up for success. I love nothing more than crushing goals. Even though I never speed, I'm the guy who has to beat Google Maps when it gives you the expected arrival time. And I have to tell you, achieving the goal of being an active cop again is huge!

You kicked butt, Tansey.

I'm full of positive affirmations as I pull into my temporary duty station—the Crime Reporting Center, also known as "The Cave." Typically, when an officer returns from a serious injury, the department puts them in the Cave to take bullshit reports like "a Nairobi prince stole my money" or "my house is haunted by evil spirits" or "my husband just farted in my olives." To summarize, the Cave has a bad reputation.

When I walk in the door I am so excited to be back on the force that I assume everything I've heard about the Cave is exaggerated. *It cannot possibly be that bad.*

However, through processing, talking to the others who work here, and fielding calls, my excitement dissipates. Something becomes very clear to me, very quickly: I hate it here.

That probably sounds harsh, but besides being a low-key position for injured officers, it appears that assignments to the Cave are more frequently used as a punishment for cops who got jammed up for too many complaints, or maybe wrecked too many cop cars, or got caught up in some civil suit or something. It is not inspiring. It's fair to say that when you are assigned to the Cave, you are working with either good cops who got hurt, bad cops who are being punished, or dumb cops who keep getting in trouble, and that's saying a lot coming from me. The place is a pit. I mean that literally. It's in a recessed part of the building filled entirely with a miserable labyrinth of dark cubicles.

Like Link in *The Legend of Zelda*, I now have a mission. To get out of here, I have to pass a physical exam that allows me to return to real duty. The test is like a poor man's decathlon. I have to do a one-mile run, a series of one-legged long jumps on the bad leg, a hodgepodge of shuffle runs and sharp pivots, and finally (and I'm not joking) I will have to take my shoes off and pick up marbles with my toes to prove that the aforementioned middle-aged man agoge didn't numb up my legs to the point where my toes won't work.

I am scheduled to take the wine test in eight weeks.

My leg is throbbing and I hurt more right now than I did after completing the Special Forces Selection Course, but the good news is that I am cleared for duty. I couldn't show the pain I'm in to the evaluator, so I kept a big smile on my face until I got to my car. Now sitting here, tears fill my eyes because I feel pain down to my bones. But fuck it.

Even though I was probably not ready for it, after two weeks of living in the Cave, I decided that I would be better off breaking the leg again than waiting it out. The one-legged jumps and the pivots weren't that bad, but that one mile of running without the muscle to support my joints was an ass-kicker. I'm gonna have to work hard to get to the point where I regain my status as the footrace king, but at least I am now back in the game.

On Monday, I am a cop once more.

11

RECOVERED

My lungs burn as I sprint through the swamp, dodging the low-hanging branches and prickly vines that have already scratched up my face, neck, and hands. That pain, however, pales in comparison to the horrific sensations running through my foot, ankle, and leg. Every plodding step into the deep mud makes me wonder if the bone is going to snap all over again, and every time I pull my foot out and hear the suction of the mud, I wonder if I'm going to leave my ankle behind.

This sucks. I guess literally and figuratively. Hahaha. I'm hilarious.

The Mohawked seventeen-year-old junkie that I'm chasing could have easily beat me in this footrace, since I'm currently only able to run at about 50 percent of my previous speed, but he made the mistake of getting off the hardtop road and entering this swamp, thinking it would dissuade me. Little did he know that I spent seven years of my life in special operations moving around in these exact conditions.

Nevertheless, as previously mentioned, this sucks. And it sucks doubly bad, because if I don't win this one, I'm probably going back to the Cave. Sunday night as I lay in bed, I was patting myself on the back for making it back to the job way earlier than expected. That was five days ago. Right about now I'm wondering if pride didn't set me up for failure.

When I walked in Monday morning and meandered into the gym, seeing Red, Serious, and Spoon in there already working out lit a fire in me. Instead of taking it nice and easy, I tried to hide my limp, and jumped on the treadmill. It's not that I went hard, but I definitely went harder than I should have. After only seven or eight minutes, I had to hop off and jump on the exercise bike, trying to pretend it was part of some kind of "routine" I was working on.

I fooled no one. My failure was partially due to my pronounced limp after my brief flirtation with cardio, and partially due to my wife's exquisite cooking, which had wrapped a nice donut of fun around my six-pack. Oh yeah, and one other little thing—my leg has swollen to twice its original size in the past twenty minutes.

As I limp to the locker room, feeling very much like a failure, I take some small solace in the moment when I finally sit down and feel the pain dissipate from my leg. I take a moment to remind myself that it will get better and concentrate on my breathing to bring my heart rate down, ignoring the jeers from Spoon and his compatriots.

"Looks like a fat guy ate Tansey and is wearing his skin as a costume!"

Yes, yes. Very funny.

"All Tansey needs is a parrot and a ship and he gets to be a real pirate with that peg leg!"

Solid 7/10 for creativity. 3/10 for clunky delivery.

As the insults come my way, I feel myself calming, but my ankle is really itchy. I reach down and pull my shoe off and my whole foot expands, giving me instant relief and sending a fuzzy feeling up and down my leg.

Damn, that does look swollen.

But the real problem comes when I try to pull my boot on. With the increased swelling, I literally can't do it. But I have to, so yanking and grunting, I keep trying. No one enjoys my suffering more than Spoon.

"Ha! Looks like it's back to the Cave for Tansey, he can't even get his boot on!" he howls out from his locker as he watches me like some sadistic voyeur. His comment brings out my greatest fear and I fire a volley back in his direction.

"No, fuck that, I will go laceless or barefoot before I go back to the CRC! Quit staring at my foot, you creeper. I'll tell your wife you've got a fetish." He laughs and tries to take a cell phone picture of my swollen foot while I swat at him from the bench.

Thinking through the problem, I loosen the laces as much as I possibly can and then stretch the boot with my hands. Finally I am able to shoehorn my boot on, but there is no way to lace it up, so I kind of tuck the laces into the boot, and since there is no way to tie it, I use black electrical tape at the very top to hold it in place. I am pleased with my handiwork and now it is time to head to roll call.

Maybe no one will notice.

Roll call is short and uneventful, until Ralph decides to be an asshole. "Hey, Tansey, show Sarge your boot!"

"Fuck you, Ralph, my boot is just fine."

"What's up with your boot, or do I even want to know?" Sarge asks.

"Stand up, Laceless Joe Jackson." Spoon snickers. Jayce starts laughing— no one loves roll-call banter more than Jayce and his laugh is contagious. When he is entertained, everyone is entertained. The room is now full of obnoxious guffawing and unruly banter. Sarge gestures for me to stand up and step away from the table where I am sitting. Now everyone can see my unlaced boot. Upon a second look, I realize that my leg looks like a really fat six-month-old baby with a slip-on shoe, where the fat rolls swell over the shoe, so it kind of disappears in the fat rolls, except my baby leg has the bonus of electrical tape wrapped around it.

The look of unbridled horror on Sarge's face gives me a hint at the words that are about to come out of his mouth. "Jeeeezus . . . you can't go out on the street like that, you need to go back to the doctor. Your ankle is not supposed to look like that, Tansey!"

"Sarge, it's just swollen . . ." I try.

"Meet me in my office. Everyone else is dismissed."

I hobble down the hall to his office. He wastes no time. "Shut the door. What's up with your leg?"

"Like I said, it's just swollen. I had to do a physical test Friday, and it took a lot out of me. I was sore from that and still tried to run a few miles on the treadmill today, and I guess I wasn't really ready for that yet. I'll be fine, though! I'll lay low and just answer easy calls. Just please don't send me back to the CRC. I can be an asset here, I promise."

There is a long pause as he considers me. I don't know what he is thinking. I hope it is about how much he respects me and desperately wants me back here. But to be honest, it kind of looks more like one of the exasperated looks my wife gives me.

Finally, he speaks. "Go disappear into the break room and don't go anywhere outside this building alone. If you get hurt, I will kill you. If that leg isn't looking normal by Friday night, you're going back to the CRC."

I can't hide the beaming! "Yes, sir! Thank you, sir! Seriously, Sarge, thank you."

"Whatever." He waves his hand at me dismissively. "Shut the door behind you."

I grab some ice and my study cards and head to the break room. I study for a few hours, then hitch a ride with Jayce to get Chick-fil-A at around 9 p.m. I tell him about my wine studies, and he is genuinely interested. Jayce isn't training anyone at this time and doesn't really have anything to do, so helping me study the rest of the night piques his interest. It is a nice little evening. Think about hitting Bed Bath & Beyond. Don't know if we'd have the time.

I lay low that Monday and Tuesday, and then on Wednesday and Thursday (my days off) I just elevate my leg and study wine all day. But there is no hiding on Friday night, and I know it. I skip the afternoon workout and get dressed just before roll call. I lace my boot all the way up and walk in tall and strong. Sarge looks me over and gives me the go-ahead to return to the street.

He does not assign me a beat. "Just be a floater and answer all the bullshit calls that flow in. Try not to get in too much trouble."

"Got it, Sarge!" I respond.

"And Tansey . . ."

"Yes, Sarge?"

"Try not to get into any chases. I don't think you quite have it in you yet."

"Roger, Sarge," I answer quickly.

"Tansey, I'm serious," he chirps, holding my gaze for almost enough time to make it romantic.

And that is my intention as I walk out of his office. By 1 a.m. I have answered all the little calls no one really wants to deal with, and I didn't have a single major incident. And even though I've barely done anything but walk around a little, my ankle is starting to complain. I have already unlaced two holes in my boot because the swollen skin was pinching up between the leather straps.

When the mild agony gets to be too much, I pull the car over, push my seat as far back as it will go, and stretch my leg toward the floorboard. I am denied the comfort I was hoping for.

Fuck. That didn't help. Still five hours left. Suck it up, Tansey!

Then the radio starts buzzing. No one answers. Everyone except me is on a call.

"Raleigh to any unit near Rogers Lane for a domestic between father and son." The radio pauses, and I know I am the only available unit. I take a deep breath.

Maybe it won't be that bad.

"Go ahead, Raleigh, send it to me."

Rogers Lane is a complex labyrinth of trailers. Nearly every street is a dead end. It's the biggest trailer park in Raleigh, spanning a road that is one mile long and a quarter mile deep, with a single-wide or double-wide, on lots sized 50 by 100 meters. Furthermore, the trailers aren't set up New York–style where you have this perfectly neat grid and it is very clear where every address is located. It's more like Boston, where every time they add another trailer, they just squeeze it in somewhere and make up some bullshit address that doesn't make any sense. Plus every trailer looks the same.

My call is for a trailer situated at the very end of the trailer park, near some woods and swampland. I vaguely remember having been there before, which is never a good sign.

As I get closer and realize it is the trailer at the end of the cul-de-sac, it comes back to me in a flash. The last time I was here was when the owner's then-sixteen-year-old son had lit the trailer on fire and then disappeared into the swamp before we arrived. The still-charred exterior confirms my flashback.

Fuck. Crazy Mohawk Kid lives here.

I know it sounds dehumanizing, but you deal with so much shit as a cop that you find a common language when you encounter people all the time. If they're nice people, they start off as "Nice flowers guy," and then you see them more and it's "Dwayne" or "Bob" and you have real human relationships. But when they're problem children that you're always fighting, chasing, or arresting, they tend to get descriptive terms so everyone knows who we are dealing with. Crazy Mohawk Kid was a problem. He was violent. He burned shit. He ran. He pretended to be hurt when caught.

I am nervous about approaching the trailer. Last time I was in it, I was investigating the arson. I remember that in the son's room, there was a samurai sword stuck in the wall and satanic symbols spray-painted all over the place. The father was an abusive alcoholic piece of shit who couldn't control the kid, but even if he could, he didn't seem to care about any sense of household discipline or pride anyway. The trailer is filled with old records, books, newspapers, and a series of half-finished models. How much of a loser do you have to be that your thing is building models, yet you've finished zero models?

Older, wiser, limping Tansey wants nothing to do with going into this place alone, and I call for backup and wait outside in the cul-de-sac. I know this is going to go poorly if the Mohawk Kid is in there, and I don't want to deal with that alone.

Backup arrives and we walk up to the house. We knock and the father bellows out, "Come on in, he's in here!"

Fuck.

We open the door, and hanging in the doorframe is a punching bag with a picture of someone's face taped on it. It startles both of us and we step back for a moment. Moving the punching bag to the side, we make our way into the living room. There is broken glass everywhere, and all the books and newspapers are scattered everywhere too. The place was already a shitty trailer that had been lit on fire, but this place looks like someone has overtly tried to make it as shitty as possible. If you paid someone to make the white-trashiest place on earth, whatever they made would not be as trashy as this house.

To add to that magic, the father is brandishing a frying pan and threatening to hit the kid with it. After a series of iterations of "Sir, I am going to need you to put the frying pan down," we get him to take it down a notch. Pleading with us, he starts to tell his side of the story, but as he does, Mohawk Boy lunges forward and thrusts his lit cigarette down into the divot between my partner's throat and collarbone.

My partner folds in pain at the shock, and using his cigarette gambit as his chance to flee, El Nino de Mohawk sprints for the gap between us. Lucky for me, my spidey sense has been tingling the whole time, and I have been watching the kid like a hawk. Diving for him, I wrap my arms around his waist and glue my face to his hips, driving with my legs and forcing him into the living room and onto the floor. The second he hits the ground, he begins theatrically convulsing and flopping around on the floor. If this is a real seizure, then there was nothing suspicious about the Trojan Horse, and Bill Clinton "did not have sexual relations" with Monica Lewinsky.

"Shit! He put a cigarette out on my neck!" my partner roars as he strips in front of me, trying to get his vest off so he can remove the cigarette that has fallen between it and his body.

"Well, shake it off and get over here and help me. Call for EMS. He's having some sort of medical emergency," I tell my partner. The second a suspect has a medical emergency, you have a dilemma on your hands. You want to be safe and protect you and your partner, but you also don't want to be a contributing factor to things getting worse. I know this and so does Mohawk.

I think Mohawk is full of shit and I want to cuff him. The Last Boy Scout does not. Against my better judgment, I defer to the Last Boy Scout and we don't cuff him.

As my partner gets on the radio, I lean down and gently whisper in Mohawk's ear, "I know you are full of shit but that's okay. After you get done at the hospital, you are going *straight to jail.* You're seventeen now, so you are going to grown-ass jail, not that pissant juvenile bullshit. And if you get convicted for felony assault, well then you are going to big-boy prison, so keep it up."

His shaking diminishes and he lies unmoving on the floor, frothing at the mouth. At this point I have seen several people take their last breath, and this isn't what it looks like. I just *know* he's faking it.

"Tansey, let's get him up and get him outside for EMS. They won't be able to do anything with him in this mess; they can't even get a gurney in here," my partner says.

"No, let's just keep him right here. He is trapped here, and I know he's faking it. He can't really go anywhere from here, so I say let's just let him lie."

But my partner is a Boy Scout and God bless him for it.

"We can't. This is now a medical emergency, we need to treat it as such," he says as the glow of the angels lights around him and gentle harp music plays to the heavens.

So against my better judgment, we carry his limp body out of the trailer and onto the grass to wait for EMS. Rogers Lane is at the far end of the district, in the opposite direction of the hospital. It is also littered with speed bumps, so I know it is going to be about ten minutes before EMS gets here—eight or nine minutes if they don't care about their vehicle's suspension. We move the young man onto his side and leave him lying there without handcuffs.

"I'm going back inside to interview the father and pick up the evidence," my partner says.

What? No. No. No.

"Bro, don't leave me out here with him! He isn't in cuffs! And he is totally faking this shit. Just wait for EMS, then we can do that," I plead.

"He isn't going anywhere. Just stay beside him and keep trying to talk to him. I need to see what-all we are charging him with before EMS gets here."

This is a dumb plan. No, more than that—this is as stupid a fucking plan as one could dream up. This is like some Day One Tansey shit.

But this guy is by the book, with no adjustment for reality. If it isn't in the manual, this guy shorts out. So you know what he fucking does? He leaves good ol' Limpin' Swolefoot Tansey with Mohawk Boy.

I try not to judge officers too harshly. That's the internet's job. But this guy works a nicer, more low-key beat than I do, and he just doesn't have a lot of time in aggressive situations. In his world, people generally comply. You would have thought the cigarette to the throat would have woken him up, but no. He is still a true believer.

The door to the trailer is spring-loaded, so when you open it and let go, it slams shut. As soon as the door smacks against the tin siding, Mohawk Boy springs to his feet as if Jesus himself has healed him. Off he goes into the night and toward the swamp at a full sprint. I run after him, wincing with every step, watching him get farther and farther away from me. I know I am not going to outrun him, and I know my partner did not hear us take off. I set my mind to just keeping my eyes on him, hoping that the swamp will slow him down.

He is familiar with the swamp and I'm sure he has a plan to lie down and hide somewhere. It is his MO, and he is probably used to cops never pursuing him into the swamp. Big mistake. As I said before, I spent four years in a Special Forces group in Florida operating in nothing *but* swamps. I am accustomed to land-navigating in swamps, patrolling swamps, and let's not forget, dodging alligators in swamps. This little marsh is child's play. Mohawk unexpectedly took me into maybe the only terrain where, in my current condition, I have a shot at catching him. I sprint into the swamp.

Which brings us to my current predicament.

I'm tired. My lungs are burning. And as the mud pulls on my ankles with each step, I feel like I'm going to leave my bad leg in the mud. But I'm staying with him. I *might* even be gaining on him!

"Raleigh, I am giving chase into the swamp adjoining Rogers Lane. Suspect has fled," I say over the radio, through labored breathing. With that I focus completely on the chase. I know he is unarmed, so I don't have to worry about a weapon. I just need to catch this guy or keep him busy until someone who is less injured can do it.

As we get deeper into the swamp, he starts to slow down.

He doesn't realize I am behind him!

As he comes almost to a stop, the slosh, slosh, slosh of my boots sticking in the mud makes the hair on his back tingle. He turns his head, displaying the full scope and breadth of his Mohawk in the gray swamp light. He looks like the bad guy in an eighties movie. The eye I can see goes wide, and he turns to sprint deeper into the woods.

But in his exuberance to get away, he doesn't notice the large drainage pipe only one step in front of him. As he takes his first big, powerful step away from me, he hits it and stumbles forward. Overcorrecting, he takes a big step forward, but his heel catches the wet swamp grass and he flies through the air, ass over teakettle, like Charlie Brown missing the damn football.

Slipping around on the wet ground, he tries to get to his feet, but I am already airborne, in what probably looks like a limping, pleasantly plump, beginnings-of-middle-age man falling on a kid, but which I like to imagine as a dynamic, awe-inspiring form tackle, worthy of Ray Lewis. I hear the breath leave his body as I make contact.

He rolls onto his back to fight me before I can straddle him to put cuffs on, but I already have a gift waiting for him. Capsicum covers his face, eyes, and mouth as I hose him down with pepper spray. The fight leaves him as quickly as it came, and he rolls onto his stomach trying to claw the pain away. I cuff him quickly and try to hop back on the radio to explain my position, but by the time I do, I see a white flashlight probing the darkness. It's my partner.

"We're over here!"

"I'm coming!" he shouts out.

On cue, Mohawk Boy starts convulsing.

"Oh my God!" my partner says as he arrives. "He's having a seizure!"

I stop him right there.

"I'm not moving him again or taking him out of cuffs. I don't care how much he carries on with this charade. They can come out here to check on his ass if they want to!"

Oblivious to the fact that this guy just literally did the same thing to get away the first time, the Last Boy Scout looks at me in horror as he realizes there's pepper spray in the air. "Oh my gosh! What happened? You sprayed him? Tansey, what the heck, man?"

"What happened? You made a terrible fucking decision to leave me alone with him, uncuffed, and obviously pretending to be a stroke victim, after I begged you not to! That's what happened!" I half scream.

Taken aback, he goes into self-preservation mode. "But you could have—"

"Let me stop you right there," I continue. "You were so worried about bullshit that you didn't back me in an area I have a lot of experience in, and we almost lost the guy in the process, and in case you didn't notice, I'm covered in fucking swamp grossness and poison ivy right now! And yes, I sprayed him! Because he rolled over to fight me thinking he was in charge, and I reminded him that King Capsicum rules us all!"

I have more in me to deliver to Officer Boy Scout, some of it out of frustration with his decisions, and some of it because the adrenaline is dumping fast and my leg now fucking hurts. Luckily, probably for both of us, Officer Quiet emerges to help us with the suspect.

Mohawk, after a few more seconds of pretending, gives up on the charade of the seizure and just starts begging for help with the pepper spray. Quiet takes him away and with a deep breath, I force myself to my feet. The pain rocks through my body as I trudge toward the car. As I clear the woods, I sense someone behind me. I look back. It's Officer Boy Scout.

"Bro, what are you doing? Go and help Quiet," I say, my ghast fully flabbered.

"Tansey! He is sprayed and in cuffs now. I need to get that cigarette before it disappears, and I need to question the father!" he says so earnestly that I hate him even more.

"Fuck that cigarette, you'll have a scar for evidence, and who cares what the dad says right now? Go back and help Quiet."

"Stop! Let go! Let go!" we hear Officer Quiet scream in the distance, breaking up our conversation. Moments later, when we arrive on the scene, Quiet is doubled over and the suspect is thrashing around. He has managed to front his cuffs and has wrapped the chains around Quiet's wrist, using it to pull him close to bite him.

I pull out my spray again and shout, "Quiet, look away!"

Every cop knows what that means. I hit Mohawk with multiple full-frontal blasts of pepper spray, just as EMS arrives. Together we all gain control of Mohawk, who kicks and screams the whole way.

We get him on the gurney, and the head medic, whom I will call Rebel, starts strapping down his arms and legs as he thrashes around like the girl in *The Exorcist*. In a final attempt to create chaos and flee, Mohawk lunges toward a female medic and bites her on the knuckles. With that, Rebel is done. He jams his finger into the space under the earlobe of the suspect, forcing pressure into his jaw and brain. Mohawk screams out, and Rebel snarls, "You can bite me, you can punch me, whatever . . . but if you bite or punch one of my medics, I will physically hurt you. Do you understand me?"

The suspect winces in agony as he tries to murmur the "yes," but that isn't good enough for Rebel. "DO YOU UNDERSTAND ME!" he snarls loudly. "Yes, yes! I understand!" Mohawk cries out in desperation.

With that, Rebel loosens his grip and continues taking vitals. I just sit there holding on to the guide rail, watching the spectacle unfold. I hate to admit it, but it is nice to see him finally get his comeuppance. Spray didn't work. Cuffs didn't work. Physical pain was the ticket, and that's not a ticket cops are allowed to write.

We get to the hospital and make our way down the ridiculously long hallway. I am limping so badly that the doctors come to me first, thinking I am the injured patient.

"What's going on, Officer? Here, have a seat. Oh my gosh! Let's get that boot off and have a look at that leg!" they say in a flurry.

"Oh, I'm fine. This is an oldish injury. That guy in the Mohawk actually needs the help," I say, pointing to the gurney. Dickhead is asleep. They look back at me quizzically.

"He put a cigarette out on my partner's chest and then tried to run, but I caught him. He began faking a seizure or something, but you know the game. Even if I know he's faking it, I have to bring him here."

He looks at the subdued teen and then back over at me. "Yeah, I'm not worried about him so much as I am about that leg. Let's take a look at that bad boy."

"Doc, I'm just recovering from a broken leg. It's my first week back. It's been a rough night. I just need to grind through the next three hours," I explain.

"I'll tell you what: he's strapped to that gurney and he isn't going anywhere, so let's get you both into a room, and we'll get your foot up and on some ice. You have three hours of shift left?"

I nod.

"Good," he continues. "We'll monitor him for the next three hours while you rest that ankle."

Even though I protest a little, I'm thankful for the kindness. The three hours pass uneventfully, and the oncoming day shift squad shows up at the jail to process the suspect for me so that I can get off on time. Back at the station, I limp into the locker room.

"Leroyyyy Jenkins!" yells what appears to be the entire police force as I enter the room. They are all laughing and looking at my leg.

"Only you, Tansey! Only fucking you could get in a foot chase with a broken leg on your first Friday night back." Spoon giggles, shaking his head in disbelief.

"Yeah, how the fuck did that go down? Was it that crazy kid with the Mohawk that lives down at the end of Rogers?" asks Officer Rabbit.

"That's exactly who it was," I say quietly.

"Damn, he's pretty fast! He's outrun us before in that swamp back there! How the hell did you catch him?"

A thousand options rush through my head. Tell the truth and tell them he tripped? Use bravado and tell them that, even injured, I'm twice the man they all are? I choose option C: keep it mythical.

"He needed to be caught, so I caught him. I guess I got lucky," I say.

"Badass, Tansey!" Spoon says, still laughing.

I get home, take some meds, and prop my leg up. My wife is not thrilled about the day's events, and she warns me that if I land back in a cast, she will deny me my God-given right to tender loving care. (That's code for sex.)

I look down at my sausage leg. "Good job holding up today, buddy," I tell it as I hop in the shower.

Toweling off, I tell myself I need to get to bed, but it's hard to relax, and I burn an hour or two tossing and turning.

Even though today sucked, I missed this.

My Saturday shift starts in eight hours.

12

CONSEQUENCES

I'm proud of myself.

It's not in my nature to hold back, to follow directions and guidance, and to take it easier than I want to, especially in the name of my own recovery, but that is exactly what I have spent the last few weeks doing.

It's not that I don't want to be in the thick of it, but after the swamp fiasco, I know how close I came to reinjuring myself, and potentially spending another six months or more healing. Hell, another major injury could end my career. Even if my department kept me around, I'm not sure my wife would!

But patience has paid dividends. While I'm not quite to the place I was before in terms of fitness, the spare tire has all but disappeared. I can see the top two abs, and the top four when I inhale, so that's pretty good. My leg is now stable. Not to say that it doesn't get sore, but it's more like an "I was standing all day without a rest" soreness as opposed to an "It might snap off and leave me with a stump" misery.

I still am not covering a full beat, but as of last week, I'm cleared to take higher-priority calls, which is exciting as hell. I'm also really appreciative of the guys and gals in the department. While they've ribbed me almost nonstop, they've also been very supportive of the need for me to step back and take it slow. I know how much it is against all these assholes' natures to do that, so I feel genuinely cared about, which has been really nice.

Needless to say, things are finally getting back to normal.

Although it has been pouring for the last few days, the clouds have finally cleared this morning, and except for a light drizzle and a whole lot of gigantic puddles everywhere, the sun is finally winning the war. I'm driving to meet Red for coffee since for once we're both on day shift and I haven't seen her much lately. It's only 6 a.m. but I'm happy to be up because the sky is pink and gorgeous as the light refracts through the haze left by the passing storm.

It's so early that the usual Monday morning traffic hasn't really picked up yet. I'm enjoying this morning's talk radio when suddenly:

"Beebooo-beebooo! Attention all Raleigh units in the area of New Bern and 440."

My adrenaline is immediately aroused from both the tone and the fact that I am actually on 440, just one exit from New Bern. Dispatchers and cops are almost always calm on the radio, even when shit is going south fast, so the fact that the tone is excited and concerned tells me there's something major going down.

"Signal 102 [shooting] possibly 103 [murder] just occurred at the Raleigh Inn Hotel. Suspect seen exiting onto 440 from New Bern towards Capital."

Oh shit.

I am literally right behind the suspect, one exit back. I activate my lights and sirens and mash the gas to the floor. As I kill the morning talk radio by jamming the volume button to off, I key up the mic. "Raleigh, this is 422. I am approaching New Bern Avenue on 440 and going to pursue the suspect unless there is someone else close to the scene," I say calmly, even as I can hear my blood pounding through my ears.

"422, continue on 440 in pursuit of the suspect. We have several units on the way to the hotel."

Game on.

As I feel my heart race, I begin to combat-breathe. I need to slow my heart rate and control my adrenaline so I can be effective, but it's hard when the speedometer now reads over 100 miles per hour. I wouldn't typically go this fast, but this is an armed suspect who has at least attempted murder and is fleeing a crime site. Of course, because it is so early, the road is wide-open and there are no cars in the immediate vicinity to deal with.

I see a car on the horizon and my eyes fix on it. I don't know if that car is the suspect or not yet, but it's a target to push for. (At this speed it's critical to keep your eyes on the horizon, or else you can overcorrect.) The car is moving, because I'm not catching up nearly as fast as I should be. Worst case, he's speeding out of his mind. Best case, I have my man.

The car buzzes by a semi and then moves back in front of it in the distance. The semi is my new target until I can pass it. A quick flick of my eyes to the right doesn't show any place where the car might exit, so it's purely about passing this truck and getting eyes back on.

As I close on the truck and pass the New Bern Avenue overpass, I see the blue lights of my compatriots taking the exit in the opposite direction, heading toward the hotel.

I'm going to get this fucker.

My speedometer continues to climb as I get near the semi. The mix of the screams of my siren and the roar of my Crown Vic's engine fills my senses. My whole body seems to be buzzing, but my gaze has to stay on the horizon.

I'm on the semi. I drift into the passing lane, just as the road changes from asphalt to concrete. Normally a car wouldn't be affected by that small a change, but at this speed, the rear suspension dumps out two to three inches, and as the wheels hit the ground again, they spin hard on the wet pavement. My rear end struggles to regain a steady posture, and as I fight to keep control of the vehicle, I hit a giant puddle from the previous night's downpours and go into a complete hydroplane. There is no controlling it. I'm going to crash.

I tuck my legs to my chair and cover my face with my arms in the "oh shit, the plane is going to crash position" as my vehicle spins wildly, finally connecting with a concrete median barrier. Thankfully, the crash isn't completely direct, so I bounce off after the initial contact and get spun around. Air bags hit me from every direction, and I smell the chemicals that propel them out. I bounce off the walls several times, with each bounce knocking me in a different direction, but also slowing the vehicle.

Please don't hit anything direct.

Somewhere in the middle of my spin, I see the semi coming my way. *Oh fuck, oh fuck, oh fuck.* Right before we connect, in what would have likely been the end of me, I bounce off the wall again, and he clears me. Finally, I come to a complete stop.

I have seen enough in my lifetime to know that now is not the time to try to bolt out of the car. Everyone has heard the stories of the guy who gets out of a wreck and thinks he's fine, and ends up dying because his spine was broken or something. I've never seen that, but I have seen a lot of people make their injuries way worse.

I wiggle my toes. Then flex my legs. Everything seems okay. I check my body, looking and then touching to see if there is anything impaled into me, anything wet with blood or urine, or any bones sticking out that I might not feel because of adrenaline. Again, all seems fine.

Normally I would call in immediately to let everyone know that I've crashed, but the last thing I want is for everyone to stop their pursuit of this piece of shit to come and help me.

Convinced that I'm okay, I slowly exit my vehicle. I move all my joints carefully and again examine my body. All seems as it should. Finally, I look up at my car. It's totaled. I give the engineers of the Crown Vic a lot of credit. Looking at the car, I would guess that the driver was dead. Instead here I stand, completely fine. Wild.

A couple of cars pull over to see if I am okay. I confirm with them that I am and spend a millisecond reminding myself that whatever bad interactions I have from time to time, people are basically decent.

A car screeches to a halt near me, then a guy rolls down the window and leans out.

"I'm fine—" I start, but he cuts me off. "That's what you get!" he chirps. "You were probably speeding to go get donuts. I hope they put you on foot patrol!"

Shocked, and then angry, I fight the urge to flip him off, but am distracted by the radio. Dispatch has blown my cover. "422, I see you are stopped on 440. Are you out with the suspect? Do you need immediate check-ins?"

"No, Raleigh, I'm good, I am no longer in pursuit. My car is code 7 [dead]."

"Ten-four, I see you on the cameras, I'm sending you some assistance."

I text Sarge that I wrecked my car but that I am fine, and let him know it is all on dashcam. Soon a tow truck and an ambulance show up, thanks to dispatch.

"Hey, man, you're bleeding," the medic lets me know.

"I am?"

"Yeah. I've got you," he says as he cleans off the side of my head. Apparently my head bounced off the corner of the cage frame and split near the temple. I didn't even know I was bleeding until just now. Maybe my checks weren't as thorough as I thought.

I watch as they load the remainder of my car onto the tow truck. I'm incredibly disappointed in myself. I was so close to catching the murder suspect. Maybe if I had been a little less overzealous . . . taken my time. If I had just a little more tactical patience, maybe I wouldn't be staring at a wreck.

Then the radio chirps up again, on all the cars now parked around mine.

"Beeboop-beeboop!! Attention all Raleigh units in the area of Capital and Peace. Signal 102 [shooting], possibly 103 [murder]. It appears to be the same suspect. Victim is 102 [shot] in the head. Suspect is leaving in a stolen, light blue, four-door sedan." As soon as the second dispatch is complete, the radio bellows out with responding units.

The sound of their responses fades into a whine as my world comes crashing down on me.

Oh my God. Someone's dead . . . I could have stopped it . . . If I had been calmer, driven better . . . if I would have just taken my goddamn time! . . . I could have prevented this—should have prevented this!

I want to vomit.

I've always feared shooting a gun without checking the depth of the shot—of being so focused on the person shooting at me that I kill a kid or another innocent person walking behind them. I imagined what that would feel like and it propelled me to train harder. I imagined that feeling of helplessness—of knowing you cannot take the bullet back once the trigger is pulled.

That's where I am now trapped. I know it's not rational, but I feel like *I* murdered the second victim.

The whole city is now trying to find the suspect: a twenty-three-year-old male from Southeast Raleigh named Kendrick Keyanti Gregory. Unlike other folks in this book, I'm using his real name, because he is a convicted felon with no redeeming qualities and I feel no need to protect him.

I want to be with my fellow officers, but here I am heading to the hospital to be examined and hopefully cleared for duty. When I am finally cleared, Red picks me up and lets me ride with her so I can be involved. I desperately hope we'll be the ones to find him. If I can bring him in, it might clear some of the pain I feel. Maybe that would avenge the victim.

But I know it wouldn't. I just don't know what else to do.

Kendrick has just become Raleigh's Public Enemy No. 1. Every cop, SWAT, and K9 unit is now looking for him. Cops quickly find the car he ditched, and they believe he is on foot, so they run dogs after him. Nothing. We suspect that he's hiding in someone's shed or backyard. It's Monday and everyone who would actually help us find him is at work, which makes things difficult because there aren't many people at home who might call in if they see someone shady running through their backyard.

Then, finally, we get a call.

It's the last call that I ever wanted to hear.

Kendrick broke into a house and raped a fifteen-year-old girl who was getting ready for school. He then stole a car from her garage and drove off, disappearing into the ether.

Tears run down my face, and I hide them from Red. The severity of my fuckup is now unthinkable. I can never forgive myself. One life ended, and one life forever damaged.

All because I couldn't keep my fucking car on the road.

The rest of the day and the week are a blur. I'm out every day, along with everyone else in the city, trying to hunt this guy down. After a forty-eight-hour all-hands manhunt, we have evidence he left the city.

He is picked up five days later in New York City, in a stolen vehicle with two stolen guns.

Here is the thing about these kinds of crimes: People always, rightfully, focus on the victims and their families. They think about how someone's life was inextricably destroyed or damaged by the evil that wanders our world. They think of the families bearing the brunt of the pain as they mourn their loved one, and at the same time try to heal those left behind. But the tragedy, unbeknownst to most, also spills onto the cop who found the victim, who saw the trauma, who didn't or couldn't stop the criminal, who fell short in keeping his community safe, and who in the end failed to serve and protect.

Many of us in the force have been in similar situations and have been weighed down by the critical events that surround us, by our responsibilities and by the instant decisions we make, sometimes in chaotic situations. Sometimes it is just not good enough and we are forever racked with guilt over our failures, our inadequacies, and our choices, and most of us spend our careers trying to do a world of good just to remove some of the residue of when we failed to measure up.

To this day, even when I see people make terrible, irreversible mistakes under pressure, I cannot bring myself to criticize them. I know how fast what seems like the right call when adrenaline is pumping can turn into the worst moment of your life. Besides, nothing can hurt them as badly as what they know deep in their hearts.

I let these innocent people down.

I wasn't the cop they deserved.

JUST A BROKEN TAILLIGHT

N ew Year's Eve is policing hell.

After a lot of hard work and pain, I am finally at 100 percent. My leg has healed nicely, the tire around my stomach is gone, and I'm feeling good. I am also supremely appreciative of the support from the whole team. They really did let me take a back seat and work the easy calls for the last few months while I recovered.

But now I'm back and I'm all in, and my return couldn't have come at a better time, because on New Year's Eve the department really needs all hands on deck.

If you take the worst Friday night you can imagine and inject adrenaline into its eyeballs and then have it do a line of coke, that's New Year's Eve. If a bad Friday night is a cat in a bad mood, then New Year's Eve is a honey badger that's been starved in a cage for a couple of days, then kicked in the balls, and then let out.

And you know why this New Year's Eve is going to have a little more zest to it? My mom wants to come on a ride-along to see what her baby boy does for a living.

Most people don't realize it, but citizens are not only allowed to but are very much encouraged to sign up to ride with an officer for a few hours. While I can't speak for everyone, my experience is that officers generally love to do it, because, contrary to what the media will tell you, most cops really do like to interact with the people they serve, and because a day in the car helps people understand what cops have to deal with on a daily basis. If you've never done it, I encourage you to sign up!

Sarge approved my mom's request last night, so she's coming along for the ride. The deal is that she can come for the first three hours, but I have to bring her back by 9 p.m.—essentially, get Mom home before everything gets nuts. I can't argue with that rationale. Things can get weird fast on New Year's, but more than that, since the killing of Michael Brown in August, two things have changed significantly in policing.

The first change is that the higher-ups, the media, and the politicians are looking with a magnifying glass at every case where a cop has to use physical force. You've all had bosses who have covered their asses no matter what, even when the stakes were easily managed and the consequences mild. But now imagine a world where if you let something go or if you make a misstep, you're going to be called racist, your department is going to be challenged at every turn, your name is going to get dragged through the mud, and you're going to have angry mobs to deal with for months. "Don't let it be us!" is what everyone in our chain of command is thinking and they've voiced that over and over again.

Don't get me wrong: Cops are supposed to do the right thing by the people. Our job is to protect and serve. I have no use for cops who overreact because they lack either the mental or physical toughness to do the job, in the same way that I am not a fan of cops who are cowards and don't get their hands dirty. But if you've ever done the job, you know how gray tense situations can be. One minute everything can be fine, and the next minute someone is trying to kill you. One minute, someone can be showing all kinds of red flags that they mean to do you harm, but later you find out they just lost their mom and are having an emotional breakdown.

Still, you have to make the best decision you can, very quickly, in situations that can lead to your death or injury or to someone else's death or injury if your assessment is wrong.

Often, these are the high-stakes situations. That's always the challenge: assessing when to protect them and when to switch gears to protect yourself. If you lean too far one way, you're a bully abusing your power. Not good. If you lean too far the other way, you are injured or dead. Also bad.

The second change since the Michael Brown incident makes finding the balance even harder: the criminals are empowered by the new pressures put on cops.

There is a misperception among people who don't deal with drug dealers and gangs that those involved in these criminal activities are not intelligent. Nothing could be further from the truth. In the same way that Al Qaeda and the Taliban rapidly adapted to the American way of warfare, they found ways to fight us effectively by learning our tactics and rules of engagement (what we were allowed to and not allowed to do). The problem children of the Southeast District have done the same.

Criminals now know that the second we put hands on them, the media and the higher-ups will look at the altercation to ascertain what the officer should have done to avoid the situation, or why the officer wasn't capable of deescalating it. The fact that a crime, often a serious one, was alleged to have been committed by that individual fades into the background.

This emboldens the worst offenders, and even basic things like asking to see someone's license will often result in answers like "I don't have to show you shit!"

Fun times.

But as Mom follows me into work, I know she's not going to have to deal with any of that.

As she walks into roll call, the team, with Jayce and Red leading the way, pour it on and make fun of me for bringing my mom to work.

The work challenges and dangers are the furthest thing from my mind. And even when they put the bulletproof vest on her and we walk over to my car, I'm in a really low-key and happy mood.

I'm healthy again. My parents are in town. My mom is coming for her first ride-along!

I'm going to keep these three hours really simple. We'll drive around. We'll grab coffee with the guys. I'll show her my beat and explain to her who all the players are so she gets the lay of the land.

It'll be cool to show her everything so when I tell her stories, she understands what I'm talking about.

And we do all of that. We even answer a 911 call that ends up just being a little kid messing around. It's a cool little day. I look over at my clock: 8:35.

"Mom, I think it's about time to head back. It's going to get busy soon," I tell her.

"Okay. But hey, before we go, could we stop a car? I want to see how you do it," she says.

Well, how can I turn down a request from Mom? I think we all know the answer to that.

I pull over to the side of the road and watch for minor infractions. I specifically want something small so that I can issue a warning and nothing more. I don't want to deal with tickets or arrests tonight. There will be enough of that when the alcohol starts flowing and the whole city starts making bad decisions. Plus, if I'm back after 9 p.m., Sarge will kick my ass.

Not even five minutes go by when I spot a car with one headlight out. The car passes me in the opposite lane, so I hit a quick U-turn and get behind him. The driver snaps his head back as he passes by, giving what we call in the biz "the ol' felony look-back."

Regular people who are just speeding or something typically look in their rearview and then turn into robots—face straight ahead, proper signaling, driving below the speed limit, and all that jazz. Regular people try to make themselves smaller. Nothing is aggressive. They want to show that they are not a threat. Criminals overreact. Quick motions. Aggressive head movement. Adrenaline spikes.

The car stops at a green light as I'm finishing my U-turn, as if to say, "Nothing suspicious to see here, Officer." I flip my blue lights on, and when I do, he speeds off.

Shit.

"Hold on, Mom, this guy's running from us."

"Oh dear, why is he running for a broken headlight?"

"I don't know, but I'm not gonna follow him too far with you in the car," I reassure her.

I hit my siren and air horn one more time in a last-ditch effort to get him to stop. To my surprise, his car jerks to the side of the road and stops. *That's odd. I bet this guy's drunk. Damn it! I can't tie myself up on a DWI right now. The squad will kill me.*

"Oh look, Eric! He's pulling over!" my mom calls out.

"Yeah, Mom. He is. Stay here. There's something up with this guy. I'm not sure if he's drunk or if he's wanted, but it's strange that he ran and then just stopped."

I'm worried. Running and stopping is a clear sign that someone is in fight-or-flight mode. Fight-or-flight is a dangerous place to be with a suspect. As they move through the time-warp continuum of determining whether fighting or fleeing is most advantageous, they become unpredictable. Things really can turn on a dime, and every cop has stories of buddies they've lost from underestimating the threat during this emotional phase.

I approach the car cautiously, moving up to the driver's-side window, and stand just behind the B pillar (the frame of the back door), trying to assess the driver. He is wide-eyed and staring straight ahead, avoiding eye contact with me. I can see the rapid rise and fall of his chest. His heart is beating through his shirt. I tap on the window with my small flashlight. The metallic sound startles the driver, and he snaps his head around to stare at me like a deer in headlights.

"Hey, sir, Officer Tansey with the Raleigh Police Department. Can you roll your window down?" I say in a kind but firm voice. He looks down and away from me, toward the center console of his vehicle. *Uh-oh.* Very often, a suspect will instinctively look at the location of where he has hidden any contraband or weapons. In many body-cam videos where we see police get shot, you can see the suspect looking at or even tapping the area on his body or in the car where the gun is the instant before he goes for it.

We all instinctively do this if we're not disciplined. If you ever find a kid with a mouthful of candy and ask them where they got it, the child will almost always look toward the place where the candy is hidden before they answer. If the candy is in their pocket, they will often tap or rub that pocket while they are talking to you (or lying to you) about where the candy stash is located. Seeing this guy look toward the center console is a major indicator that there is something questionable inside it.

I don't want this to go there, so I try to divert his attention with another question. "Hey, sir, can you please roll your window down? I wanted to let you know that your headlight is out," I say with a little smile on my face.

The man shuts the car off and then turns the key halfway back to get the window down. I see him working through his fight-or-flight response and I hope it doesn't land on fight. I can see his brain trying to formulate a plan, but my questions and requests, coupled with his rising adrenaline, are making it difficult for him to even focus on the simple task of rolling down his window. When people are having trouble with simple tasks like this, especially when you see them physically breaking down (sweat, heart palpitations, etc.), they are either high as fuck or in fight-or-flight. This dude is in great shape and he is pretty damn big. I don't want to deal with him high, and I definitely don't want to fight him. Neither of those situations tends to work out great for cops.

When he finally gets the window completely down, he again glances back at the center console. *No, no, no, buddy. Let's not do that.* Again, I divert his attention. "Sir, I just wanted to let you know that your headlight is out. Were you aware of that?" My distraction works and he looks back up at me. Beads of sweat are building on his forehead, and one droplet hangs precariously off his brow, deciding if it's going to ride the lines of his nose or drop into his eye. He hasn't said a single word. He's just staring at me, with the exception of a handful of glances to the center console. There has to be a gun in there.

I need to get him off that idea. Speaking calmly, I choose my words carefully. "Sir, is everything okay tonight? You are not in any trouble. I just simply wanted to inform you that your headlight was out."

The man begins to whimper aggressively in what I can only describe as the most stereotypical flamboyantly gay voice that you can imagine: "Oh my goodness, Officer! I'm so sorry, but I'm fucked-up. I'm reeeeally fucked-up." The voice throws me. I was not expecting that at all.

I quickly get brought back to the present when I see him grab his keys and attempt to turn the car back on. I reach through the window and grasp his arm. As I start to say, "Sir, I need you to get out of the vehicle," the man's head snaps back and I see rage through his tears.

Oh shit.

"Sir, pull the key out of the ignition and hand them to me, right now!" I command.

Glaring at me, he pulls the keys out of the ignition, reaches his hand out of the car, and as I reach for them, pulls his hand back and drops them purposefully onto the passenger seat.

Double shit.

"Hey, man, you're scaring me. Put your hands on the wheel for me," I command.

If there is a way for him to take his "gay voice" to another level, he does it right now. "I'm scaring you? You're scaring me! Cops are out here killing niggas like me, just like y'all killed Michael Brown. And there ain't nobody stopping them!"

This language, from the voice he's using, to the racial slurs, to invoking Brown, is all meant to elicit a reaction from me. And you know what? They are jarring. I have to fight the urge—whether it's to get angry or to be more lax—and just focus on the job at hand. Emotion is dangerous for everyone involved—for the officer and for the suspect. We're human, however, and it's a constant battle.

His eyes are filled with fury, and I know I need to take this down a notch before something supremely stupid happens.

"Hey, young man, that was Ferguson. This is Raleigh. We haven't had an unjustified shooting in over a decade. We don't roll like that. I'm just stopping you to let you know that you need to get your light fixed. That's all. But you're acting all weird and it's really bothering me, okay?"

He stares at me, considering, and then stares back at the compart-ment. I don't want that, so I play the only card I think I have left.

"Look, I know that you have a gun in that compartment, and I don't care. I'm not out here looking for guns tonight. It's New Year's and I don't have time for misdemeanor gun charges. I'll tell you what: how about you step out of the car, away from the compartment, and we can talk like adults about a headlight violation," I say in the most mild-mannered but firm voice I can muster.

Now, to be clear, I'm totally full of shit right now. I care greatly about whatever the fuck he has in that compartment, and I absolutely want to know who this guy is. Based on the way he is acting, it wouldn't surprise me to find out that he just murdered someone and I'm the unlucky bas-tard who happened to stop him at his worst moment. But one thing is for certain: I have no intention of just letting him go with a headlight warning. I need to detain him, because he is very clearly unstable and we don't need citizens running into him on New Year's Eve.

"Officer, why are you making me step out of the caaar?" he asks, really sounding out "car" so it lasts for four beats.

"Because I don't want to get shot over a headlight violation. Just step out, away from the compartment, and let's work this out." I'm not play-ing around anymore.

He looks back at the compartment and then back at me. He hasn't denied my accusation about there being a gun in the car, so I have to as-sume there is one.

"Come on, I'll even open the door for you," I offer.

As I begin to open the door, he stares at me, confused. He still has no idea what he wants to do.

"Ooooookkaaaaay, Officer! But don't you touch me," he says, wag-ging his finger at me. "I don't consent to you touching me."

"No problem, just get out slowly and keep your hands where I can see them."

Now, it's important to note that I have *never*, in my entire career, al-lowed someone to get out of their car without my assistance. It's a huge safety issue. Letting someone get out of their car hands-free gives them an open opportunity to run, or to punch you right in the face, or to create space and draw a weapon. None of those things are good.

However, in this scenario I know that he wants to fight, and I don't want that, so I am hoping he runs. Chasing someone is much easier than wrestling with them in the streets on the hard pavement. Not to mention that if he wins the fight, I might end up dead or seriously injured, leaving him alone with my mom. So, my plan is to give him a free exit strategy. He gets out, runs, and then I catch him, preferably on some soft grass, but in either case, away from my mom. Or maybe he's too fast and I don't catch him and we pick him up later. Either way I get the gun off the street, and he has warrants for his arrest. All I need to do to win this one is to get him to run, because I know he's not going to follow my instructions.

The second he's out of the car, he backs away from me.

Yesssssss! Let your anger flow through you. If you run, I will become more powerful than you can possibly imagine.

Okay, it's possible that I don't sound like the Emperor from *Star Wars* in my head at that moment, but that's the way I remember it. In either case, my plan seems to be working. The only missing indicator is that he isn't looking off in the direction he wants to run. Instead, he's still eyeing the center compartment in his car. This guy really wants to stay close to that compartment.

It's a weird feeling when you realize someone wants to kill you. I don't know this guy and he doesn't know me. But he is willing to take my life if it gets him out of trouble. That's not normal, even for criminals. When you give them running as an easy option, they almost always abandon the idea of fighting. Running from a cop could get you in trouble, sure, but not as much trouble as killing him. Not even close. I don't like this.

Making sure I am outside of "get quickly punched in the face" range, and with his eyes darting back and forth between me and the compartment, I try to get him refocused on me. "So, what's up with the light?"

That does the trick, and he drops back into the outlandishly high-pitched flamboyant voice that doesn't seem to match his body. "Welllll, you see, Officer, this car isn't mine. It belongs to my cousin, and she . . ." As he continues his lengthy soliloquy, I'm not really listening. I'm developing a plan of my own, and it starts with gently keying my radio. "Raleigh, I need a T-78 [check-in] to my 22 [location]," I say calmly. As I release the key, he pauses.

"What was that about, Officer?" he asks, his brow furrowing.

"Oh, they were asking me if I was okay, because I've been on this stop for a few minutes. I just told them I was fine," I say with a smile.

He stares at me for a moment, looking upset that I used the radio—as if I have broken some trust with him, the guy who wants to kill me. I see him considering me. I know he's wondering if I'm full of shit. Did I really just say I'm fine, or did I just call for backup? He doesn't know.

Quickly, he moves to the back of the vehicle as if he is going to run, but instead he stops by the trunk and spins to face me. Anticipating his run, I had already closed the space, and am now blocking his path to the driver's-side door. I've separated him from his gun.

Instantly, he looks defeated, like I have beaten him. But just as quickly as he seems to give up, he finds renewed energy. He looks confused and angry all at the same time and keeps pacing back and forth behind the trunk. Then his eyes brighten, and his fists clench, and he looks at me with vigor.

"Yo, man . . . Officer . . . let me show you the inside of the trunk. I can show you the wiring for the lights. Just let me pop the trunk."

Awww, hell no.

"Nah, man. You're good. I don't need to see the wiring. Just come over here and talk to me," I reassure him.

"Nah, I'm gonna show you my trunk," he says, determined. He walks over to the trunk and pops it. I quickly unholster my gun. "Sir, shut the trunk now!"

He flings it open and steps back. I'm now ready for a gunfight with my pistol at the low-ready carrying position. He glances down at my pistol and then back up at me, but doesn't follow my commands.

"Sir, that's enough! Sit down right now!" I command as my tone shifts from easygoing and humble to stern.

He looks pissed. "Yooo, I knew you was gonna shoot me. I want my dad! I want a black cop out here right now!" he wails.

"Sir, have a seat! I won't ask you again." Finally, the man puts his hands up and lowers himself onto the curb. *Thank God.* "Thank you, sir. Now, what is going on, my man? Why are you acting like this? I know you're thinking about running and I'm gonna tell you right now that it ain't worth your trouble."

He puts on a face that looks genuinely insulted. "Man, I would never run from the police! My dad's a general at West Point, and he's gonna kill me for running into the police tonight."

The situation is unnerving. On the one hand, he's saying a lot of the right things that tend to indicate he is not a threat, but on the other hand, he's setting off massive alarm bells. I calm myself a little more and try to appeal to him.

"Man, he doesn't even have to know. What's in the compartment? I know there's something in there. If it's a gun, just tell me. I'm just gonna seize it until I run it to make sure it's not stolen. If it isn't stolen, I can simply give you a ticket for having a concealed weapon if you don't have a permit. That's it. No big deal. It's up to you to tell your dad you got a ticket, okay?" He nods at me. "How old are you?" I ask.

"Twenty-nine," he responds.

"Yeah, you're a grown-ass man, so it's up to you what you tell your old man," I say, trying to reassure him that this situation isn't that bad.

In the back of my head, I'm pretty pleased with myself, because I know that I've called for backup and they should be here any minute. If I can stall this guy just a little longer, I won't even have to chase him, let alone fight him. What I don't know, however, is that the dispatcher mistook my calm voice to mean I was fine and not in any imminent danger, and had asked me if I needed a unit to come out my way. When I didn't respond, she assumed I was fine.

No one is coming to help me. It is me and him and a long dark stretch of road. So dark a stretch, in fact, that I have not seen a car pass by during our entire interaction.

"Sir, just tell me what you have in the car, and I'll get you back on the road. No drama, and no problems. I don't have time to arrest people tonight. The city is about to blow up with serious calls. Help a brother out," I implore.

"Okaaaay, I'll tell you the truth," he says flamboyantly in a way that is still unnerving. Looking over his shoulder and then back at me, he lowers his gaze to the road. Defeat seems to fill him. His hands are drooped over his legs, his shoulders are relaxed and hunched over, and his head is now bowed. There is nothing but silence.

"Hey, man, it's fine, whatever it is we can work it out like gentlemen." He mumbles at the ground just as the corners of my eyes squint as a car's headlights enter my periphery. *Thank God, backup is finally here.* I return my focus to the young man on the curb. "Hey, man, I can't hear you. What are you saying?" I ask as I lean in to hear better.

In my eagerness for my backup to arrive, I missed a tiny detail. As I had looked away to see the lights coming toward me, he had drawn his legs in toward his body, loading his weight on the balls of his feet.

Rather than stop, as I had expected, the car passes us by. It is not my check-in. *Where is my backup?* As I spend too much time watching the car disappear with 70 percent of my vision, I catch movement in my periphery.

I turn just in time to see that the man has launched his body into my torso. *Fuck.* He drives me back into my patrol car hard, bouncing me off the hood, and then using my bounce to pick me up and slam me down onto it. "How do you like that, motherfucker?" comes a deep, powerful bass voice. The "gay" voice was all pretense. But I can ponder that if I live. Right now I'm bouncing off the hood of my car, having just been hurled through the air like a child. Since this is a new experience for me, I am ill-prepared when he starts raining fists down on top of me.

I eat the first one hard in the face, and my vision blurs and sparkles tingle throughout my vision. The second one connects, but without the same oomph as the first one because in his desire to do massive damage to my face, he overextends himself. Feeling him stumble, through my blurred vision and the ringing in my ears, I shoot my arm past his extended shoulder and around his neck, trying desperately to choke him. My choke isn't good enough to stop him, and he doesn't have enough leverage to throw me again, so we sit for a moment in a lethal stalemate.

Action is better than reaction.

I let go to try to get the advantage before he resets. As I loosen my grip, he frees his head and hand and delivers a hard jab to my chin, right on the button. My legs go limp and I fall to my knees. Everything goes fuzzy, but somehow need keeps my eyes on him, even from the ground. He swings again, and for some reason known only to God, he misses, likely saving my life.

I lunge forward and wrap my arms around his knees, pulling his legs out from underneath him and driving him to his back. Through the haze, I crawl on top of him and establish the full mount position, known worldwide to jiujitsu practitioners and childhood bullies. Now, finally in the dominant position, I rain several blows down onto his face and head. Left hook, right hook, left hook, again and again, all the while yelling, "SIR, PLEASE STOP! SIR, STOP RESISTING!"

Whether it's from skill on his part or lack of orientation on mine, he deftly covers up and avoids most of my strikes. I probably only land 5 percent of everything I throw at him. The combination of my adrenaline burst, my many punches, and the ass-kicking I just took has me breathing hard. I stop swinging for an instant. "SIR, PLEASE COMPLY! WILL YOU PLEASE COMPLY?" I scream.

For one instant, I think it's over. He stops. Then, as quickly as he stopped, he grabs my wrist and rips it toward his face, sinking his teeth deep into my forearm. "Fuck!" I howl in pain. "SIR, STOP BITING ME!" I half command and half beg.

His bite gambit works. Instinctively, to flee the pain, my body comes off him just the slightest bit—just enough to create space. He uses that space to bump me off with his hips, and still holding his bite, starts to roll me. *Fuck! He's fucking gator-rolling with my arm still in his mouth.*

My choices are to maintain the full mount and lose all the muscle in my forearm to his bite, or follow the roll and give up my full mount position. As I roll through the dark night, I finally feel my arm tear free from his mouth. I know there's skin dangling, but I think the muscle is still all intact. I'm fucking pissed. Immediately I rain punches on him, delivering a haymaker to the back of his head, which rocks him but sends a snapping sound ricocheting off the cars and dissipating into the night air. My hand is numb and I now know it's completely broken.

Injured, but still in the fight, I watch as he gets to his knees and then to his feet, as I hopelessly try to hold on to his waist. Years later, I'll reflect on this moment and wish I had taken more wrestling and jiujitsu, but right now all I know is this guy can easily stand up, even when I'm holding on to him with all my might. Stumbling forward and dragging me across the pavement, he turns and begins pummeling me, trying to force me back onto the ground.

I know that if he gets me to the ground, I'll be dead. He's the better athlete and the better grappler. I have an almost impossible time holding him down in a dominant position. I will not recover if he gets one. I have to take the risk of leaning forward so I can get my feet under me while he throws uppercuts into my face. Tucking my chin, I explode up to my feet, eating two shots in the process.

Back on my feet, I go into boxing mode. Here I am his equal. We trade blows back and forth, and when the moment presents itself, I reach for my mic and attempt to scream into it. "Raleigh, I need help and I need it now!" But as I key it, he rips it from my hand, ripping my shirt in the process, leaving half of it dangling from my body like a budget Chippendale dancer.

Finally, the asshole takes off running. I tear the radio from its holster and, fumbling over the loose mic cord while I chase him, I repeat my plea for help through it.

But just when I think we're finally going to get the chase I so desperately wanted, he stops at the fucking car door and goes for that center compartment. *I'm not dying here!* I smash him through the open car door, keeping him from getting the compartment open. He turns toward me to fight, but this time I'm ready, blasting him with pepper spray. As I watch it go up his nose and into his eyes, I grab his hair, yanking his head back and pinning his chest to the compartment, so there is no way in. I jump on top of him so that he is pinned between my body and the console, placing us in another stalemate. Despite the misery of the pepper spray we are both bathed in, this time I'm fine with waiting.

After a few seconds, he tries to grapple his way out. I've had enough.

"Hey, asshole, I'm gonna get off you and just shoot you, okay?"

His weak, aw-shucks demeanor returns, but thankfully not his fake high-pitched voice. I'm happy to see that charade die. "No, man! Please! Please! I give up! My hands are up! Please, I'm done too! Don't shoot, don't shoot!"

I wait a moment, and before I move I find the right voice inside me so that when I deliver this message, he understands that I mean exactly what I am saying. "Listen to me. I'm gonna get up. I expect you to stay there until I tell you to move. When I do, if you do *anything* but back up slowly, I'm gonna shoot you. Do you understand?"

He nods from underneath me. "Okay, okay! Just don't shoot me, okay? Promise? Promise you won't shoot me," he begs.

I'm unwilling to commit to that. At this point I feel as if admitting I won't shoot him could put me at a disadvantage if I have to shoot him. I don't want to have to overcome any mental obstacles.

"I'm not promising anything unless you comply. Just get out of the car and onto the ground," I bark.

Slowly I release my weight, watching and feeling for even the slightest tensing of his muscle. He keeps his hands up. "Slowly start to move out of the car. Those hands better stay up!" I tell him. He complies. In fact, he complies so well that he almost falls down as he keeps his hands up even while he is trying to stand. As soon as his head clears the doorframe, I drag him by the head to the ground.

"Don't shoot me!" he screams again.

"Lay on your stomach!" I scream back. As he does, I straddle him in a "rear mount" position. I see my own blood dripping on him and fumble with my handcuffs, but the combination of adrenaline and my broken hand leaves the cuffs a puzzle I can't seem to solve. I look for my radio. It's five feet away. I have to get up.

"Look, I'm going to reach for my radio, and if you so much as blink while I do that, I'm going to permanently part your scalp. Do you understand me?"

"Yes, sir. I'm so sorry. Please don't shoot me."

As fast as I've ever done anything in my life, I dive for the radio, key it up, yell for help, and return to my rear-mount position on the suspect, the whole time screaming for him not to move. I cannot afford for him to find a second wind, because I will not be able to keep up with him a second time, and I do not want to shoot him, even after everything he's put me through.

In less than a minute, I hear the sound I've been yearning to hear all night: the sweet sound of sirens piercing the night air, wailing across the city. A few moments later they will be converging on my location, blue and red lights cutting through the night.

The first officer to arrive on scene is an older sheriff's deputy who was just down the road serving subpoenas. As he exits his vehicle and moves toward me, he sees the blood running from the bridge of my nose, and realizes that the suspect is not secure. He immediately sprints toward me, changing his demeanor, and as he takes in my battered face and my half naked torso, he realizes that this is a dangerous situation. As he arrives, he pins the suspect's face into the pavement with his forearm so that I can cuff him without the threat of losing control.

"Man, I'm so glad to see you," I wheeze. "My hand is fucked, and I can't get him cuffed."

He nods, eyeing me up and down, wondering what the hell happened here, and knowing it couldn't have been fun. "I got him for ya." He moves quickly to control the suspect, and as I hear him ratchet the cuffs down, I finally let myself relax. The ordeal is finally over.

On cue, many moments after I needed them, the blue wave swarms in from every direction. Officer Jayce jumps out of his car and yells, "Leeerrroooy Jenkins!" Sarge is close behind him and lets out a chuckle as he takes in the scene. Shaking my head, I make my way back to my feet, still panting. The whole fight lasted just under two minutes, but it feels like I went a full thirteen rounds.

"So, what happened?" Sarge asks.

I can't catch my breath because my lungs are full of pepper spray. "He was going for a gun in the center console," I wheeze.

"So, you boxed him instead of shooting him?" Jayce asks, perplexed.

"Yeah, something like that," I mutter.

Jayce shakes his head and says, "Hey, Sarge, that's all well and good and all, but I'm tired of Tansey's unprofessionalism. He isn't even wearing a tie!"

"Yeah, where is your tie?" demands Sarge.

I know they're in on some joke right now. Too tired to care, bent over with my hands on my knees trying to clear the snot and blood from my nose and face, I render the one-finger salute. Finally, I realize that the joke is that Jayce has once again cut my tie in half, the same way he did when I shattered my leg. *Yes, yes. Very funny.*

Sighing, Sarge says, "I'm glad you didn't lose, but in the future, he should be bleeding a lot more than you. *And* you should have more clothes on."

"Thanks, Sarge, I'll keep that in mind." After a moment, I hobble over to the suspect, who is now sitting in the patrol car. I open the door, lean in, and say, "I don't know what your deal is, man, but what you did right there—that's how Ferguson happened. You're lucky I didn't kill you tonight. We both are. Think about it."

I shut the door and stumble back over to Sarge and Jayce, who are taking pictures of my broken gear and the chaotic crime scene. It looks like a war zone, the ground littered with an empty bottle of pepper spray, half of my uniform sleeve, my radio, half of my clip-on tie, one of his shoes, and his broken watch and cell phone, all being lit up by the red and blue strobe lights of about eight different cop cars and an ambulance. Jayce's voice cuts through all that noise as he blurts out, "Hey, Tansey, good thing your mom wasn't with you tonight!"

My eyes go wide. *Oh shit. My mom!*

I run for the car. To paint a full picture, you should know that my mom's name is literally Patsy Thelma, and she is the sweetest woman on the planet. She is as doe-eyed as they come. She loves a little bit of excitement—but preferably from playing cards or bingo.

When I arrive at the car, my mom is sitting frozen, staring straight ahead out of the windshield. I gently pull the door open and ask calmly, "Mom, are you okay?"

She slowly turns her head toward me. "Did you shoot that boy?"

"No, ma'am."

"Did he shoot you?" she asks, tears in her eyes.

I chuckle. "No, Mom. I'm fine. He's in a cop car and he's cuffed now."

"I want to go home," she says clearly.

"Okay, Mom, I'll get you home."

A paramedic tugs on my shoulder. "Hey, Tans, come on over to the meat wagon and let's have a look at you."

"Yeah, okay. Hey, Mom, come on. I want you to stay with me." We all walk to the ambulance and climb inside. One of my favorite medics, Pete, is on board, which makes me happy.

"Tansey!" He smiles. "Good to see you . . . in one piece. Now, what hurts? Let's go head to toe, since we have a lot going on." He dabs the bridge of my nose with a wet bandage. It stings enough to make me jump. "Hold on, buddy. Almost done." He removes the wet nap and shoves two pieces of tissue into each nostril. My eyes swell up instantly. Even though the pepper spray has dried them out, they are now watering again. I lean forward, needing to sneeze, but my jaw hurts so badly that I know sneezing is a bad idea, and so I attempt to hold it in. That actions turns my slightly painful sneeze into a violent cough, filling my mouth with gritty saliva, mucus, blood, and some remnants of the spray.

I begin to spit out gritty specks from my mouth. "Ugh, what did I do? Lick the pavement?"

"No, buddy, I think those are bits of your teeth or something. Here, rinse your mouth out and spit in this," Pete says as he hands me a bottle of water. After I rinse, he feels my jaw gingerly and peers into my mouth. "Well, your back molars are a bloody mess, but your jaw seems to be intact. Just keep rinsing."

Just then Jayce opens the back door to the ambulance. Sarge is standing next to him. "Tansey, we finished searching the car. No gun in that center compartment."

I'm dumbfounded. "What? No gun? What the hell was he going for?"

Sarge holds up two large bags of powder cocaine. "Looks like he was trafficking some coke—and get this, he has no record and no warrants. This was his first arrest."

I'm in shock. The guy himself had alluded to there being a gun in that compartment. Why would he do that? While I ponder that mystery, Pete moves to my arms, where both elbows are bleeding from the rough pavement. My knees are also exposed and bleeding through what's left of my pants. When he's done cleaning those out, he grabs my wrist and I grunt out in pain.

He nods, and when he starts talking, I'm not sure if it's to himself or to me. "Yeah, it definitely looks like a boxer's break. We will need to go get that X-rayed." I figured as much, but I had been hoping for better news. I reach into my pocket to grab my phone. It's shattered. I sigh. "Hey, Mom, can you call my wife and let her know that I am going to the hospital and that we're going to get home late?"

By the time the ambulance is about to drive away, I get my adrenaline dump. But instead of shitting or puking, the dump comes out as a full-on Tourette's episode. "Fucking motherfucker! That cocksucking fuck broke my fucking phone! All because of a couple bags of fucking coke?! What if I shot that motherfucker in the back over that shit?! People would burn down this whole fucking city and some fucking asshole DA would make me out to be a fucking monster! Fuck this bullshit! MotherFUCKER!"

Sarge just stands there smiling with his arms crossed. I think he knew Jayce would have something witty to say about my rant, and he did. "Hey, um, Tansey, don't forget your tie!"

Just before he closes the ambulance door, Jayce throws a piece of my tie at me. I can't help but smile.

Almost as quickly as it closed, the door opens back up. It's Red. "Hey, Tansey! Daaaamn, that guy did a number on you! You look like shit."

"Thanks, Red. I hate you too."

"Seriously though, I'm going to take out the charges. What do you want me to charge him with?"

"Everything you can. Fuck that guy. He could be dead right now over two bags of coke. I could be dead. I've never seen anything like it. What a fucking moron! Plus, he broke my fucking phone!"

"Ten-four. Copy everything. Roger that," she says, mock-saluting me as she shuts the door. Pete taps the driver's window, signaling that it's time to roll out.

My mom's voice brings me back to the real world. "Hey, Ash. We are on our way to the hospital. It seems like it's only minor scrapes and probably a broken hand. I'll keep you posted."

I can hear my wife laugh on the other end. "Yeah right, Patsy! Come on home so we can watch the ball drop." I have just recovered from my broken leg. I can't be hurt again. As Ashleigh laughs, my mom starts to weep. I can hear my wife asking her to put me on the phone, but my mom loses all control, holding the phone to her lap, crying. I try to comfort her and tell my wife I will call her back.

Later that night they will confirm that my hand is broken and they'll put a cast on me, and when I get home, my wife will stare at me like there is something wrong with me for doing this work. But right now I can only look at my mom—sweet Patsy—and realize that she will never forget watching me almost die.

I love this job, but my family is clearly suffering and carrying a heavy burden because of it. I guess they always have, but this is the first time I'm really seeing it clearly.

I push that to the back of my mind—at least for now.

The next day I am not even halfway through breakfast when I am called in by Internal Affairs. They claim they need a report right now. Up until this point, I have dodged the cancer that is our department's IA.

Contrary to what the movies tell you, most IA officers are excellent. They have high standards, and they want to make sure cops do the right thing.

Not so with our department.

Our IA officers are more like the kids who got bullied in high school, joined the police force so they could bully citizens and power-trip, and then when they didn't cut it on the street, joined IA to bully the cops who *did* cut it. We referred to them as the Karens™. The Karens' whole goal in life seemed to be to nitpick, harass, and harangue officers that they selected until they destroyed them. A real fun bunch of guys and gals. And the head of this organization was a lady who was transferred here from the Parks Police! No kidding!

I have avoided the cancerous IA office up until this point, but there's always got to be a first time, and this is mine. Truth be told, I'm not sure exactly why they made me come in. The whole fight was captured on multiple cameras, and according to everyone, both my camera and mic make it very clear I did the right thing.

When I sit down, the IA officers are glaring at me as if I am a dirty cop who has killed someone.

"Hey, Officers, how can I help you?" I ask.

"Officer Tansey, we are really disappointed in your behavior last night. We are writing you up for discourteous behavior."

My mind races. I literally have no idea what they are talking about. "My apologies. I may have forgotten something I did last night. Was I discourteous when he was body-slamming me into the hood, or when he was trying to bash my face into the pavement?"

"Officer Tansey, we are not writing you up for anything involving your altercation with the suspect," they say, cold as ice.

"Then what am I getting written up for?" I ask, perplexed.

"When you got in the ambulance, your mic was still on. We counted hundreds of F-bombs during the forty-five-minute ride to the hospital."

I can't believe it.

"But there were no civilians there. It was just me and my mom and Pete, and I was coming off an adrenaline dump! You know how that is," I start, but I can see in their eyes that they don't know how it is. These nerds sat there and listened to forty-five minutes of conversation, in the ambulance, immediately following my ordeal, and counted F-bombs! Swears that were being delivered to no one, moments after I had fought for my life!

But they don't care, and I shouldn't be surprised.

It is common knowledge that the Karens always get involved with high-profile incidents. It doesn't matter what the outcome of the case is, if you go to IA for any reason, it seems they make sure you leave with some form of negative paperwork—some way they would have done it better. It is a total power flex.

As I drive home that day, fuming at the interaction with IA, wondering if IA parents go home and tell war stories about counting F-bombs or checking to see if officers have properly shined their shoes, I come to a realization.

Maybe the job is wearing on me a little too.

14

TUBE TOPS AND PUSSY BELTS

E verybody loves a raid!

Now, I know I've gotten all kinds of injuries, like broken bones, and been beat up. I've upset my family, and generally have been having a hard time lately, but tonight, only a couple of days out from getting my cast off, I got assigned to a raid!

SWAT is the main effort for the raid, with support from federal agents. We're hitting a nightclub that has been secretly operating as a strip club and brothel, with drugs being sold over the bar counter. You know . . . just to stack up another criminal charge.

The operation plan is simple enough. Undercover agents are walking in, buying some dope, getting a lap dance, and recording a *spoken deal* for a blowy or a handy. They don't get to actually go through with it, because undercover work isn't quite that fun, but still . . . it could be worse than a free lap dance. Once the deal is struck, the SWAT team will make entry and detain all personnel inside. I'll be in the back door (that's what she said) in case anyone tries to squirt out (that's what she said). Once we have the situation under control, the detectives will go through the monumental task of interviewing everyone and determining who gets arrested and who gets to go home.

The undercover guys have been in there a little while, so our team meanders to the back of the building, trying to generally be innocuous. It doesn't take long for the drugs to be purchased and for a couple of nice young ladies to agree to some illegal sexual activity. Sadly, no one makes a run for it, and in short order the whole thing is over, leaving us with 113 people detained inside.

Now we have to identify every person present, determine their involvement, and check to see if they have any outstanding warrants. Basically, we need to figure out who is a criminal, and who is just a person hanging out at a club that happens to also have an insidious and dark criminal underbelly. That last line was overly dramatic, but I enjoyed writing it.

Due to my experience working in the SED with prostitutes on the daily, I am assigned to question the ladies suspected of prostitution here. For me this is an easy task, and not awkward, but for a lot of people it's challenging. People are people, and sometimes cops forget that. No one starts out wanting to be a prostitute, and everyone is the hero of their own story, so being kind and professional is critical. Otherwise you will absolutely offend people and then they won't want to talk to you. From experience, I know the right questions to ask and how to use the proper lingo.

A detective guides me through the club, down various hallways and up a small flight of stairs to a half wall balcony. The room is set up with shitty drywall cubicles, built as sort of a poor man's series of private rooms. This is where the private lap dances and more nefarious activity take place. Each cubicle has a lady or two in it, waiting.

If you've ever been in a club at the end of the night when the lights come on, you know that the illusion of cool and fancy disappears. All of a sudden you see the spills, the grime, and the mess. The pictures that looked so cool under dim lights and black lights are actually pretty basic and cheap. Even the people look different. The dim light made their skin look perfect and smooth, but with the lights on you see the bags under the dudes' eyes, and makeup caked on the girls. The illusion is busted. So it is with these ladies. There's lots of flesh, very little clothing, and even fewer teeth. I feel bad for them, and whatever happened along the way that got them to this point. I'm sure they did not plan on ending up here. But here they are.

I escort the first two ladies, who are both wearing tube tops and "pussy belts" (pussy belts are glorified tube tops that strippers wear to barely cover their nether regions), outside of their cubicle so I can question them privately in the presence of a female officer. My partner for this interrogation is an officer from the Downtown District, who thankfully is also used to dealing with prostitutes.

Separating the women so they can't influence each other, we sit down and talk to each of them about what has been happening. They both admit to lap dances, but not to prostitution. The first woman immediately pops up on our system as having warrants out for her arrest. We cuff her and escort her to the team outside. The second woman, however, is a ghost. Not only do we not see her in our system, but we don't see her in any system. No license. No data. Nothing.

Typically, when we come up with nothing, we suspect they are giving us false information, but hey, maybe we made a mistake. "Ma'am, can you give me your birthday again? You're not coming up in our system, and I may have heard the date wrong," I say, knowing I did not get the date wrong.

"Sure," she answers. "February 19, 1987." That's absolutely not the date she gave me before. In fact, the only thing that is the same as the first time is the year. Now I know she is lying.

I take a deep breath as I stare at her. I'm not in any way frustrated, but I am using it to build tension for the moment.

"Ma'am, I'm not a rookie cop, and this is not my first rodeo. I know you aren't having a good night but let me assure you, it can get worse. I know you gave me a fake name and birth date. I've got a detective bringing me a fingerprint reader, and if it comes back that you aren't who you say you are, I'm gonna tack on the charge of Delaying an Investigation to whatever pending warrants you may have. So, I'll give you one more opportunity to come clean and give me your real name and info. Really, there's no reason to take on any additional charges. Do you know what I'm saying, ma'am? The game is over."

Fidgeting around and looking from me to my partner, she makes her decision. "Okay, I'll give you my real info. My name is Crystal Honeycutt. Honestly, I'll just tell you . . . I got warrants out for my arrest . . . for assault."

Crystal Honeycutt? Sometimes, when I meet people in bad situations, I blame the parents. You're gonna name your kid Crystal Honeycutt and not expect her to end up a stripper? Why not Chastity Sugarpants? Why not Cherry Loverboy? Why not Stripper McStripface?

"Thank you, Crystal. I appreciate you being honest." We run her name and date of birth and her name is, in fact, Crystal Honeycutt. Once we see the warrants pop up, my partner pats her down, cuffs her, and walks her to the patrol car as the van is already full.

On the drive, as we head to the jail for processing, Crystal explains to me that this is the final straw. She's done living the life of a call girl and stripper. "I have a daughter and my biggest fear is that she will end up like Mom. I don't want this life for her . . ." she says, trailing off, reflective.

I look at her in my rearview mirror. She's about my age. I know the challenges of paying the bills, especially with kids, and I'm lucky enough to have a tremendous wife and a good job. It's still hard sometimes. I have tremendous empathy for her, and if I were a betting man, I'd think she truly believes that this is the end. Whether she lives up to her promise to herself, I can't tell you. Criminals tend to go back to crime. Nevertheless, she's very polite and courteous, and seems like a decent person. I'm rooting for her.

When we get to the jail it's a fucking madhouse. It's Friday night, and a full moon, so all the crazies are out. That probably sounds silly, right? It did to me the first time another cop told me that full moons bring scary results. Now, I'm not into astrological mumbo jumbo, but ask any cop and they will confirm: full moons bring out some real shit. Not werewolves crazy, but dudes who think they're werewolves! Oh yeah, I've seen that.

I sit Crystal down on the center row of stainless-steel benches so that I can get going on my paperwork.

"Officer Tansey? I need to pee," she calls out in her dripping-with-honey stripper voice. As I said earlier, this is not my first rodeo.

"Okay, Crystal, no worries. This paperwork will only take me like two more minutes, then one of the jail staff is gonna give you a quick search and take your cuffs off. But we can't take your cuffs off until you've been searched here. That's the rule, okay? So just hold it for like five more minutes."

The jail staff supervisor meanders over looking at me like I'm a douchebag, and then she chimes into the conversation: "She ain't wearing any clothes! Take that poor girl's cuffs off and let her go to the bathroom. What could she possibly hide in that outfit?"

Every nightmare story that you hear as a cop starts just like this—with an exception to the safety protocol because you don't believe there is a threat. Now, don't get me wrong, I don't think Crystal is going to do anything, but why take that risk? "Um . . . I'm not going to take off her cuffs and break *your* policy but if you want to, by all means do. This is your world, I'm only visiting."

The supervisor starts to walk over to Crystal and fidget with her cuffs.

"Thank you, Deputy. This officer's been a real asshole to me all night," Crystal fires at me.

My jaw hits the ground. "What? I was nothing but polite and courteous to you this entire time!" I say, completely flummoxed.

The supervisor smiles at her sweetly. "Well, we aren't assholes here, and we will get you out of those cuffs so you can use the restroom."

Just like that, the supervisor has won over the whole room. Every arrestee is now staring at me like I am a huge dick. I feel their silent applause as the deputy, reveling in undermining me, removes the keys from her waist to free Ms. Honeycutt from her cuffs.

Jail deputies have a reputation for hating their jobs, especially the in-processing deputies. And who can blame them? They constantly deal with intoxicated jerks and tweaking, agitated asshats. Crystal seems harmless, and this is her chance to get a little positive feedback in her miserable job while flexing a little power. This is her world, after all, not mine.

As she finds her key, she holds it up for all to see, like He-Man summoning the power of Castle Grayskull. *I HAVE THE POWER!* With a dramatic flourish, she uncuffs Crystal, looking around the room so she can absorb their adulation. Then, taking her eyes off Crystal, she grabs her radio. "Can I get two female deputies over here to escort a detainee to the restroom?"

Whatever. Let me finish this paperwork and get out of here.

As I get to the last page, a gentleman from the third row pipes up. "Excuse me, Officer?"

Oh here we go! Everyone is going to have to pee now. Great job, lady. I hold up a finger to pause him. "One sec, man." He pipes up again, this time urgently. "HEY, COP! This woman is tryna do something!"

I look over just in time to see Crystal pull a pistol out of her hair. I see her. She sees me. Her eyes go wide. She tries to draw on me, but the gun is stuck in her weave. *Oh fuck, oh fuck, oh fuck!* I have no options. I don't have my gun because no one is allowed to have a gun in the jail. I have to close the distance or get shot, and I am not about to have "Officer Tansey was killed by renowned low-budget stripper Crystal Honeycutt" in my obituary. The inmates scream, trying to get away from her, as I lunge toward her. I have no plan other than speed. To borrow from everyone's favorite naval aviator, Maverick, "You don't have time to think. If you think, you're dead."

I'm almost in arm's reach as I watch her free the last of the gun from her hair. With every ounce of energy I have, I try to beat that gun from pointing at me and let my hands fly. A punch would take too long from my running posture, and since my hand is already swinging up as I sprint, I use the momentum to let loose the biggest slap I can muster. My hand makes a loud, fleshy smacking sound against her cheek, propelling her violently off the back of the bench and onto the ground. The gun launches out of her hand and slides across the room, right past every inmate in the place, their eyes following it the whole way, until it finally comes to a standstill.

Oh shit. Now, I have no idea who is in this room. Are they here for just being drunk, or are they drug dealers, or are they murderers? I have no idea. What I do know is that in a room like this, where no guns are allowed and no one wants to be here, a gun just lying there on the ground is like a raw steak in a lion's cage. I run toward the gun and dive down on it like a football player trying to recover a fumble. Relief fills me as I feel my hands wrap around it, and, returning to my feet, I shove the gun into my waistband, scanning the room in case any of the other arrestees have the brilliant idea of getting to it and killing me.

But no one moves a muscle. They all just stare at me in shock. Finally, a deputy's voice rings out: "Who searched her!?"

"No one searched her in here. We patted her down on the street, but we didn't search her hair!" I half scream, frustrated as hell.

"Well, who searched her in here?!"

"No one! Your supervisor just took her out of cuffs so she could pee! You guys haven't searched her yet!"

It is too late. The supervisor has already dipped out of the room and, literally as I was fighting for my life, was on the phone with our leadership, putting all the blame on us to cover her own ass. This was a dream call for the Karens. I am already smoldering with anger, at her, at the conversation I know I will have with them. I'll bet my next three paychecks that not a single Karen has ever had to search a half naked girl's hair even once in their careers, but I'm sure they will have tons of opinions about how it should have been done. But that's not even why I hate them. Good cops make mistakes every day. The job moves too fast for them not to. But the Karens delight at the opportunity to punish them for it.

I spend all night expecting a call from IA. It never comes. Instead, when the news comes on the next day, my female partner from the raid is on the news, being dragged. There is no mention of the club raid, or the many charges brought against it, only that a police officer allowed a suspect into the jail with a gun. No mention of the fact that the jail staff failed to search the suspect before uncuffing her.

Why wasn't I named as well? Guilt washes over me. I feel terrible. I find her phone number, as she had listed herself as the arresting officer on our documentation, and give her a call.

"Hey, what the fuck! I just saw the news. They outed your name! Why didn't they list my name, or the jail staff? What can I do to help?" My voice is cracking, because this is so unjust.

"I knew if I mentioned your name to IA that they would call you in too, and you would try to take all the responsibility, because that's your MO. They'd just write us both up, and they already don't like you. I figured there was no need to bring two of us down for something so stupid, so I left you out of it."

In the world of policing, I know a lot of good cops. But even the best cops don't like to take blame they don't deserve, and certainly not all of it. In a perfect world, would she have found the gun in her hair? Yes, of course. But in a perfect world, there wouldn't be one female cop searching every woman we detained in front of the club. Also, do you want to be the person asking someone to remove their wig so you can search it? Would that be seen as offensive? Nothing is easy in this line of work, and at the end of the day, she was cuffed and ready for the jail search when we handed her over. And the jail is tasked with a deep search starting from the hair and going all the way to the toes. They didn't do it.

The amount of blame that my partner deserves is minimal at best, yet here she is, shouldering all of it. By doing so she brings a dark mark on her name, prolonging any future promotion and putting her in the crosshairs of the Karens and the city manager. She could have thrown me or the jail supervisor under the bus, but she chose the "death before dishonor" route. It was utterly selfless, kind, and full of character.

She's incredible. They'll never promote her.

15

THE WAR WE CANNOT WIN

The sun warms the back of my neck as I hit the second mile of my run. It's an absolutely beautiful day, and the light breeze in my face fills my lungs with air just crisp enough to make me feel good about life, and just warm enough that I'm not feeling the burn, even when I push up the hills. I'm feeling particularly good about life today, so I'm timing myself for the first time since the broken leg. My robotic ankle has been getting the job done, and it's finally time to see where I stand.

As my phone tells me I'm at the 1.25-mile mark, gently interrupting the motivating beats of Rob Bailey and the hustle standard that I'm listening to, I get ready to push even more. I'm feeling great! Then the music stops. I look down and see that Bruno is calling me. I ignore it and get back into the moment. *He probably wants to link up tonight for a K9 mission. I'll call him back after my run.*

Moments later, the call pops up again.

Aggravated, I answer the call, about to tell him I will call him back, but before I can say anything, he blurts out, "Tansey! Where are you?" There is a decided note of panic in his voice. Something is wrong. I stop running.

"I'm on a run near my house. What's up?" I ask, concerned.

"Thor is in a shoot-out on Bragg Street. Sounds like he has one suspect down, but I don't know anything else. I'm en route to him now, as is the entire city."

Not good.

"I'm like a mile out, but I'll get moving and see you soon." Not waiting for a response, I end the call and don't even bother to put the music back on. I just put my head down and run as hard as I can, beating my run out by almost ninety seconds.

I throw the door open to my house, soaking wet, and still gross, sweating and breathing hard, I throw my uniform on in the middle of the living room while I simultaneously brief Ash about what is going on.

Thor is my boy. His children are my godchildren. His family is my family. And I don't know where he's at, if he's hurt, if the threat has passed, or anything.

Thor is a member of C-squad, our sister squad. I don't know how other police departments do it, but in the SED, you and your sister squad share a work calendar. If we are on nights, then C is on days, and vice versa. We patrol the same streets, know the same members of the community, deal with the same criminals, relieve each other daily, and back each other up in times of emergency. C-squad is the other side of our coin.

Think of it like when you're in a restaurant and the nice lady who has been serving you is replaced and you get the ol' "Hi, I'm Jennifer, and I'll be your new server for this evening. Mary's shift ended." It's the same with us, except it's more like "Hi, I'm Officer Tansey, and I'll be the one taking you to jail. Thor's shift has ended."

I'm naming him Thor for this book because if they hadn't picked Chris Hemsworth to play the God of Thunder in the Marvel movies, he would have been their next choice. He's insanely fit, is of Nordic ancestry, and looks like he could very well be the Thunder God. Also, he has a tattoo of Thor's hammer on his arm and is enamored with all things Norse. So much so that the last time I was at his house, his daughter was brandishing a toy Shera sword and playing "Berserkers."

Thor had just been picked up for SWAT but hadn't officially transferred yet, so he is on the line for just a couple more weeks. Most officers take it easy and fly under the radar until a transfer is complete, but not Thor. He's always all in. If there is a bad guy to catch, he will give it all he has to catch him.

And if there was ever a man that God designed for the purpose of hunting bad men, it's Thor. At 5'9" and 198 pounds of pure muscle, he looks every bit the part of the Hunter. But it isn't just looks. He's a competitive CrossFitter. He did Strongman for a few years, then, realizing it wasn't as valuable to his chosen profession as it could be, switched his focus to jiujitsu.

Thor is so good and so focused on being a great cop that if he wasn't such a good guy, we'd all hate him. He's the dude who works out three times a day every day, and incorporates dry-fire gun drills into the mix. Like, he'll do a hundred push-ups, then sprint, then throw a live ox over a ravine, then draw his weapon and dry-fire to a target. Okay, I may have exaggerated the ox-throwing, but the rest really happened on the regular. He knows the law. He's courteous. And he only goes after the real bad guys. I doubt he's ever given a ticket in his life. He doesn't want to hassle regular citizens. He wants to put away the rapists, the killers, and the dealers. If you're interested in hurting people, then Thor is interested in finding you.

As I finish my synopsis to Ash and she gives me a quick kiss, I jump into my car and head toward the Southeast District station. On my way, I call Thor's wife, Leslie.

"Hey, Leslie, are you all right?" I ask.

"Yeah, I'm fine. I'm on my way there," she responds.

"Do you know what happened?"

"Thor shot someone and killed them. There was a chase. Thor's fine." Her tone is distant, distracted. Later she will have no recollection of our conversation.

"I'm on the way. I'll see you there."

Moments later, as I pull in, I can tell this is going to be a shit show. The station is full of people. I learn that the guy who got shot was Randy, a well-known gang member in the SED. Although Randy was hated by his immediate community, the department knows an uproar is coming, from the broader "community." Attorneys from both sides, command staff, and union representatives are shuffling around the station, either to get their pound of flesh or cover their asses, or both. Uniformed officers are corralling witnesses near a conference table. Radios chirp everywhere, and cell phones cut shrilly through a thousand simultaneous conversations.

Gross.

I slowly back away from the crowd. I want no part in this circus. Sarge sees me through the window of his office and waves me in.

The second I cross the threshold, he jumps right into it. "Hey, once they're done interviewing Thor, I want you to stay with him for a couple days. He is gonna need another cop around, especially since they're going to take his gun for evidence." He pauses, doing some kind of Sarge calculus in his head. "We'll count it as alternate duty. Don't bother with your regular shifts."

"Ten-four, Sarge. I'll head that way."

"Hey, Tansey!" He stops me, calling for me seconds after I walk out, realizing he may have been too forceful in his command. "I'm sure you have time to grab some clothes or whatever. Bring your family if you think that will help."

"Um, yeah, no problem," I reply.

"And Tansey?" he says, his voice stopping me again. "*No drinking.* There will be reporters banging on the door, friends and family to navigate, and the possibility of gang retaliation. You need to stay frosty, okay?"

There is no reason to warn me of that. I'm an idiot from time to time, but not that kind of idiot. My MO is to be a smart-ass right now, but I see the very real concern on his face as he runs through the checklists in his mind. The risk of hurting my feelings is far less important than the risk of me screwing up because he didn't warn me, so he had to warn me. Period. So I let it slide. "Yeah, Sarge, no sweat."

Before leaving the station, I get the story of what happened. Thor saw Randy on the corner, hanging out with several gang members. Thor, like all of us, knew Randy well. He had been arrested sixteen times on twenty-six different charges in 2011 alone. Those charges included assault on a female, possession of a concealed firearm, and possession of cocaine with intent to sell. He had nine misdemeanor convictions and had an outstanding felony warrant for cocaine possession.

Thor called it in, got out of his car, and approached, calling out Randy's name. Randy took off running and jumped a chain-link fence. Thor gave chase, but as he jumped the first fence he fell. When he stood up, he saw that Randy had stopped and was now facing him, trying to pull a gun out of his waistband. Thor drew faster than Randy and managed to get off the first shot, his first bullet actually striking the gun in Randy's hand. The next few rounds walked up through Randy's torso, chest, and shoulder, killing him instantly.

Thor's training and meticulous practice saved him today. All those gun pulls between workout reps, all those exercises drummed into us at the academy—they paid off. One millisecond slower and Randy would have shot Thor instead of the other way around. Thor's situation was a textbook example of perfect police work. He should be getting a fucking award. But I know that won't be the case.

I pick up the wife and kids and head to Thor's house later that night. My awesome wife makes dinner, and after we have all eaten, we send the kids upstairs to play. But the night is awkward, like conversations at a funeral or visiting a sick relative—you don't know exactly what to say. Do you act like everything is normal? Do you talk about the elephant in the room? So with that hanging over us, Thor, Leslie, Ashleigh, and I are all sitting quietly at the table when finally Thor breaks the awkward silence: "Hey, you know what? You know what I'm gonna do?"

We all look at him curiously. I'm wondering if he is okay. He took a life. I know it's not easy to deal with that, even when the guy is a piece of shit. Or maybe he's rethinking his career. Or maybe the whole thing has given him some great wisdom he has to espouse. We all stare as he seems to be choosing his words, hoping we all react correctly so as not to do him any additional emotional damage.

"I'm gonna have a bowl of ice cream tonight." Thor, the guy who works out relentlessly, counts his macros, his micros, his sleep, the time between meals, and anything else that might optimize his fitness, wants ice cream?

For a second, we don't know what to say, but when he finally smirks, we lose it. The laughter melts away the awkwardness, the stress, and the uneasiness as we all realize that after the fight of his life, maybe some ice cream sounds pretty damn good.

Once he opens up the floodgates of humor, I jump right in with him. If you've ever been around soldiers, cops, or first responders—people who routinely see danger and death—you will realize how dark their sense of humor becomes. After a few zingers of my own that are not really fit for mixed company but had Thor rolling, my wife throws up her hands as Leslie yells, "Tansey!"

Normally I would stop there, but Thor is laughing his ass off, and I know he's in for a long road. Deep into the night we joke about everything, up to and including death, and as the night winds down and we're about to go to bed, our wives look at us in utter embarrassment.

"Who did we marry?" Leslie asks Ash as she shakes her head and begins to clear the table.

"Winners," I reply. "You married winners."

———

The media does in fact show up—every single day for a solid two weeks. The knocks come day and night, without any respect for the family that lives inside. At first they identify themselves readily and park in the cul-de-sac in front of Thor's house. It starts civilly. The knock comes and when I answer the door, there's the "Hello, Mr. Thor? This is Anna Asshole with DEF News Raleigh. Can we talk for a second?"

When that doesn't work, they get sneaky. They park out of sight. They knock gently and have no identifying elements about them, pretending to be a neighbor or curious citizen. They even try to act as salesmen or utility workers. It is absolutely disgusting.

Contrary to the story they hide behind, they are not looking for the truth. They are looking for anything that makes Thor look like a loose cannon. They want the sound bite. They want the angry wife. They want the cop to say something that paints him in a bad light. They want something they can bend or twist. They want the town to burn so they can cover it. They want, no, they need THE story!

And I hate them.

Is that fair? Maybe not. People who hate my profession like to say they've never met a good cop. Well, that's been my experience with journalists. That's my story and I'm sticking to it.

But I will give credit where credit is due—they are great at finding the story they want to tell. The news teams lean hard into civil unrest, literally using the tools that are meant to report news to create it. They stir up locals and try their best to pit the community against police officers. Headlines from around the country and across the world read, and I quote (minus real names):

> Randy, who was black, was shot and killed by Raleigh Police Officer Thor, who was white, on Monday . . .
> White Officer Shot Black Man in Self-defense
> NC Police Shoot and Kill Black Man
> Randy, a Black Man, Shot Dead While Trying to Run Away from White Cop
> Officer in North Carolina Fatally Shoots Black Man During Chase
> Raleigh Police Shooting: Man Shot, Hundreds Protest

It goes on and on. One newspaper does some particularly nasty work. They disclose Thor's church, where his kids went to school, where he and his wife were married, what gyms he attended, and his home address. His life becomes complete chaos. Even after he is exonerated, the persecution will endure.

Thor and his family sell their house and move to another town. They had to buy their new home through a third party just to keep their names off the mortgage records. They spend a small fortune just to protect themselves.

Local activists hold protests in the neighborhood where Randy was shot. A famous footballer has Randy's name stitched into his Hall of

Fame tie, along with the names of eleven other black men and women who were shot by police. It could not get any crazier, but while I wish this situation on no one, it is oddly perfect that it is happening to Thor. His record is flawless and untouchable. He has no prior complaints. His career is a model of professional policing. Among his co-workers, he is known throughout the department as a family man who is both humble and proactive. He pushes himself as an athlete and as an officer.

The community appreciates him because he focuses on hunting bad people—he doesn't write speeding tickets or mess around with "quality of life" issues like vagrancy, prostitution, or homelessness. He looks for felony warrants and violent crime warrants, to work against the evils of this world. His reputation in the community and in the department is that he is the guy you call to get the real bad guys—the ones who are really dangerous to society: the men who will rape your daughters, rob you in the night, pistol-whip you for a laugh, or slit your throat to show their mettle. He only pursues the men who choose to do evil.

But the media doesn't care about that, or about the community. If they did care, they would report about the hardworking black folks in the area, their investment in their community, and all the good that is happening in the SED. You would see stories about kids thriving, people starting businesses, parks being cleaned up.

But they don't want you to see that. They prefer the racist trope that everyone who lives in black neighborhoods is like Randy. The interviews they take aren't with intelligent business owners, parents holding down two jobs to get their kids a better life, or teachers pushing to get their students resources that come easy in places like Cary or Chapel Hill. No, they interview the idiots—the ones hanging with the Randys of this world, and they garner the most inflammatory quotes they can get. They need the story!

It reminds me of their storm coverage. You'll get the guy who finds the one ditch that is overflowing and shoots a close-up of it and reports the mild storm like it's Hurricane Katrina. It would be funny to me if so many people didn't fall for it. I cannot believe the news anymore; I'm too close to a lot of it. I don't care what they report: I always ask the question, "Who is trying to make me feel what and why?" It's a pure propaganda operation. If there is one group of people whom I hate even more than the Karens, it's 99 percent of the media. They both share a love of propagating drama, no matter whose life they ruin in the process.

Why report a story when you can create a better one?

16

US AGAINST US

The treatment of Thor·by both the leadership and the media gutted the Southeast District. If you ask a person, even perhaps one who doesn't like police, "Should a cop be able to shoot someone actively trying to kill them?" most people would answer in the affirmative. And certainly after an investigation occurs, and everyone involved agrees that the officer did everything right, there should be no issue, correct? Well, just the opposite is true right now.

The chief and her upper-management cohort completely cowered to the demands of local "social justice warriors." They were forcing us to partake in roundtable discussions with activist individuals who you could tell absolutely despised us, who offered up solutions like "stop arresting people" or "we need to create a dialogue." These things all sound great to people who have never been shot at or assaulted, or had a gun pulled on them by a stripper in a holding cell, but to those of us who have been on the job for more than a week, the world they are describing is an absolute fantasy. The deeper the discussions go, the more it seems like their core argument is that the police are too tough on criminals. *Do they want more crime?*

Don't get me wrong: Activists are gonna activist. And there are plenty of examples when activist work has led to changes that are good for society and policing. And if we had just been found to have done the wrong thing, and abuse had been uncovered, then I'd be the first in line to say, "Hey, we fucked up, and shit needs to change around here," but often quite the opposite occurs.

Our organization has a reputation and a history of not going too far, of not being violent unless violence comes to us, and of not shooting people. Our incidents of deadly force are shockingly rare. Considering how rough the SED can be, I am sometimes surprised at how clean we are! But so what!

Everyone on the line is about to learn the same valuable lesson that so many employees have learned over the years—under pressure, most bosses will throw you under the bus if they think their ass is on the line, even if they know you did the right thing.

Chief Antoinette is such a boss. She's either genuinely incompetent, fooled by them hook, line, and sinker, or so fearful that she is going to end up on the wrong side of the media that she caves to and implements their ideas without hesitation.

Her changes to policing procedure almost immediately cause violent crime rates to skyrocket in the city from 17 percent annually to 29 percent annually in each of the next three years. While I know it's probably unfair to assign all the blame to her, at the line level, we all feel like she is trying to actively ruin Raleigh. Here's why:

Our search policy is the first one she attacks and changes. Prior to Whitegate, verbal permission was the only thing necessary for a search. You would simply ask, while your mic was recording, "Sir/ma'am, do you have any illegal weapons, drugs, knives, anything that could hurt me, poke me, blow me up? Do you mind if I search you real fast for any of those things?" They would simply answer yes or no. If the answer was yes, we would conduct the search. But the chief changed the procedure and mandated that we do "consent searches." So we now have to print a form, read it aloud while filming the subject, and then finally ask them to sign it.

Guess how many people sign it?

Some of you out there might be saying, "Good, whether they are criminals or not, they should have the clear opportunity to not incriminate themselves. Good police work should make up for it if they really are guilty!" While I personally disagree, I can definitely understand that argument. Unfortunately, however, we'll just need to significantly upscale our covert operations and covert vehicle presence, so that we can watch people and catch them committing a crime as it is about to happen, rather than search people for illegal weapons and drugs.

Which brings me to the second change from Whitegate. The civil board spoke out against covert vehicles and covert officers, so except in the rarest of cases, our ability and budget to use them were eliminated. Now we have to wait for crime to happen and respond to it, rather than be proactive in any way to prevent it. And, in case you were wondering, when crime happens, criminals tend not to stick around and wait for us to catch them.

The combination of those changes gave the civil board exactly what I believe they wanted—the inability of police officers to weed out criminals. And as I've said numerous times, criminals are very smart and adapt quickly. News spread through the SED, and in less than two weeks, drive-by shootings and gang fights became standard fare. We went from one of the toughest departments on crime to maybe the weakest, and that created additional problems. The promise of unbridled criminal enterprise brought in rival gangs from Durham and Rocky Mount, North Carolina, and their behavior went unchecked.

In case you were wondering, the chief is not yet done with her "cleanup" of our police department. Our department has a gang wall spreadsheet from the Southeast District. The gang wall is probably the best tool the SED has. Think of it as one of those murder boards from cop shows like *Castle* or *Blue Bloods* where the cops stare at it to solve crimes. Instead of solving a particular crime, however, it's a who's who of gang members and their known associates, broken down by gang affiliation. Members are listed under their gang names, but also under the sect or subsect of that gang, as well as by rank and position.

The gang wall is an amazing resource and visual guide to what is going on in the world of gangs in our district, at any given time. It allows us to quickly figure out where to go if we need to serve a warrant, allows rookies to get schooled up on the world they're entering, and is an amazing way to communicate across shifts.

We leave sticky notes on individual faces to share valuable information with other officers so they don't have to wait for formal reports. For example, if you run into an unfamiliar guy on Star Street with a spiderweb tattooed on his face, you can walk over to the gang wall while on potty break and look for his picture. Or maybe you see that Fred is a Crip from Bragg Street, but you saw him on Star Street, which is mostly Bloods. You can leave a note saying that you saw him there. Then later there's a drive-by shooting on Star Street that night, after your shift is over. Well, the oncoming squad sees the sticky note about Fred hanging around Star Street earlier that day, and now they know that Fred should probably be located and questioned. A low-ranking gang member bebopping down a rival street hours before a shooting would be a great person of interest.

The gang wall is absolutely invaluable to us.

Chief Antoinette says it has to go. Why? The supervisor tells us because there are too many black people on it, and the perception is bad. Now, just in case you've missed this critical detail throughout the book, almost 70 percent of the SED is black. Which is why about 70 percent of the gang wall is black.

People cooler and smarter than me try to convince her and her team that we need this critical tool, so painstakingly constructed and maintained over the years, in order to be at our best.

The wall is torn down.

Suddenly, without the three critical tools that we have used to combat gang violence, it feels like we're being asked to do chemistry without the periodic table of elements at our disposal. It became impossible.

But the chief has an answer to all our problems. Sure, she is removing the tools for proactive policing, but she is giving us the Special Project Squad, or, as I like to call it, the dumbest possible idea in the history of policing. The SPS goes to rough areas (like my beat) armed with happiness, joy, and hope. They are specifically asked not to police, not to arrest, not to do the work the community expects, but instead to reach out and talk to the local citizenry and garner their views on how we should be policing. Now, to be very clear, they aren't hiring more officers to do this. No, sir. Instead they are going to take cops away from their beats to build out the SPS, which means there will be fewer cops policing. *A real win-win for the civil board activists.*

SPS is the last place on earth that I would ever want to be, and I've been in combat and a Waffle House after 1 a.m., so naturally that's where they put me. I know for a fact that I was added to the squad because I was on a list of go-getter proactive cops who need to be "retrained." The rest of the squad is mostly made up of guys like me but also has a sprin-kling of "true believers." The true believers are the ones who agree with the civil board. The way I see it, they're the cops who hate cops. The way they see it, they're here because they believe that the worst members of our society just need to be shown a little more respect and then they will see the error of their ways.

The one bright spot on this squad is the sergeant they put in charge of us. He's coming from SWAT, so he's coming in with a warrior's mentality. If he hates the assignment, I don't know it because he's too professional, but I at least know he's not going to let us be sitting ducks. Having a good leader goes a long way.

Nevertheless, day one on the job is humiliating. During our brief beforehand we are reminded of the chief's mission. We are not here to stop crimes. We are only here to report them, while maintaining friendly faces. *I don't have it in me to do this. What am I supposed to do if some woman is getting mugged? Call a real cop? What the fuck?*

My partner is excited to be here. He's a true believer, but he's also super interesting. He's a black Muslim, which is not particularly com-mon in North Carolina, and he's intent on fixing the police force and bringing justice to all people. He's extremely noble, and I cannot knock him for that at all. The problem is that he hasn't really worked the street. He's been a cop for a little while, but he's been solving "my husband far-ted in my olives" kinds of problems, or he's been in positions that were public relations–worthy because his combination of race and faith is the modern press's wet dream.

As we visit house after house and store after store, I feel like a bastardized Jehovah's Witness. *Hiya! My name is Officer Tansey. Please note my long-sleeved shirt and tidy necktie! How can I be of service to you today, and have you heard about the good message from our Lord and Savior, Chief Antoinette?* The fact that my old squad makes endless jokes about it when I get back only adds to the brutal humiliation.

There's a house that has always made me curious, and I decide to use this opportunity to visit it and figure out the mystery of it once and for all. Located across from a mini-mart that is known as an open-air drug market and prostitution hub, and the site of hundreds of violent crimes, it somehow sits nice, clean, and untouched by the crime that happens all around it. (Fun fact for any nineties rap aficionados: This particular mini-mart, which is basically the capital of my beat and district, was featured in the music video "Raise Up" by Petey Pablo.)

Anyway, back to the house. It is the only house in the area with a manicured lawn. An old 1970s Buick sits in the driveway, kept in pristine condition. A little old man sits on the porch each morning with a cup of coffee before disappearing inside for the rest of the day and night. I have worked at least two homicides right in front of that house, and each time the little old man knew nothing about them. The guy is an absolute mystery. He's in his eighties and very quiet. Peppered-gray hair graces his head pretty robustly for a guy his age, and he always maintains a perfect clean shave. His impeccable manicuring is completed with a collared shirt and pressed slacks.

The man is dressing up for no one, in the middle of the epicenter of crime in the Capital City, and is not getting fucked with. If you did a plot graph of murders in the past ten years, his house would be bright red like the sun, so how in the world does this guy maintain his sanity, and his innocence? I've always joked with other officers that he must have been a real badass back in the day, and that's why they all left him alone. Kind of like Clint Eastwood in *Gran Torino*.

We walk gingerly up the stairs and knock gently on the door. It's all so nice compared to the rest of the area that neither of us wants to be the one to disturb anything. He answers with a light smile on his face. "How can I help you, Officers?"

"Sir, we are part of a community-focused police squad tasked with speaking to people about how to better serve the community," I say as respectfully as I can.

"Well, come on in, gentlemen," he says in a very kind voice. It throws me. Inviting a cop into your house is a big deal. In this area of the city, you aren't allowed to talk to the police. There are consequences. It's a really good way to end up dead. Street justice is real.

Now I'm convinced that this guy is mafia or a war hero, or a literal vampire who feeds on gangbangers at night.

"Sir, are you sure you want us to be in your house?" I ask, trying to get a read on him.

"Oh yeah, you're fine. I'd rather them not hear what we talk about anyhow. Please, have a seat."

"Thank you," my partner and I say simultaneously as we sit down.

"So, what can I do for you officers?" he asks, staring at us intently.

"We just want to know how we can be of more service to this community. With everything going on in the world, we want to take a step back and see if there is anything different we could do to better serve your neighborhood," I say, and even though I hate this bullshit assignment, as I look into his eyes, I mean every word.

The old man sits down in his rocking chair and chuckles. He looks from me to my partner with a spark in his eye, then lets out a long sigh, glancing back and forth at us a couple more times before fixating on me. Leaning forward, he looks me dead in the eyes. "Young man, I have lived here for over fifty years. I have seen it all. I watch you fine gentlemen drive by here all the time. You make an arrest, and within the hour those same people are back out here dealin' the same dope, pimpin' the same hos, and stabbing and shooting each other. I have seen police arrest one man twice in one day—in the same damn day—and that night he was back out here dealin' in the same spot you arrested him from.

"I gave up a long time ago worrying about these folks out here. I was a pastor for thirty-some-odd years and I pray, Lord, I pray for these streets, but that's all I can do. Sometimes y'all work real hard out here and the crime stops for a bit, but as soon as y'all slack off, it just picks right back up again. You asked how you can be of service out here? I'll tell you how: You stay on 'em. You stay on these streets all day and all night, and you don't leave. If you're here, they can't commit those crimes. They can't hurt nobody. If you wanted to really stop crime, you'd put a cop out here all the time."

The words cut through us both. Me, the hard-edged street cop, and my partner, the true believer, were equally rocked by this gentleman's pointed statement. We knew he wasn't wrong about any of it.

It's so simple; so breathtakingly simple. I'm baffled that despite all the political changes in the last fifty years, not one chief, mayor, or city manager could fix a few blocks of city streets, especially when the answer is so obvious and easy to execute: put cops on that street all day and all night.

My partner is wrestling with the internal views he brought into this room, his eyes almost pleading with the soothsayer we have unwittingly come upon, to ratify his worldview in some way. "Sir, what about the people who say it looks bad to have cops focusing on one place? Who say it appears that we're controlling a neighborhood, rather than policing it?"

With that comment, the old man laughs out loud, and it takes him a moment to recompose himself before he speaks. "Young man, these folks out here got everybody fooled. They're just spoiled kids that never got the rod. If you don't discipline your kids, *that's* how they'll turn out." He points outside as a crackhead strolls by like a zombie. "They have no rules out here, and when someone tells them no or they simply don't get their way, they resort to violence, or they have a meltdown in the streets. Binge drinkin' and druggin' until they are so high they pass out or kill somebody. I watch 'em. I've watched 'em for years, out there acting like little children that have no parents. They're out there acting like fools, and you know what? Some of them got kids of their own, and them kids are even more lawless.

"Those younger ones are even scarier than the parents. They out here real young trying to rob folks, but even after they rob 'em, they still shoot 'em, or pistol-smack 'em, even if they ain't done nothing to 'em. Their parents had at least a few rules back in the day, like they didn't shoot folks who give up their cash without a fight . . . They also didn't deal on Sundays until church was over and they didn't flood these streets like this on Sundays . . ." The man stares out the window and takes a moment before returning to us. "Now there ain't even one rule out here no more. Yeah, they got you all fooled all right. They ain't had rules for fifty years, so they ain't *ever* gonna listen now."

My partner's mouth is agape, and when I see him, I realize mine is wide-open too. The man continues.

"I seen a real bad fella out here, for a long time. He was always out here dealin' and bullyin' folks. He was a very disrespectful boy, and if you even looked at him wrong, he'd be threatening to shoot ya. He got shot a while back by another bad fella and died right down the street from here. Young man, you woulda thought that boy was some kind a hero. Whites, blacks, everyone, all out here holdin' hands and singin' songs, chanting hate about police and puttin' their fists up, talkin' about stoppin' racism and such." He shakes his head sadly. "Yeah, they got y'all fooled. They're playin' you folks good. That boy got shot by another real bad fella that didn't get his way some way or another. Ain't no police problem, or no race problem. They're just bad kids out on the streets being bad. That's all it is."

The room is now quiet and neither my partner nor I know what to say. The young man he's referring to went by the name Angel. He died in a drive-by shooting at about 3 a.m. one morning. He still had a bag of cocaine in his mouth and a gun in his hand when the police arrived on scene. The initial rumor was that police shot him. Then the truth came out, but people ignored that so they'd have a reason to march, and so they did. I remember it vividly. It was the first time I saw so many white people in the inner city, acting like they gave a shit. One white hipster college student from Durham took the colored gang flags of all the different gangs in the area and sewed them together like a mini quilt. Soon the popular topic was uniting the gangs to decrease gang violence. White kids marched up and down the road waving these "unity gang flags" above their heads, yelling "Fuck the police!" as we drove by.

Good times.

I was embarrassed for them. These young, would-be activists out there marching down the road with men who had over fifteen domestic violence and sexual assault charges, plus a slew of other felonies. What a slap in the face to all the victims. Could you imagine being a rape victim of one of these gang members, and now a bunch of woke white folks are holding hands with them and flying their gang colors? It was surreal.

The "Angel" movement lasted for all of about three days, and then the white people fled back to their safe, cushy lives. The unity gang thing didn't work out so well, and that Friday night we had five shootings on one street as rival gangs lashed out against each other over Angel's death. It got so bad that we had to have the SWAT team go in to disperse the gang members who were lined up against each other like a scene out of *Gangs of New York.*

The old man has seen it all firsthand. He needs no explanation as to why his neighborhood is such a dire place to live. He has held firm, an island of tranquility and manicured plants in a sea of crime, swelling and festering over generations of lawlessness. He knows the truth. He knows his home. And he just confirmed what I felt from the start, and my partner was only now just realizing: Expecting our little unit of community-based police to solve a problem designed for proactive policing was as senseless as sewing together the flags of violent street gangs and calling for unity so that order and calm can be restored to the community!

———

You know what's worse than being tasked with walking around town talking to people who don't really want to talk to us? Driving around town looking for dark places where the city could install better lights to stave off crime. Yup, that's what I'm doing on a Friday night, formerly the night where I would be busiest. *How the mighty have fallen . . .*

The radio suddenly lights up with members from my old D-squad in a foot pursuit. I'm jealous and a bit depressed, listening to the radio traffic as they chase a known gang member who apparently tossed a gun as police approached him and is now running toward some apartments. The radio perks up again with a report of shots fired about five blocks from the foot chase. I've seen this before. I grab my radio.

"Raleigh, there is an active foot chase blocks away from that shots-fired call. That is likely a decoy call to distract police attention away from the foot chase. I'll head to the shots-fired call and handle it. I don't need a check-in. I'll advise," I say quickly to free the radio up for the chase.

I'm not allowed to get into a foot chase (how dumb is that?) but I desperately want to help in some capacity. Taking a shots-fired call that is likely bullshit keeps the officers focused on the foot chase. Plus, I'm less than a mile away. For once, the stars are aligned for an easy call. I close in on the area.

"9-424 David, be advised we are getting multiple calls on this shots-fired call. I'm sending you check-in units."

"Raleigh, hold those check-ins and have them continue to the foot pursuit. This is going to be a decoy—" Before I can finish the sentence a car runs the stop sign right in front of me and spins sideways as I smash the brakes. The car's back window is shot out and I can see bullet holes all across the trunk. The car speeds back up, squealing its tires and fish-tailing over the road as it leaves a cloud of smoke from the burnt rubber in its wake.

"Raleigh, 9-424 David, I just had a car take off on me that appears to be shot to pieces. We are headed towards New Bern." I'm now in pursuit. As we approach a large intersection, the car makes no attempt to slow down, ignoring the red light. I call out on the radio that we have passed through the intersection and are heading toward St. Augustine College. The driver tries to make a left turn onto a side street but loses control and hits a telephone pole, just as blue and red lights fill the night and another cop car pulls up.

The driver jumps out and runs. I immediately give chase. For once, before the chase gets out of hand, Sergeant Tom and the Professor (I'll tell you more about him later) cut him off and tackle him to the ground. As I help them get him into cuffs, I realize that I'm covered in blood. My hands are painted in the red sticky substance, and my pants are too. For the first time, I take in the suspect. He looks like he just walked off the set of *Carrie*. Not one inch of his torso or head is dry.

"Tansey, roll him over and find the bullet holes," Tom commands.

I roll him over, pull out my knife, and begin cutting off his shirt and pants so I can quickly find his wounds and apply first aid. "Sir, where have you been shot?" I ask. He screams and wails and provides me with no information. "Sir! Calm down and tell me, where have you been shot?! Holy shit!" I pause, taking him in. There is a translucent substance running down his face. Then it hits me. "Sir, is that brains on your face?" I know the answer. It looks like someone puked up ramen noodles on his head.

Tom asks sternly, "Sir, whose fucking brains are on your face?"

The man screams, adding crying to the mix, "IT'S MY FRIEND'S BRAINS!" As soon as he finishes yelling, he pukes all over himself. I roll him to his side so he won't choke.

Tom is completely unaffected by the vomiting and the rivers of blood on this guy. "Where is your friend?"

"He's in—" *Hhhummmp!!!* He vomits again. Tom grabs him and looks right into his eyes, and that focuses the young man. "He's in the car!"

I look up at Tom and the Professor. The Professor speaks up, still searching the guy for bullet wounds. "Hey, Sarge, I ran by that car and I didn't see anyone in there."

Sarge nods, but we all know we have to check again. "Tansey, go check that car real quick."

I walk down the road toward the car with my flashlight out. A crowd is already starting to gather around the wrecked car. "Back away from the car," I order.

"Fuck the po-lice!" they respond, aggressively letting me know I am not welcome. Knowing there is a tiny window of time before this gets unruly, I close in on the car and see a stream of blood flowing out from the bottom of the closed door. My flashlight pierces the darkness to find an eyeball and its stringy attachments hanging from the ceiling. My eyes follow my shining light, on particles dancing in its beam, then fall on a headless person in the front passenger seat. Well . . . mostly headless. The bottom part of a jaw is dangling from a collapsed neck, with the rest of the head scattered across the driver's seat like a smashed pumpkin.

"Um, Sarge? I found him." I yell over my shoulder.

"And?" he asks, knowing the answer.

"Yeah, he's dead," I reply, maybe too matter-of-factly.

"Stand by and don't move."

"Roger that."

"Fuck you, cop!" the crowd screams at me. "You killed that nigga!" "You shot that dude in the face!" Obviously, nothing is further from the truth, but nonetheless, the crowd is accusing me of shooting the poor bastard who's now sitting headless in front of me.

"That's my son!" one lady yells as she falls to the ground pretending to have a seizure, looking like a bad actor on the set of *The Exorcist Part 7*. I can hear sirens in the distance, but as we are already short-staffed and half the squad is on a foot chase, they may be coming from far away, maybe neighboring districts. It will probably be a while before they arrive, and that could be a real problem.

I assess my situation. Tom and the Professor are standing with the man they have detained, waiting on an ambulance. I'm a block away from them, standing next to a headless person, being yelled at and accused of being the cop who shot him.

"Yo! Daaaaamn! What's goin' on?!" one gentleman shouts out.

"I saw it! That cop shot a nigga! Nigga's dead in that car!" comes the call from an honest bloke to his left.

"Man, fuck these po-lice, they out of control," adds a voice that I can't quite place, but who is certainly of the same fine upbringing as his compatriots.

"I did not shoot this guy! I repeat, I did not shoot this guy! BUT . . . if anyone has information on who did, please come forward!"

To my surprise, a small voice comes from inside a row of bushes, just behind the crowd. "I have info but please don't shoot me!"

I yell to the bushes, "Come on out and chat with me!" Emerging from the hedge is a young boy of only about fourteen years, covered in a mix of blood and dirt. It's smeared on his arms, face, shirt, and pants. "Officer," he whispers timidly, "I was in that car when they shot Marcus. I'm scared." *Poor kid.*

My friends in the crowd waste no time. "Don't you tell that cop shit! We seen him shoot that boy!"

Ignoring the rabble, I sit him down beside me, moving my body to obscure his view of the headless body in the front seat. The blue wave finally arrives and they are quickly followed by some local protesters and rioters. Ambulances arrive from all sides. One ambulance is for the convulsing lady, who is still claiming it was her kid and I shot him. The other two ambulances are for the other two guys who were in the car. The fourth was for another woman who had been across the street from the shooting and had initially been reported as shot, but thankfully, she wasn't. Oddly, it was worse. She was just an innocent woman who had sent her daughter into the kitchen to fetch some ice from the freezer. The little girl opened the door just as a stray bullet ripped through the door and into the bag of ice. Thank the Lord, the girl was fine, but the poor lady, stricken immediately with guilt, fear, and anxiety, suffered a heart attack.

The swarm of blue and red lights acts like a bug zapper without the zap, drawing in more and more spectators. The crowd is not friendly. A man sprints at me, throwing his hands up over his head dramatically. Looking at me with more hate in his eyes than I have seen in a long time, he screams, "You killed my cousin! You killed him! He's dead and you killed him, you fuckin' pig! Get this pig outta here!"

I know this isn't his cousin. And even if by some random chance it is, there is no way he has identified him by his teeth and lower jaw. And it isn't like you could see anything else clearly through the gore. I can't even tell what color shirt he is wearing and I'm the one with the flashlight. The crowd has entered the bullshit phase. Every clown here is now trying to outdo the other with theatrics and unruliness. *What a shit show.*

The crowd gets bigger, and it gets angrier as bizarre rumors course through it. Officers start arriving from neighboring districts to help hold back what is now a mob. If there had been any evidence outside of the wrecked vehicle, it's worthless now. Calling the crime scene contaminated would be an understatement. There is no crime scene. It's a battleground.

The horde chants, "No justice, no peace!" followed by "Fuck 12!" Meanwhile, some poor human is lying headless inside a car. Some person—a son or father, husband or lover, friend or partner—is dead now, and in the same way the media doesn't care if the news is true, the mob doesn't care how or why this man died. They just want to vent their anger and add to the chaos.

A beige sedan begins inching through the crowd and finally stops in the middle of the street, just shy of our police line. I stare at the car, hoping it isn't gang-related, anxiously waiting to see who is going to get out of it. The crowd's curious too. They even stop their incessant chanting for a moment. The door creaks open and an older woman steps out. She's alone, wearing a white nightgown over some jeans and slippers. She walks toward the line and speaks softly to an officer. My heart sinks, because I know what's coming.

"Officer, I'm from Knightdale. One of my grandson's friends called me and told me to come here quickly. I'm afraid that . . . I have this awful feeling that . . . something bad has happened." I can see a dark fear in her eyes—a fear every parent or grandparent has had at one point or another, worrying about their child. I can feel her fear and her knowledge, somehow, that the worst has happened. Her shoulders are slouched, her arms crossed tightly, and her head hung low. Sorrow and defeat seem to embrace her. *How many battles has this poor woman gone through to try to keep this kid on the straight and narrow, only to have it all end here? I hope it's not her grandkid.*

I draw her quickly through the line and gently guide her to a crime scene vehicle, where she sits down in the passenger seat.

"Ma'am, I don't know who your grandson is, but if you wait here I'll find whatever information I can about him and let you know." I know that she is truly afraid, and not like the rest of the crowd. She isn't looking for attention or trying to add to the chaos. She wants the kid she raised to be safe, like we all do. "Ma'am, could you tell me what your grandson looks like, and maybe describe any clothes you think he might have been wearing?" I ask her as gently as I can.

She quickly describes him and his clothes. She knows every detail. She's folded those clothes hundreds of times. As I walk away, she stops me. "He's only thirteen years old."

"Yes, ma'am. I understand."

"He's been hanging out with a nineteen-year-old gang member . . . but I don't know his name . . ." Her voice trails off.

"Okay, ma'am," I say, and walk over to the detectives who are photographing the scene, to pass on the information.

"Oh shit," the detective sighs. "That clothing description matches our deceased. Go stand by her, but don't tell her anything about the victim. Let's pray that it's all just a coincidence."

I walk back over to the car. Her eyes follow me the whole way over. The tiniest glimmer of hope is in them. "Is my grandson okay?"

"I hope so, ma'am," I reply. I feel awful and awkward. I know there is almost no chance that her grandson isn't dead, but that's not news you want to give someone and be wrong. We've already had one heart attack tonight, and once you give that news, a person is never the same. So we stand there together, both hoping.

In front of us is a wall of cops fighting to hold back the mob. Their chants, temporarily stymied by this lady, are once again cutting through the night. She finally breaks our silence.

"What's wrong with these people?"

"Excuse me, ma'am?"

"I feel bad for you boys out here. Y'all don't deserve all this madness. Don't these people have jobs or something better to do than standing out here acting like fools? I hope my grandson is not out in that crowd acting like that because if he is, I'm gonna give him the belt. He has been needing a good whippin'. He's been running with this older boy who is nothing but trouble, and ever since he's been hanging out with that boy he has just gotten more and more disrespectful. He was supposed to be home a long time ago, and his phone is off. When I get ahold of him I'm puttin' a stop to all this. He don't need to be hanging out on this side of town anyway, with all these people acting like this."

I know her grandson is dead. I can just feel it, and I think she can too. I've seen this before. It's so awful that her brain needs to focus on something else—something she can control. And to have the kid die the way he did—having his whole face blown off.

What is wrong with this world?

I keep up the small talk and try to keep the conversation light. Suddenly emotion hits me hard. My heart grows heavy, and my soul feels drained. It is the same feeling that I had after wrecking my car while chasing Kendrick, who went on to murder one more person and rape another.

The detectives start to walk over. Their body language tells us everything we need to know as they approach, looking down at the ground, building the courage to talk to her. When they finally look up, a few paces away from us, the first detective asks, "Ma'am, can you come to the station with us?" I watch the light leave her eyes, and her face go completely dark. Not a muscle moves. The lines that hold our expressions—smiles, frowns, and even grimaces—are cleansed completely. She is a statue. She knows.

The detectives slowly move her to their car, but it's not her anymore. Her soul has left her. She sits in the passenger seat and they close the door behind her. Another officer will bring her car to the station.

Later, we'll get the story from the two surviving boys. The thirteen-year-old victim was in the front passenger seat. The driver was nineteen and a verified gang member. The boy in the back seat was fourteen and already wearing gang colors. They were parked on the side of a street. The nineteen-year-old was recruiting for his gang, and his rivals had a hit out on him for it. They saw his car parked on the street and ran up to it with an AK-47, unloading an entire magazine into it point-blank. The thirteen-year-old, the one who was excited to have this new nineteen-year-old looking out for him, took all of the rounds. The large, 7.62-millimeter bullets exploded his skull like a watermelon and opened the flesh of his torso, emptying nearly every ounce of blood from his body.

Everything he was and ever will be was gone in an instant, taken by gang violence over something as simple as recruiting grounds.

Of course, what happened that night didn't fit the current narrative, so it only made the third page of news with the headline RANDOM ACT OF GUN VIOLENCE LEAVES THIRTEEN-YEAR-OLD DEAD. The article never mentions that it was gang-related, or that there has been a major spike in gang violence because a turf war is growing.

That isn't a story that you can sell on television. Nor is it a story that allows leadership to pat themselves on their backs.

So it doesn't matter. Except to the grandmother who lost her grandson, and the child who lost his innocence and then his life.

17

THIRSTY LIEUTENANTS

As the weeks go on and the SED is inundated with shootings, stabbings, and a slew of other crimes brought on by the increase in gang power, I grow increasingly frustrated with the policies and my lot in life. Our Special Project Squad is a half-assed attempt to appease social activists who will never be appeased. Trusting that these professional protesters will ever be happy is like trusting a two-year-old to eat only one piece of chocolate out of the bag you leave him.

I know many think (and say) that people become cops because they want to bully others and feel important. Don't get me wrong, those people exist. They exist in every profession, and yeah, in police work, they are a bigger problem. But the cops who work places like the SED don't tend to do it for anything other than service. They are sincerely trying to make the community safe. The job is hard and most times it is thankless.

So watching the chief and her posse of sellouts put their heads in the sand and brag about their vast improvements while the good people of the SED are suffering, gangs are getting away with literal murder, and cops are placed in increasingly dangerous situations from the gang activity and lack of support does not make me happy.

Sarge is frustrated too, but he is freshly promoted and he's still finding his way. Becoming upper management in the department is not a job I would ever want. Once you're promoted, the politicians of the cop world expect you to fall in line. If you don't, you don't get promoted, or you get put in a shit job, or you get fired. So, more often than not, after a few years of being upper management, they wear you down and you become a yes-man.

Now, you don't go from warrior to yes-man overnight. They chip away at you. One minor concession at a time, they start to add up and before you know it, you're using the pretext of "once I get to the top, I'll be a good one" as the reason why you're going along with bad decisions. But in doing so, you become that which you once hated.

Not everyone falls into the trap, but it's a rare specimen that stays true to him- or herself, manages to stay effective by looking out for the men and women on the ground, and succeeds with the political body. To be a good officer, you need to do both. To get promoted, you only need politics. You can see the problem.

As I said, with rare exceptions, the worst become vultures, feeding off each other in a race to get to the top. The people who become that way were always that way. The others suffer more of a quiet death of their former self. They attend courses that mock who they once were. They're surrounded by people who paint the picture that the proactive approach is one meant to oppress, and find themselves biting their tongues until they feel comfortable espousing the same ideologies because everyone around them already is doing the same. And at some point, they're speaking the same jargon and making PowerPoints and trying to get some love from the press so they can get an attaboy from the mayor.

Sarge isn't quite there yet, but I can see them trying to pull him into their world. He spent his early career as a warrior, chasing bad guys on a daily basis, so the promotion to sergeant hasn't turned him to the dark side yet. But he's been forced into a position he hates and has no control over, and since this project is the chief's baby, he's forced to just say "yes" or his career, at least in Raleigh, is effectively over. In the chief's eyes, our

Special Project Squad is the most important thing going on in the city, and that means it has to succeed.

When all eyes are on you, out come the bloodsuckers. Lieutenants far and wide descend on us, scurrying around like suckling pigs trying to get a teat. It is nauseating to see so many grown adults fighting to get in line to kiss some ass. I'm honestly embarrassed for them. Sarge knows it too. When he sees us cracking jokes at their expense, he tries to protect us and himself by pointing at us silently, like a scolding father in church, just to let us know that he knows what we're snickering about.

Now, I want to be painfully clear: There is nothing special about these briefings. They exist solely to inform the sergeant and captain what magical tidbits o' knowledge we learned that day, and to explain how we plan to use that information. And for a short period of time it was, in fact, just that. But as more and more lieutenants start showing up to be close to the "action," these meetings are starting to feel more like press conferences. But in classic officer form, rather than ask us questions, it becomes more about giving long soliloquies about how they would handle all these pesky SED problems, even though not one of them has worked there a single day in their careers.

Even in a group of vultures, though, there is a leader. (Actually, I don't know if there is. I don't know anything about vultures, but go with me on this one.) And their Vulture Queen is a woman that I'll call Lieutenant Queen Bee. By my estimation, Queen Bee is the most insufferable and incompetent of them all, and I need you to understand the full weight and breadth of that statement. She works the downtown district, which neighbors the SED, so she should be somewhat competent, because while downtown isn't the SED, it's no joke either. But no. She's a total basket case with a history of being extremely overdramatic at crime scenes. None of us really know how she made rank.

For anyone jumping to the conclusion that she pulled it off because of sex, race, or something like that, I won't deny that there is certainly an advantage to being anything other than a white male when it comes to promotions, but even for these politicians, they typically weed out the totally inept. Queen Bee, much to her credit and our chagrin, somehow made it through.

Queen Bee heard through the political grapevine about this new project that 1) didn't involve any real-life, dangerous policing, and 2) was the chief's new thing. So she just kind of started showing up and acting like she ran the place. She seemed to force her way into the project and then took it upon herself to write operation plans, pretending to be a subject-matter expert on SED policing even though I have never seen her work here a day in her career.

It would have been a real help (to her and *maybe* us) to have . . . I don't know . . . a gang wall to educate her before she started writing standard operating procedures, but what do I know?

The politics and the ineptitude combine to turn my life into a waking nightmare. I now hate my job, and nothing wears me out more than that, other than perhaps seeing my old D-squad buddies living their best lives actually fighting crime and talking about it every day in the locker room. Personal feelings and misery aside, we stick to the chief's agenda, canvassing door-to-door and reporting back what the community has for us.

Most of the complaints we hear are things we really have no control over, like trains going by or the sun rising too early, or things where people have conflicting opinions. "We have too many cops around here!" "Well, if there were cops around here, this wouldn't happen!" Making it more complicated is the fact that some people have those same two opinions at once, depending on how it affects them.

Except for one bright blemish in a city full of blemishes: There is one zit that everyone, young and old, black and white, gentile and Jew, Blood and Crip, wants popped. That zit is the homeless block that is two streets away from the old man's house. To put it in perspective, a local church has been complaining about the street for years! You know it's bad when even Jesus is like, "Hey, guys, get the heck out of here." These guys don't just beg. They aggressively beg, usually while drunk or high or both. Crack pipes and human dumps are everywhere, even or maybe especially on the steps of the sanctuary.

To be fair to the church, they did what they could, often feeding or providing blankets to the homeless, but these guys aren't there for salvation. They show up to get what they can, when they can, and show no respect to the church or to God, and use the times when the congregation shows up to worship as an opportunity to block people away from the doors until they give up some money. They take begging as close to assault as you can without getting arrested.

Most cops, myself included, avoid this block like the plague. The homeless there are less people who have fallen on hard times and need a hand up than they are people who have completely embraced the lifestyle of the street. They party all day, drinking and drugging into the wee hours, only taking short breaks to head downtown to beg until they get enough money for more rocks, malt liquor, and maybe some quarters to gamble with.

So, at today's briefing, when we cite that block as the main complaint during The Meeting™, every lieutenant races to get their two cents in. Naturally, Lieutenant Queen Bee gives us all the great opportunity to hear her wisdom.

"It's important that we remain a symbol of kindness to these people and that we don't make any arrests. We need to treat them with respect and dignity. We need a plan to get them to voluntarily leave the area."

The other lieutenants in the room break their necks nodding vigorously in agreement. They aren't going to argue with her. There's no upside.

I know I sound really negative here, but fuck it: These people aren't here to really change things in the SED. They're here for an attaboy or a medal or plaque at the end of the project. Departments love handing out medals and plaques for this kind of thing, because it makes for good publicity and media exposure, which is the real endgame for these leaders. All they have to do to get their names on the project roster is to stay low-key and not ruffle any feathers.

My favorite part of this plan is that these people think we've never thought of this. "What? Ask the homeless people to leave? Brilliant! Thank you for your insight and tremendous leadership, ma'am!"

Of course voluntary compliance is always the goal, but getting an entire block of lifelong homeless people to disperse on their own accord is a completely fruitless endeavor.

Although anyone with any sense knows how this is going to go, the lieutenants now have a problem that their leadership requires solving. They posture. They give speeches. They meet in secret—in the halls, in the break room, in the bathroom—whispering among each other, fighting for position. Whose team is he on? What does she think? Do you think he'll go along with us? It's like watching *Survivor* but instead of a lot of hot people in bathing suits trying to win a million dollars, it's a bunch of middle-aged people in uniforms that are a size smaller than they should be, trying desperately to win a pat on the back.

My aggravation about their politics aside, the extra leadership is nice. Who wouldn't want to have a seven-member squad with fifteen bosses?

Finally, the brain trust tells us what to do: We will escort them down there so they can personally assess the challenges and make a difference in the lives of the homeless and the community. Fantastic. And I'm not being sarcastic. I'm actually really excited to bring these people there because I'm pretty sure none of them have met a homeless person before, let alone the crew we are about to meet.

When we depart, our convoy of leadership vehicles is so vast it looks like we're in *Swingers*. It's embarrassing, but no one wants to cede control and ride together. As we pull in, the neighborhood obviously thinks there is a murder or something, but then quickly realizes this is some dumb cop bullshit when we all exit the vehicles in clean blue uniforms, shiny shoes, and gleaming gold badges.

The objective today is to do a simple foot patrol through the area and inquire about behavior on the block. It is supposed to be a friendly recon so that these leaders can gauge firsthand what we are up against, so they can form an effective plan later.

As we turn the corner onto the block, we encounter what I can only describe as a scene from an eighties gang movie. We hear the bass of music blaring from an old-school boom box—*thump, thump, thump*. Beer cans and cigarette butts line the gutters. The sweet stench of fresh piss hovers in the air. The vacant buildings were boarded up to keep trespassers and squatters out, but the boards have been yanked off so they can use the houses to shit and do drugs. I don't think anybody sleeps in them, or at least I hope they don't. The smell from outside is enough to send any man packing.

We pour on the schmaltz as we stroll through the camp, greeting folks kindly and extending open hands for handshakes. We make it clear that we are not here to enforce any laws. "Hello, nice to meet you! We just want to learn about your neighborhood! What a lovely backpack! Is that your shopping cart?" We regular cops are all unfazed by this, but the looks on the faces of the captain and the horde of lieutenants from other districts following close behind us, laying eyes on the block for the first time in their careers, are priceless.

But when one of the lieutenants from a normal district sees a crack pipe out in plain sight, things get spicy. Seeing a crack pipe in the SED is like seeing a girl named Ashleigh wearing long brown boots and drinking a pumpkin-spice latte in the fall—they're everywhere. But for this lieutenant, it may just be the first time he's ever seen one outside of training. Rather than ignoring it and just taking note like they ordered us to do, he seizes it dramatically and starts to question the man. "Is this yours, sir?"

"That ain't mine."

Thinking he's going to show off in front of everyone, the lieutenant continues. "If this isn't yours then why did you have it on you? Huh?"

The guy doesn't answer and begins to walk away, which embarrasses the lieutenant. "Hey, I'm talking to you!" he shouts.

Wrong tactic.

In the same way that a warthog doesn't bow up to a lion, a soft-ass desk jockey can't bow up to a hard dude who survives on the streets without repercussions. There's a reason real street cops tend to be way nicer than cops who have it easier—mutual respect is better for everyone.

"Excuuuuse me, Officer? I know you're not talking to me like I'm some punk-ass bitch!"

The lieutenant has no idea what to do. He clearly is used to regular citizens who just comply. Welcome to the SED, broseph. "Well, no . . . I'm just saying . . ."

Sensing weakness, the guy begins to lay it on thick. "You come down here and mess with us even though we aren't doing nothing wrong? You cracka-ass, racist motherfucka! Fuck you! You can have that pipe. Arrest me for it! Come on now! Arrest me, cracka!"

Now homeboy has a dilemma. He knows we aren't supposed to arrest anyone. Hell, I've been struggling with that pain in the ass for months. But he's being talked down to—his authority has been questioned in front of other officers, and I know his ego cannot handle it. He has to save face. Turning toward us, he commands with his deepest tone of voice, "One of you come over here and take this evidence, and give this gentleman a citation."

Now the man glares at us. "Yeah, you rookie-ass bitches! Come over here and give me a fuckin' court date. It ain't even a ticket, bitch! You gotta pay a ticket! All you can do is give me a court date and guess what?! I ain't even gonna go to court anyway. So come on over here, bitch, and give me that paper!" He lets out a wheezing chuckle as the lieutenant stares at him incredulously.

I can't help myself. I try to stifle the laugh, but it comes anyway. Taking the bullet for the team, I walk over to the lieutenant and reach out with bare hands to grab the pipe from him. He's pinching it between two gloved fingers like he's a Frenchman from the Middle Ages about to get into a slap fight. As I reach for the pipe, he pulls it away from me. "Don't you need gloves before touching this evidence?"

"Um, no, sir. We aren't going to send it out to get fingerprinted or anything. I'm going to just put it in an evidence bag, fill out the evidence paperwork, and write a report about how you saw this gentleman with a crack pipe sticking out of his breast pocket, and seized it from him. Then I'll seal the evidence bag and place it into a locker. From there, eventually, an inner office evidence mail clerk will file it in a massive warehouse after she processes it into her computer. Right now I'm gonna walk all the way back to my car—about a quarter mile away—type out a citation, and issue a court date just as the gentleman described. A year from now, after about three or four continuances, he'll get his mandatory community service from the judge. The lady up the street, who has a fake nonprofit set up, will just sign off on it for him. I don't *think* I need gloves for all that but if I do, I know where to find some." I deliver every word with a smile and a cheerful, pleasant, and humble tone, so that even with my dripping sarcasm, it's hard for him to get mad at me without overreacting.

The fire in his eyes could melt the polar caps, but he's already looked the fool twice now, and if he blows a gasket on me, he's really going to have egg on his face, especially because everyone here knows everything I said is factual, and there wasn't a hint of malice in my voice. The homeless guy nods with a smirk. He and I are fully aligned on this.

————

It only gets worse after the citation. The other homeless guys walk up and launch salvo after salvo at the lieutenants until finally they are overwhelmed and we all beat a hasty retreat back to the station. We officers use all the self-discipline we have not to laugh about it. It's not that we want all lieutenants to suffer. We just wanted *these* particular lieutenants to suffer.

The situation rocks them, and they want some kind of vengeance for being made mildly uncomfortable for an hour or so. Queen Bee, previously very focused on treating everyone with dignity and respect, now wants to break up those rapscallions.

"We need to get No Trespassing signs up right now! I didn't see a single No Trespassing sign up! Who are the beat officers for that street!?" she yells in her best command voice, treating her peers like she is the captain.

Dear Lord, thank you for this gift. I will use it well.

Clearing my throat loudly and raising my hand like a schoolkid, I interject: "Ma'am, technically that street is in your district. So whoever you assigned to that beat would be responsible for it."

You could hear a pin drop.

She glares at me, rage in her eyes. Snapping her fingers to herself several times like she's having some kind of episode, she finally squeezes out some words: "Excuseee me, Officer . . ." She leans in to dramatically read my name plate. "Tan-ZEE. That is *not* Downtown District!" She bobs her head back and forth, jabbing her pointer finger into the air. "That is Southeast District, thank you very much!"

One of the other lieutenants interrupts: "Lieutenant Queen Bee . . . he's right. It is actually Downtown District. It's the far corner of it, but it is in fact Downtown." Now her glance cuts from me to him. It's the same lieutenant who was just made to look like a fool out on the street. He's just passing the shame from him to her like some kind of lieutenant hot potato.

Unable to admit she's wrong, she twists and contorts the world so that she remains right. "Well, it's closer to Southeast, so I just *assume*, since their officers handle most of the calls there anyway, that one of them would have some sense! I guess not! They need to take it upon themselves to put up some No Trespassing signs!"

I let out a laugh, then immediately try to disguise it as a cough, which only makes it more awkward and obvious.

"Well, Tan-ZEE, do you have something to add?" Lieutenant Queen Bee snarls.

"No, ma'am. If you want me to manage one of the beats in your district, I am at your service . . . ma'am."

She stares at me with the fiery intensity of a thousand suns and brings her voice to a climax. "We are going back out there today, and we are putting up signs!" Even though she is not in charge, everyone kind of goes along with it.

Looks like we're putting up signs.

Half of us leave the station to go and pick up a few signs from the supply warehouse. The other guys stay back and research the names of the homeowners so we can get a No Trespassing letter on file in case the signs disappear.

As we arrive back at the street, signs in hand, we are greeted by our new and greatest fans. "Look who's back! They sent the rookies back out to hang some signs!" They are laughing their asses off. "Looks like I'm getting me a new sign!" "I'm gonna take a shit on that sign, pig!" One gentleman walks up to me and says, "Hey, boy, what do you think hanging those signs is gonna do?!"

"Oh, I don't know, sir. Maybe it will act as inspiration and will guide you from your troubled ways towards a fruitful and meaningful life, full of purpose and prosperity . . . But truthfully, I really have no idea if it will work." The laughter goes cold as he tries to process my sarcasm.

We hang the signs and head back to the station. Sarge is waiting there for us. "Did you accomplish your mission?"

"Roger, Sarge," I reply quickly. He nods and we disappear into the back. Once there, we shut the door and turn the lights off so the other 116 supervisors that we now have won't know where we are until our shift is over.

The next day we all gather around for the morning's brief. As with the previous day, all the supervisors argue with each other, trying to coordinate the day's agenda and be the top dog. The first thing on the to-do list is to return to the homeless block, this time with a megaphone so that Lieutenant Queen Bee can give the occupants a loud warning and explain how the No Trespassing signs can lead to future arrests if they are not adhered to. All five of us are sent out to find one megaphone for her, which is a phenomenal use of taxpayer money.

In the Army, there is a thing called the E-4 Mafia. E-4s have no real formal power, but they are the building blocks of all tasks. To get something done, you need to have E-4 buy-in. So when a leader sucks, be it a low-level sergeant or a high-level officer, the E-4 Mafia has a way of well . . . getting their way. Parts will disappear from vehicles of leaders they don't like. Maybe a unit will fail a critical task that a leader would be graded on after excelling at it for years. Maybe they'll just work a little slower every day. The E-4 Mafia excels at passively resisting bad leaders.

As a man who had once been an E-4, I suggest that the first place we look for a megaphone is Starbucks. I can tell we all need a coffee break and a chance to vent a little before the stupidity begins again. We return to the station about an hour later and I can tell that Queen Bee is frustrated at how much time it took us to find one megaphone. "Where have you been?" she snaps. "Ma'am, you'd be surprised how hard it is to find a megaphone in this town. Everyone buys online now," I answer. *You treat us like children, and we will act like them.*

We arrive back to the block, this time with Queen Bee leading the way, megaphone in hand. As we turn the corner, my smile creeps to the edges of my eyes, it's so big. There is not a fucking sign in sight. Queen Bee is pissed. "I thought I told you to hang up signs yesterday?! Where are *my* signs? Where are my signs that I requested?"

I immediately answer, "We hung up ten signs yesterday, Lieutenant. I don't know what happened to them, but we hung them with a stapler."

"How can I make an announcement about the signs if there aren't any signs!" She pouts a moment, and then, as if a revelation has struck her, she turns the megaphone on. "EXCUSE ME, folks. My name is Lieutenant Queen Bee. We are a community-based policing project for this area, and we have been tasked with making the streets and community a safer place. We are trying—" She is abruptly cut short.

"You don't do this shit in the white neighborhoods! Why you comin' down here and botherin' us!" a man screams.

"Now, sir. That's not . . ." she attempts before she is hit with a barrage of insults. They come fast and furious and she has no retort for them. It's so bad that once again we retreat.

Lieutenant Queen Bee is furious, and her wounded ego dictates her next plan. "I want you all to go back out there and find the tallest ladder you can find, and I want those signs posted so high that they cannot be taken down!"

Oh, fuck yeah. This is going to kill an entire day. I am now in full E-4 mode. In sharp contrast to my last job, where I would do anything I could to get better and be better, I now find myself happy anytime I can waste time and kill as much of the day as possible. And no one has dropped a time waster like this on my lap . . . well . . . ever!

First we drive across the city to find the largest ladder available. Then we have to find a truck capable of transporting it. Now it's time for a late lunch. When we finally roll in with our forty-foot ladder in tow, we get a standing ovation and boisterous laughter from our local squatters. To be fair, if I were them, I'd be doing the same fucking thing. Regardless, we climb the giant ladder and hang the signs up as high and as visible as possible.

The next day, Queen Bee once again leads the entourage into the block, certain that this time they will see she means business! And you know what? Those crazy motherfuckers have taken down all the signs!

I don't know how they did it. I don't know if they made a human pyramid. I don't know if one of them is a former lumberjack. I don't know if they have a firefighter buddy who did them a solid. I have no idea how they did it, but I absolutely love it. It's a phenomenal fuck-you.

Don't get me wrong. They aren't in the right living on this street and harassing people, but if I have to choose between people who take shits on the street and people who are full of shit in the precinct, I have to tell you, I prefer the former.

As Queen Bee looks around and realizes what has happened, fury fills her, but then it dissipates.

She leaves the project shortly after, and one by one, so do the rest. You see, these guys all thought this was an easy way to move up the ladder (see what I did?), but once they saw that there would be real work involved to make even the tiniest of improvements, they were out.

With all of them finally gone, life gets better, and Sarge has a new plan.

"Three of you will work days, and three will work nights. You gentlemen can rotate that as needed. Violent crime has actually gone up during this project and now that the bullshit has subsided, we are gonna get back to real police work. Monday, we'll have a conference with the technical unit [a group of nerds who can set up cameras, track phones, etc.], Drugs and Vice, the Alcohol Law Enforcement agents, and the Gang Unit. They are gonna brief you guys on how they can help with this project. We'll get bad guys off the block, but we'll do it quietly, outside the limelight. We won't go in there arresting guys and chasing them through the streets, causing a scene. Instead we'll watch them, monitor them, set up fake buys with confidential informants, and take out warrants.

"As far as the homeless camp, we'll roll down there with the van and fill it up every morning. We will go down there, jump out, grab as many as we can, get 'em in the van, and process them. We'll do that every morning, first thing, until they get tired of it and leave. No drama, no arguing, no bantering, we already gave them warnings so now it's game on. The main thing is that we aren't just hitting blue lights and screaming on the radio every five minutes. This project is just a political shenanigan. They don't want a lot of noise from us . . . At the same time, though, we aren't going to just shake hands and kiss babies all day while violent crimes are skyrocketing in the area. Any questions?"

"Yes, if that starts Monday, what do we do today?" I ask.

"Go post up No Trespassing signs one more time and take note of any asshole that talks shit. Monday morning, they'll be the first in the van. After you finish that, grab you some lunch and disappear back into the office. Stay out of trouble. We'll take care of business come Monday."

"Roger, Sarge!"

Now *this* is a great sergeant. He's a go-getter, and still hasn't drunk the political Kool-Aid. I'm excited to see what Monday will bring.

————

After making our first van of arrests bright and early Monday morning, we meet down at the special operations building. The conference room looks like it belongs in an episode of *Law & Order*. Maps and computer graphics line the walls and a large oval table with tall leather chairs sits in the center. The walls are glass, with automatic shutters to conceal the occupants when needed. Bearded men in ragged clothes chill in one corner of the room, while men in suits and fresh haircuts sit in the chairs. A couple of nerds stand in another corner, gathered around a laptop on a wheeled base. We are the only guys in the building wearing standard police uniforms, so actually, maybe we're the nerds here.

"Come in, gentlemen, have a seat," one of the suited men says and gestures. We take our seats and the briefing begins. One of the bearded dudes raises his hand to go first.

"What's up, fellas! We are the Drugs and Vice unit. If you need an informant or want to flip someone as an informant, come see us. You need to set up a prostitution sting? Let us know. For now, here are some drug test kits so you can do field tests. This will help you get informants more quickly, without waiting on lab results before signing them up. Also, if you need help with search warrants and big-picture stuff, we can help with that too."

The nerds are up next. They brief us on how they can set up cameras on light poles or street signs. They show us an undercover van that, from the outside, looks like a work van with ladders on the roof and a dashboard littered with fast-food wrappers and empty cigarette cartons. There are rolled-up site plans squeezed into the front seat just like every stereotypical work van on the planet, but if you slip through the tiny door that leads to the back of the van, it is like entering a spaceship. There are monitors, radios, audio-level lights, headphones, and a desk. There is even a toilet, and if that isn't cool enough, the desk's bench folds down into a bed. It is a surveillance van that can sustain two detectives for forty-eight hours.

Each rung of the ladder on the roof houses a small camera with night-vision capabilities, giving you 360-degree eyes night or day. They give us a quick class on how to record video and audio from it, then hand us the keys! They plan to set up a computer in our office with access to any pole cams they set up for us. We will literally be able to sit and watch suspected dealers on a street corner from the quiet of the office. *Incredible*. All we have to do is tell them where we need cameras, and they will do all the paperwork to make it happen. This is wild.

The Gang Unit strolls in late (with the ultimate "cool guy" vibes) and gives us an amazing crash course on gang activity in the area. We already know the gang names and have a basic understanding of their current rank structure and the key players, but the Gang Unit takes us to a whole new level. They explain problems in the rank structures. It probably will surprise no one to learn that just like in the police department, or really any organization, the gangs have leadership issues, with various members lobbying for power. They have guys snitching on other guys to snatch their positions from beneath them, guys taking out hits on rivals, and a really impressive mountain of treachery and dissension.

Once we're up to speed there, the Gang Unit plays audio from jail calls that indicate possible hits that are scheduled to go down in the area, and they bring us up to speed on several guys who are flipping gangs. This last detail is especially important, since the thirteen-year-old who was shot in the face is directly tied to gang-flipping.

In my entire career, I've never had the tools and freedom that we have just received. My job has gone from the absolute worst to "holy shit this is cool" in the last five minutes.

The obvious place to start our surveillance is the mini-mart. We get a hidden camera installed on a light pole across the street and use the camera to document crack buyers. Once we have enough buys on camera to have a reasonable chance at an indictment, we spring into action.

Our process is awesome. A buyer approaches the dealer and makes a buy, and then when the buyer gets down the street and away from the dealer and any possible witnesses, we arrest them. The dealer has no idea the buyer was arrested and continues to deal until he needs to re-up his supply. When he does, we follow him to the resupply point and hopefully find a big stash.

Now, it sounds perfect, but there is no perfect plan when the enemy is smart, as ours is. These people are career criminals. Sometimes a small resupply gets delivered to them by a car or scooter so that they never have to risk someone tailing them to the mother lode. As if their tradecraft weren't enough of a challenge, we also need to be cautious because we still can't get into any big chases or uses of force while on this "community-based policing project." As an example, trying to take down cars is a huge no-no.

After a month of cherry-picking dealers and working days, my life is getting tedious. I need some action. I need something. A half mile away, violent crime is through the roof, and ideally, I'd like to be helping there.

"Sarge, are we ever going back to nights?" I ask, like a child asking if we're almost there on a long car ride.

"As a matter of fact, yeah. They just found a dead fifteen-year-old behind a house. Looks like he was the victim of another drive-by shooting last week. Some kid cutting through a backyard on the way to the gas station found him. What's even crazier is that the victim was missing his shoes. But it turns out, the kid who found him admitted to stealing the shoes before reporting the body to the police."

The SED never ceases to amaze me. "Holy shit, how old was the kid who found him?"

"Eleven."

"That's gross! He took the shoes off a dead body that's been rotting for the last week?"

"It was only out there from the weekend, so more like three days."

"Oh, okay. Well, in that case, it's totally reasonable. I can absolutely see taking shoes off a three-day-old dead body. But I draw the line after that."

Sarge ignores my banter and continues with important information.

"Well, regardless, that's like the twelfth shooting on that block in the last month, so we're going to switch gears over there and just be a presence in the area at night, to hopefully deter some of the shootings. We'll still play it low-key. Only make a traffic stop or jump out on someone if you know they are a gang member, *and* you have a good idea that they're on the street to do violence. We have to stay out of the limelight or it's back to going door-to-door . . ."

Sarge looks me in the eyes for a while during that pause. He wants it to sink into my brain that no one wants that. He then continues: "At the same time, the district needs help getting the violent crime down."

So, in case you haven't been keeping up: Upper management eliminated proactive policing, causing an increase in crime. They then created community policing to combat the crime. When they saw firsthand that it didn't work, they fled from the program. Now they are looking the other way so that we can begin proactive policing once again, but if we get caught doing it while in this capacity, they will have full deniability. In other words, we are tasked with solving a problem they created, but we have to do it with our hands tied behind our backs, and with some more gadgets. Wild.

The following week (finally!) we go back to nights, and I am paired up with a younger officer we'll call Officer Major. Major is a go-getter and a nice guy. He plays politics a little bit, but he's a good egg. We get along pretty well, but I keep him at a distance, because fair or unfair, I have a feeling he's going to cause me problems. His uniform is always perfect, his boots are always shined, and he always sports a fresh professional haircut. Me, on the other hand, well, my hair is too long, my uniform is wrinkled, and I can't remember the last time I shined my boots. I'm not saying that I'm cool or anything because of that—I'm just saying, the two of us have the makings of a good buddy-cop movie.

After a quick coffee stop, we notice a small sedan parked between a house and an apartment building with its engine running, but its lights off. As we pull in behind it to run the tag, the car takes off without turning on its lights, running a Stop sign in the process and aggressively speeding up after it. We drop back and hold off turning on the blue lights, in fear that the car will run; we do not have permission to chase it. We continue following from a distance until it turns into a large neighborhood. Finally we hit the lights just to see if the car will stop. It does. We look at each other in surprise, and slowly get out to carefully approach the rear of the vehicle. We can see two men sitting in the front seats.

Major goes to the driver's side and I go to the passenger's side, stopping just behind the rear-door pillar. I can tell that the passenger doesn't even know I am standing there. His eyes are fixed on Major. "Hey there, sir. I'm Officer Major. Did you know you were driving with your lights off, and that you ran a Stop sign a little ways back?"

As he speaks, I watch the passenger. There is just something not quite right about him. I can see his jugular vein pulsing. His right hand is shaking, and his left hand is slowly inching up his thigh toward his pocket. I can see a bulge in that pocket but the low light makes it hard to tell what it is. I interrupt his movement by tapping on his window with my flashlight. His head snaps around and he has deer-in-the-headlights eyes as he peers into the beam.

"Hey, young man! Do me a favor and roll your window down." The teen complies and then huffs at me, "Yo, bruh?! Why you sneakin' up on me like that?"

"Oh, I'm sorry about that, buddy. Can you do me a favor and place your hands on the dash?"

"Why you want me to do that? Am I being detained?"

"Yes, sir, this is a traffic stop, and I see you have something in your pocket. Since I don't know what it is, I want you to place your hands on the dash until we finish up the traffic stop."

He fires back, "You can't tell me what to do. I wasn't even driving! I ain't detained for shit. Matter of fact, let me outta this car." He reaches for the door handle.

"Young man, place your hands on the dash and just relax," I say sternly. We lock eyes, and I can see fight-or-flight rearing up in his brain. I know this look well by now, so I decide to nip it in the bud.

"Young man, you have something in your pocket, and I perceive it to possibly be a weapon, so for my safety and for yours, place your hands on the dash and do not reach anywhere near your left pocket."

"It's a fuckin' cell phone, RoboCop! Calm the fuck down."

The kid continues to stare at me, and I stare back. The hostility between us is building and I don't feel this is going anywhere good. Finally, reluctantly, he places his hands out on the dash. I try to ease the tension with a polite "thank you" but he isn't having any of it. He looks down at his pocket and then back at me. "Fuck this! Get me a black cop out here! You niggas out here murdering kids like me over fuckin' cell phones! I don't trust you! Get me a black cop right now!"

"Sir, if you keep your hands on the dash, we won't have any issues, but if you move your hand and go for your pocket, I will act accordingly."

"You're going to shoot me! Over a fucking cell phone!"

"Major, go ahead and step the driver out of the vehicle for his safety. This guy has something in his pocket, and I don't want the driver in my way." I can feel Major staring at me, but I never take my eyes off the passenger, not even while speaking. Major steps the driver out of the car and sits him on the curb.

"Now what, Tansey?" he asks.

I lean down into the window opening and speak softly. "Young man, what is in your pocket? And I know it isn't a phone."

"Yo, you crazy as fuck and you know you gonna shoot me . . . I see it in your eyes." He screams out, "Get me a black cop now!" He takes his hand off the dash, so I reach in and pin his chest to the seat.

"Put your hand back on the dash." His hand freezes, hesitating, hanging in space. "Okay, I'm taking you out of the car, and I am going to remove whatever is in your pocket so tell me now, IS IT A GUN? If it is, it is not a big deal. I will remove it from you and give you a citation for misdemeanor Conceal Carry. I have a body mic on and a car camera watching us, so you don't have to worry about me shooting you as long as you comply. If it's a gun, it's really not that big a deal, but you need to tell me now."

"Fuck you! It's a phone, you fuckin' cowboy!" he screams directly into the microphone that is attached to my belt. It is glowing green, indicating that it is recording. "You are violating my rights and calling my phone a gun so you can violate my rights even more and probably shoot me!"

"Okay, listen very carefully. These instructions will be the most important instructions you may ever get. It is of the utmost importance that you obey them directly." I pop the door open. "First, I want you to slowly take your left hand and place it on your head." Surprisingly, he does so. I continue: "Good, now place your right hand on your—" He lunges outward, jamming his shoulder into my waist as he tries to charge his way out the door. I use his forward momentum to sling him onto the ground by his shirt. His left hand disappears under his waist as I dive down on top of him, using my full weight to pin his hand under his body. Major runs over and begins plunging his hands under the teen's body to secure the hand.

"GUN, GUN, GUN, TANSEY!" Major yells.

I rear back and punch the teen in the side of the face as hard as I can. He lifts his head and attempts to pull farther away from me so I can't hit the same spot twice, but I come down hard with a second blow. His skull bounces off the concrete, and I feel his body stiffen. He turns his face toward me and looks at me with a blank stare as I deliver another punch, connecting with his mouth and chin. His head snaps back and then falls forward hard onto the pavement. He is out cold.

Major pulls the gun out from under him, prying the teen's fingers from its handle. I sit up and call for an ambulance and a supervisor over the radio. *Fuck! I did it again. Here we go.* To be clear, we didn't do anything wrong if this was a regular beat, but this wasn't exactly a low-key traffic stop.

My mood is instantly glum. I expect to get kicked off the squad and sent back to regular duty. I don't care if I do—in fact, that would be a blessing. I just don't want to return in failure and embarrass Sergeant Tom. As the EMS truck arrives, the suspect regains consciousness. He howls repeatedly that we beat him up over a cell phone. Regardless of the evidence and the fact that he just tried to kill us, he never stops calling it a phone. The gun comes back stolen and attached to another strong-arm robbery. These guys are young gang members, doing gang member stuff.

We transport the suspect to the hospital to treat the gash on his forehead. Once it has been bandaged, we take him to jail. Sarge calls my phone and wants me to immediately return to the station to download the video from my dashcam and microphone. I know I am toast. I am going to be scorned for causing chaos and punching a seventeen-year-old in the face. I sit down and type out my report, then turn in the paperwork before clocking out.

The next night when I return to work, I know the Karens will be calling at any moment. Sure enough, Sarge calls me into his office right after roll call. The captain and lieutenant are both standing in his office too as Sarge takes a seat behind his desk.

"Shut the door, Tans."

I do as I'm told. As soon as the door closes, I begin. "Look, Sarge, I'm sorry. We tried to just chase them off Star Street and question them about why they were there. I didn't know all that shit was gonna go down! It's not like I plan any of this shit!"

The captain laughs. "Calm down, Tansey. Please, have a seat." I once again do as I'm told. "The reason you're here is not because you did anything wrong. We just need to ask you some questions. That's all." Sarge turns his computer toward me and hits play. I watch and listen to the footage. I hear myself speak calmly to the teen, and then watch as he violently tries to charge out of the car, and I punch the shit out of him over and over again.

Sarge stops the tape and asks, "Do you think you did anything wrong?"

I answer confidently, "No. But if I could go back in time, I probably wouldn't have encouraged Major to pull the car over."

"Do you think you used the necessary amount of force?"

Shocked that they were asking me if I went too far with a guy trying to kill me, I get a little pissed-off. "I mean shit, I could have punched him one time real hard instead of three times kinda hard, but he had a fucking gun for fuck's sake."

"That's our point! Watch the video! Major yells 'GUN GUN GUN' and moves aside for you to shoot him. Instead, you go all Chuck Liddell on his ass. What if your punches hadn't swayed him from getting the gun out, and he shot Major? Or you!? You took a gamble with your fist, and we want to know why."

You've got to be fucking kidding me.

"Wait. Am I in trouble because I didn't shoot that motherfucker?! Unfucking believable! Screw it, I'm done with this bullshit. Send me the fuck somewhere else!" In my entire time policing, I never yelled at a superior officer, but this was re-goddamn-diculous.

"Calm down, Tansey," the captain interrupts. "You aren't in trouble, but this is serious. We need to know the psychology behind it. We want to write this up and have higher management review it so we can address it as a department. We can't have officers being afraid to use deadly force just because society doesn't like it. And furthermore, we can't have officers successfully fighting suspects over guns and automatically think they're in trouble for something. Now, let's sit down and discuss this."

We go over every second of the video. I am asked to analyze every action I took, over every second of tape. It is helpful, though. They show me several key points to improve upon for next time, but I am still upset, and the stupidity of the entire situation has really sunk in, from every level.

The department warns us constantly that if anything happens, we'll be dragged publicly by the media. The department shows us through actions that they will not readily have our backs, and if there is an opportunity to blame an officer for political gain, they will. They take actions that give criminals the upper hand and blame us for trying to combat crime, and then they have the fucking audacity to ask why I didn't shoot?

On the other hand, this fucking kid is ready to die at the age of seventeen over what? A stolen gun?

I drive home that night wondering what the fuck is wrong with everyone—these idiots in the gangs, my chain of command, and one last person: me. *What am I doing in this fucking job?*

18

SENIOR OFFICER REAPER

The project finally wraps up after about five months, and sure enough, we receive some attaboys and a commemorative T-shirt. It was a great learning experience, despite my best effort to try to hate everything about it, but it's a relief to be back to doing real line work again. Red and I pick up right where we left off, and immediately we are back out on the streets hunting bad guys together. I am on night shift today, which, if you haven't figured out by now, is my favorite. Just as I sit down in the squad room, Red calls me on my cell phone.

"Yo, we just sat down to eat, where are you?" I ask her.

"I just got a call about a body or something behind Wee Bob's store. Can you come check in with me?"

Say no more. I wrap up my sandwich and head out to meet her at Wee Bob's, a local convenience mart just off MLK Boulevard. The store is surrounded by thick woods on three sides, and there is a short trail behind it that leads to some apartments. When I arrive, I find Red out front.

"Hey, Tans. It says in the call notes that there was a Facebook post about a dead body behind Wee Bob's."

It's just after midnight. Although there are a few people hanging around outside the mart, there isn't anything too peculiar going on. We approach the handful of guys standing there. "Hey, gents, have you heard anything about a body behind the mart?" They snicker and say, "Hell nah." We return to the cars and grab our flashlights.

"So, how long ago did the Facebook post go out?" I ask Red, thinking about my uneaten sandwich and wondering if we are on a wild-goose chase.

"I don't know. They emailed me a screenshot of the post, so let's see." She brings the email up on her phone. "There is a body behind Wee Bob's," it reads, with sixteen or so comments under it. The Facebook post had gone up almost an hour before the call. It took that long for anyone to bother calling 911.

We walk around the back of the store, and as we approach the dark corner that leads to where the body is allegedly located, anxiety builds a little. You just never know what you're going to get with this job. Finally we arrive at the corner, turning sharply to see . . . nothing. There is no one back here.

There is a nearly overgrown trail that leads to the apartments. It doesn't look like anyone has traversed it in a while, though, and at night it looks like that trail in every fantasy movie that leads to a big fucking problem, like a witch or a giant spider that will eat you or something. It's creepy.

We begin walking down the trail and sure enough, there it is: a body lying face up with a bullet hole between the eyes. At first glance it appears that the man had been coming from the apartments when he was shot in the head, and our best guess is the suspect left back toward the apartments. We're pretty sure this is the case because the grass is not at all agitated between the body and the store, whereas we can clearly see that it was in the other direction.

We set up crime scene tape and call for detectives. Soon a wave of suits shows up to gather info, interview people, photograph the crime scene, and collect evidence. In what seems like only a few moments, the crime scene is packed, with agents from the City-County Bureau of

Identification (CCBI) and detectives spread about. Red was the first to find the body, so she is the one briefing the agents. Since I'm just standing there while people work around me, kind of in the way, I decide to wander back to my car to ride this call out and wait for her.

While sitting in my car pretending to type but really watching *Drinkin' Bros* on YouTube, a man approaches and asks to speak with me. I get out of the car to talk to him, and he leans in and whispers to me, "I might know the victim."

My spidey senses start tingling. "Why do you think you know the victim?"

"My brother-in-law left a few hours ago to go to Wee Bob's, and he ain't back yet. He has been beefin' with some gang kids down the street. I told him to knock that shit off. He was yelling on his phone at one of 'em when he left the house."

I ask him for his brother-in-law's name and description. When he proceeds to describe the outfit of the dead man to a T, I call the detectives to let them know what I have learned. They ask me to try to get the man to go with me voluntarily to the detective's station for questioning. I ask him, but he refuses.

I don't want to let the detectives down, so I improvise. "Sir, let me be real. Your brother-in-law matches the description of the body I saw."

He begins to lose it, stomping his foot and crying out, "No! No! I don't believe you! I knew it! I knew he shoulda left them boys alone!"

"Sir, I know you're mad, but we need you right now. You have information about these gang kids that we need to bring them to justice."

"Fuck that, your justice ain't our justice! I ain't saying shit, and you'll know who did it when you find them dead on Corey Street!" This is another street that is predominantly occupied by gangs.

"I know you're mad, heartbroken, and I can't even imagine what else you must be feeling. Let me drive you down there, and you can just tell them what you told me. You don't have to tell them anything else, but if you could just tell them what you told me, that'll be your golden check mark on civil duties and good deeds for the week."

He paces for a moment, then he comes back to my car. "I'll come with you, but can we stop by my apartment first so I can tell the baby-sitter I'm gonna be late? And I need to grab my phone charger."

"Sure, man, that's fine, where's your apartment?" He points, and I realize that his apartment is literally right where the trail comes out from Wee Bob's. I am shocked at the proximity. I pull into a space but before I can get the car in park, he opens the door and takes off running toward the stairs. I jump out, confused and unsure what to do.

"Yo! What are you doing?" I yell. He yells back for me to hold on. I sit by the car and wait, thinking that he is probably going to ghost me. I must have spooked him. *Damn it.* But then he pops out of the stairwell and runs back to my car. We both get in and shut our respective doors. The situation gives me pause. "What was that about?"

"I ran up there to tell the babysitter I'll be right back."

"Did you grab your charger?"

"Nah . . . I lost my phone."

My heart sinks. Something is wrong. The man had his cell phone in his hand the whole time he was talking to me. He was even texting on it. Why is he now claiming to have lost it? And why did he run like that up the stairs? I haven't searched him or patted him down, and now he is going to be sitting in my car for the next twenty minutes on the way to the detective station.

This is a bad plan, Tansey.

The drive is quiet and awkward. He answers every one of my questions with a single-word response. We get to the station and I pat him down before going in. *Phew! Clean.* I place him in an interview room, then shut the door. As I brief the detective on what just transpired, I can see he's more than a little interested, and immediately goes into the room to have a chat with the man. Less than thirty minutes later, he comes out in somewhat of a panic.

"Tansey, where did you take him before coming here?"

"Some apartments by Wee Bob's," I say, already feeling like I had fucked up before, and now getting that gut feeling confirming it.

"Shit, you dumbass, take me there right now. Come on, let's roll."

As the car doors close and we head back to the apartment, he jumps right into it. "That guy is the murderer. He shot back into the apartment to dump the murder weapon. You'd better hope the gun is still in there, Tansey."

I don't hope the gun is there. I pray it is. The last thing I want to do is be the guy who ruins a murder case. Professionally, I'll be a laughing-stock for getting played, while personally I will know that I prevented the victim and their family from ever getting justice. The drive feels like an eternity.

When we finally arrive at the apartment, I scale the stairs, bounding up as fast as I can, skipping every other step. I take a position to the side of the door with my gun out while the detective knocks on it. A petite, friendly teenage girl opens the door.

"Hello, miss. Did a gentleman come in here and leave a gun and a phone?"

"Yes, Officer. He ran in here quickly and threw his gun and his phone on the couch. I didn't want them hanging out in the open room, so I put them in his room. As far as I know, they are still there." The detective and I are both kind of shocked she is being this forthcoming and kind, but we'll take it. We quickly secure the apartment and call for a search warrant, which we get. The gun and phone are both recovered from the bedroom, and I breathe a huge sigh of relief.

The detective, relieved himself, pats me on the back. "So, Officer Tansey, did you learn a lesson tonight?"

"Yeah, I did. Holy shit."

"Good, I won't tell anyone you drove the suspect around and helped him dispose of a murder weapon as long as you promise to never let any-one in your car ever again without a proper pat-down first."

"I promise."

It's been a while since I've been tricked like that, but it's a good reminder of how quickly you can get yourself in a bad situation. The guy had really good control of his fight-or-flight and he threw me off the mark by offering up information. He put himself in the position of being the helpful family member, instead of a suspect, so I lowered my defenses. I could have ruined the case, or even got myself killed. I got lucky this time.

The sun is cracking the horizon now, as night becomes early morning. Red and I head to a spot behind a church where we do most of our paperwork.

"Was the guy you let in your car the murderer?" she immediately asks me.

"You swear it stays between us?"

"No, but go ahead anyway," she says with a smile.

As I tell her the story, she cries with laughter. I am not amused. "Red, shit! Come on!"

"No, Tansey, you're a fucking idiot and that shit's funny! You could have gotten shot in the face!" She is laughing so hard that she begins to cough.

"And that's funny . . . me almost getting shot in the face?"

"Yeah, it is, it's funny, and I'm telling everyone. What an idiot!" she cackles.

"Well, I'm never checking in with you again. I wish you were that body with a hole in the head behind Wee Bob's," I snap, half joking and half bitchy.

"Whatever, you love me."

———

"424-David, shots fired, multiple victims, 454 Dacien Road behind the apartments."

Shit, I'm only two blocks from there. "Raleigh, I am en route, thirty seconds out."

While it's good to be back on the street, lately the string of gang violence has been overwhelming for everyone: the people of Raleigh, the cops, EMS, everyone.

I pull behind the apartment buildings and my eyes dart to a man covered in blood and waving me over to a white pickup truck. Jumping out of my car and sprinting toward him, I see a body, crumpled under the tailgate with part of his scalp missing. There appears to be a bullet hole in his head.

The man in white is waving his arms and screaming in a thick Spanish accent as blood gushes from a wound above his face. "They shoot 'em, man! They shoot 'em and hit my head with *pistola*! They rob the money!" He is standing over another Hispanic male who is lying on his back and trying to cover a gut wound with his hands. The man bleeding from the gut is in dire straits. He stares up at me with wide eyes that have a thousand questions in them. I kneel beside him, ignoring the man with the bloody face.

"Who shot you?" I ask.

The man just stares up at me, slightly arching his shoulders back as he tries to gasp for breath. He is leaving this world and can't communicate with anything but his eyes. I slide my hands into some latex gloves, move his hands aside, and put pressure on his gaping wound. His hands drop, limp and nearly lifeless. His eyes never leave mine.

I speak again, gently. "Hey, señor, it's going to be okay. I can hear the ambulance. Can you hear it?" I place my left hand to my ear and cup it to show that I can hear the ambulance. He just blinks and arches his shoulders back for another breath. He isn't getting the air he needs and arches his shoulders even more, his lips parting. I watch as panic and fear set in; his soul cries out through his eyes, soundless, but I can hear him, nonetheless.

When someone is dying of cancer or another illness, they have time to put things in place. They have time to say goodbye to loved ones and friends. This poor man does not have that time. Lying in a dark parking lot, bleeding out from his stomach, his eyes communicate a lifetime's worth of unknown questions. Maybe he is asking me why he got shot? Or maybe he is asking for his mother, or father, or wife, or children? Maybe he is begging for more time. Whatever questions he has, I don't have the answers.

An even greater panic sets in, and his pupils darken. "Hey, you are okay. It's all okay. *Un momento, por favor.* They're coming." He arches his shoulders back again, his mouth wide-open as he fights for his soul. I know, and he knows, that this is the end. "Hey! Hey! Don't you do it, brother, you look at me." My face is inches from his, my right hand sinking into the bullet hole in his gut. I can feel the warm pool of blood oozing against the palm of my glove. I sit back to ease the pressure on the wound, never taking my eyes from his. Then his eyes roll gently back.

I want to cry.

He is so scared, and not ready to die. An EMS worker runs up and pushes me out of the way, saddles up on top of him, and starts chest compressions. I know it is over, though. I can just tell. And I hate that I've seen it enough that I can tell. They load him up onto the ambulance and I jump in next to him. On the way to the hospital, they shock him several times and pump his chest without a break. Minutes later, they pronounce him dead.

I wish this is the end of my night, but we're just getting started.

The district is blowing up with calls, and we only have one sergeant on. He calls my cell. "You stay there with the doctors to tell the family he's dead. You were with him at the end, so just be gentle. Be there for them. Do you have any questions?"

"No . . . well, yeah: Do you know what family he has?" I ask, trying to get myself prepared for whatever is coming my way.

"No, but whoever it is, I'm sure you can handle it," he answers gruffly. He's having a long night too.

I put my phone away and walk over to the doctor. "I'm the only officer here, so I'll be here with you when you tell the family."

He eyes me up and down, oblivious to the night I'm having. "Okay, great, we're just waiting for the nurse and chaplain."

I am emotionally exhausted. The bridge of my nose feels like a dam holding back a flood of tears. I've seen a lot in my life, between combat and policing, but I cannot get the image of that man out of my head. He didn't want to go. It was just a normal day for him, and now he's gone. *I hope I made it just a little bit better for him.* I am not sure I did.

Once the nurse and chaplain arrive, we walk down a series of hallways until we get to a small room. The doctor knocks softly before opening the door. Inside is an older lady and a girl in her twenties, about the same age as the victim. The girl has long, black hair and freshly painted red fingernails. Despite the time of night, her makeup is fully done. The nurse interprets in Spanish as the doctor gives out a quick "I'm sorry, but he's dead." The first time I experienced one of these moments, I judged the doctor for not handling it perfectly, but with time, I've come to realize that there is no perfect way to handle it. It's always bad. Some doctors explain everything. Some try to be kind and reassuring. Some just rip the Band-Aid off.

The news is obviously a shock. The girl falls violently to her knees, letting out a wild sob on the way down. Although I don't speak Spanish, I innately understand every word she says, just as I had understood the victim's silent pleas. She crawls over to me and grabs hold of my ankles, looking up at me, yelling and weeping. I look down at her, unable to speak, completely unable to help her, the same way I was unable to help the love of her life. The older lady is slumped in a chair, crying softly into the thick sleeves of the priest's arm.

The nurse sits down, and the doctor slowly backs out of the room. I don't know what to do, so I just stand there while the young girl weeps at my feet. She grabs on to my knees, shaking, then twists a ring off her left ring finger, sobbing in Spanish. She eventually lets go, and I move to a chair. She lies on the ground for over an hour, crying and stroking her wedding band.

I try to be the rock in the room. The older lady, who I have to assume is the victim's mother, comes over and hugs me, crying into my shirt. I reach out to pat her back, but suddenly notice there are splatters all over my right hand. The victim's blood must have seeped into my gloves. I become hyperfocused on the blood-spattered hand, trying to hide it behind my back.

In these moments you are forever intertwined with the family. I will always remember them, feeling their pain, imagining it was my wife or my child that was now gone forever. And they will always remember me, the stranger who was there when their world fell apart. It's a relationship that neither of us wants, but I must do my part.

The girl gets off the floor and moves to the bench I am on. She punches me in the shoulder. I wince, as it catches me off guard. She hits me again in the same spot and then stands up, looming over me, striking me repeatedly and yelling. The older lady steps in to block her. I lower my head like a shamed pup that has just been caught peeing on the rug. She finally sits back down, sobbing uncontrollably into her own hands.

I leave the room. I want a full retreat, to go hide and cry for a solid hour, but I can't. I am stuck in this hell. I stay at the hospital for hours as waves of emotions pour through me over and over again. I stay until a group of family members arrives to relieve me.

Daylight is just beginning to show outside, and my shift is over. When I get back to the locker room, the other guys are already gone, and C-shift is gearing up for the day.

"Hey, Tansey, busy night?"

"Yeah. It was."

"Heard some thugs popped out of some bushes and smoked some Mexicans who just got off work. Were you working that?"

"Yeah, I worked it," I whisper.

"Fuck, heard one dude took it to the face and the other in the stomach."

"Honestly, man, I was at the hospital all night. I never got the full story." I'm hoping he gets the hint that I would like to go home.

"Well, I heard from Officer Quiet that the three Mexicans were doing a drywall job at a store after hours. They finished up and were sitting on the tailgate of their truck when two black teenagers jumped out on 'em from the woods. They shot the first guy in the gut and then the second guy in the head. Their piece-of-shit gun jammed, so they just smacked the third guy. They got two hundred dollars off 'em, or some small shit like that. Not even sure if it's gang-related this time. Can you believe that shit?" He doesn't realize he has just ripped my heart out. I know the world can be a bad place, but sometimes I want to live in a bubble like everyone else.

"No. No, I can't . . ." I whisper, trailing off. The young widow's face pops into my mind. Then the mom, hugging me desperately, trying to hold on to a small piece of her son. Then to the man. His fear. His pain. The life leaving his eyes, and all his questions left unanswered.

Their whole lives were destroyed . . . over $200.

———

"You're being promoted to senior officer next week. And you're going to Field Training Officer (FTO) school and Taser school. Congratulations. Now get out of my office," Tom barks at me.

I am speechless. The promotion to senior officer is not a huge surprise, because it's just the time in my career when I'm supposed to be promoted, but I was not expecting to be an FTO. The last four years have flown by, and somehow, some way, Leroy Jenkins is now considered to be a pretty hardened officer.

So here I am at FTO school and I'm not super excited about this prospect. In fact, I think I'm the only guy in my class who doesn't want this duty. It's not that FTO school is hard or anything. It's basically five days of learning all the ways that a training officer can get sued, and reminding you that you are almost completely responsible for the safety and actions of your rookies. The challenge is that at the end of it, you have to babysit another person. And yeah, maybe I'll get someone awesome, and my days will be filled with laughter and joy, but I could also end up with someone who loves the idea of being a cop more than actually being a cop, and I'm just the wrong guy to deal with it. My feelings notwithstanding, Tom told me to do it, so I do it.

Immediately after FTO school, I have five days of Taser school. The Taser course is another "here are all the ways you could get sued" course. Basically, you learn how hitting someone with a Taser can completely fuck up your life, then you learn how to Tase someone properly, and then the course ends with you getting Tased yourself. The tradition in the SED is that your FTO gets to Tase you, so Jayce shows up on my graduation day just to shoot me in the back. He shoots me right in the ass, and I drop like a sack of potatoes as he stands there laughing like a troll. As I sit on the ground shaking from the prongs in my ass, I realize that maybe the one upside of being FTO will be Tasering some cop in a few years.

After Taser school I take a week off before returning to the squad for a new night shift. I walk in as a senior officer and new FTO for the first time. I have to admit, it feels different, and the tiniest bit of pride seeps into my ego.

Night shift never disappoints, and this one starts off with a literal bang. Minutes after I pull out of the station, the radio chirps, "424-David, shots fired, Star Street and Cross Street."

That damn block is going to be the death of me. I turn on my blue lights and head that way. "Raleigh, I'm en route, about one minute out." It takes me no time to arrive, and as I do, I notice two guys squatting in a ditch. Our eyes lock, and they take off running, as if to say, "Nothing fishy to see here, Officer. We're just a couple of dudes hanging out in a ditch, living our best lives, and now we want to go for a jog."

Their totally normal behavior aside, I slam on my brakes and lurch the vehicle into park, hopping out to chase them. "Raleigh, I have two running from the Motorcycle Club toward Cross Street." I cross the sidewalk and head down the embankment. Just as I am beginning to slide down the hill, I notice a man lying on his belly in the little ditch. I pull my gun out and shout, "Hey, you! Show me your hands!"

"I can't! I've been shot, man! I'm fuckin' dying!" he whimpers.

I walk over and cautiously try to roll him over as he squeals in pain. I see a tiny amount of blood on the waistline of his jeans. He must have been shot in the upper pelvis.

"Raleigh, I need an ambulance. I have one shot in the stomach here. The scene is secure. Victim is conscious and breathing."

"Ten-four, 424, we have EMS en route," comes the prompt reply.

"Hey, man, who shot you?" I ask him.

"Fuck you! I'm dying, and all you care about is who shot me?" he snaps, anger in his eyes.

"Sir, I've seen what dying people look like and you don't look like that, so hold tight. EMS is on the way. Now, who shot you?"

"I'm dying, yo!" he moans.

"No, you're not. You are gonna be just fine. Would it feel better if you rolled over? I can help."

"Nah. I don't want to move, man. Fuck, it hurts."

"I know, my man. Just hang in there. I hear the ambulance. I'm gonna run up the hill to flag 'em down just to make sure they don't miss us." I run up the hill just as EMS is pulling in behind my car.

The EMTs jump out and run up to me. "Hey, Tansey, another gut wound?"

"Ha, yeah, this one doesn't look that bad. It seems like more of a pelvis hit."

"Where is he?"

"Down the hill," I say, pointing to where the wounded gentleman lies. They run off in the direction of my finger. For my part, I stay up top near the vehicles, waiting to bring them whatever they might have forgotten from the truck.

"Tansey! When did you last speak to this guy?!" comes a shout from the ditch.

"Like thirty seconds ago!" Walking over, I crest the hill and see the EMS workers giving CPR. *What the fuck? This guy can't be that bad. I was just talking to him!* After several minutes of CPR and lots of other medical voodoo, a sweaty EMT stands up and walks over to me.

"Damn, Grim Reaper! Weren't you working the night shift when that other guy died from a bullet hole to the stomach?"

I can't believe it. The dude was fine a minute ago! "Yeah, but . . . what the fuck! He was just talking to me and telling me how bad it hurt, but he did not have the voice of a dying person."

"Tell me, Reaper, what does the voice of a dying man sound like?"

"Ugh . . . I got shot in the stomach but I'm not going to tell you who did it because FUCK THE POLICE, ughh." I drop my head and pretend to die.

"Damn, that was cold, bro. You're fucked-up."

"You asked, asshole."

I've become cold to a lot of things since I started this job. The innocent Mexican guy who died last night is dead because of assholes like the gangbanger wearing Crip beads who died today, using his last words to tell me I suck. In my calmer moments, I will have empathy for the kid he once was, but I don't feel sorry that the man he became is gone. I can still see the Mexican guy's face. For all I know the guy in the ditch did it.

I return to the station to begin typing out the murder report, as detectives again flood the crime scene. My phone rings and a guy from the Gang Unit is on the other line. "Tansey, what did this guy tell you before he died?"

"Jack shit, he didn't even give me a clue. "

"I know the kid. What the fuck was he doing over there on Star Street?!"

"I have a few guesses, but they're insensitive, and you're on a work phone."

"Ha, yeah, you're probably not wrong with your guesses. So, we're starting out with not too much for this case."

The night ends with the SWAT team raiding a house full of rival gang members a few blocks away. They are separated and questioned individually. I watch one of them as he sits on the curb, waiting his turn to speak with detectives.

"Hey, man, did you know that cat who died tonight?" I ask. He stares at the ground and doesn't say anything back. "Did you kill him? Is that why you aren't chatting with me?" I press.

"Fuck you, dog. I don't speak Pig Latin," he says with a glare.

Death is the norm for these guys. Everything in their gang culture revolves around darkness. The movies they watch and the music they listen to are all about rape and murder, guns and drugs, madness and mayhem. Gang culture is disgusting; it is the sheer definition of evil. But I understand why kids are attracted to it in communities mostly bereft of healthy home life and family stability. It's something to cling to.

What I cannot understand is why so many movies and celebrities glorify it. I've seen a professional football player throw gang signs behind another player during a TV interview. I've seen rappers and musicians flying gang flags from their pockets while onstage in front of thousands of people. I've seen community leaders shaking hands with high-ranking gang members. Why?

Why do we pretend it is okay? Why do we pretend it's cool?

In the movies, there is always some kind of honor among the gang leaders. They're portrayed as complex individuals, who could have been anything, but for their place of birth. That's not the reality here. Here it's much grosser than the movies. There is no empathy. There is no humanity. There's just evil.

19

A SOVEREIGN CITIZEN, AND BEYONCÉ

I AM A SOVEREIGN CITIZEN! You are not an elected official, you have no power over me, and you do not have the right to talk to me!"

Well, this is a new one.

I'm here responding to Red's request for an assist, so ignoring the insanity that is this very serious man with dreadlocks, I walk over to Red's car. She is in the front seat, just belly laughing like she always does.

"What's up with this guy? What do we have here? Is this the call that came in?" I ask her.

"No, the call is down the street. I have no idea who this fucking guy is. He just flagged me down and told me I can't come down his street because it's a Sovereign Street or some shit."

Now, I have heard of sovereign citizens, but I always thought they only existed in places like Montana, you know? Places where you can have a ranch and kind of be away from the law and civilization. It's kind of hard to be a sovereign citizen in a place that is nothing but infrastructure created by the government, but shit, what do I know? Regardless, we are not listening to this clown.

"Well, fuck this guy. Let's go around him. Just follow me."

I get into my car and hit the gas, heading right for him for a split second, causing him to think I'm going to really hit him. He dives out of the way, and we both speed by him. We drive about three blocks before we get to the domestic call. A man and a woman are standing in the front yard of a house, screaming at each other. I don't know the address of the call, but it doesn't take a detective to see that this is it. Red and I both get out and begin to mediate the lovers' quarrel. It's a pretty typical argument, without any violence.

"Sir, I know we all have tense moments in relationships. Lord knows I have. Do you think we can work this out?" I ask.

"Yes, Officer. I just need a little respect in my own home, you know?" he whimpers.

"Respect goes both ways!" she counters.

These aren't bad people. They're having a bad night. We've all been there. They just chose to have the argument out front, and the neighbors were worried it was something more serious. After a few minutes of Red and my intervening, they're pretty calm, and we're close to feeling good about leaving. That's when the strange man from up the street comes stomping up the driveway.

"Did y'all call these motherfuckin' police to my street!" he screams.

The woman pipes back with the attitude of a honey badger. "Who. The fuck. Is you?" I now realize that she really likes her husband, because the heat this guy just got is at a whole different level than the shade she was throwing at her husband earlier.

"Bitch, I am Eric L.! Sovereign Citizen of the Moorish Nation!" he proclaims, like he's Xerxes from the movie *300*.

Now the husband is pissed. "Did you just call my girl a bitch? Imma fuck you up!" Red grabs him to hold him back and steps between them, while I grab Mr. Sovereign Citizen.

Just at that moment, our district lieutenant happens to be driving by and sees the commotion. He gets out and begins trying to calmly mediate the five of us. It doesn't take long for the lieutenant to figure out what the problem is, and he orders the Sovereign Citizen to leave the property. "Sir, these people want you off their property, and therefore you are, at this time, trespassing. You must leave this property now, or you will be arrested." He puts enough bass into that command that I think about leaving the property, but good ol' Eric L. is not swayed.

"Fuck you! You have no authority over me! You are not an elected officer, and therefore you are impersonating a law enforcement officer. I am placing you under citizen's arrest!"

The lieutenant is already done with this bullshit. "Tansey, arrest this man."

Rolling my eyes, I reach over for him. I know the man is completely unhinged, so I know he is going to swing at me. My eyes are on his hips as I reach out and grab his wrist. His hips turn inward and as he swings at my face, I've already slid my head back, causing his fist to whizz by my chin. I'm only pleased with myself for a second, because I underestimate his athleticism. He ducks through the motion of his swing and takes off sprinting up the driveway toward the house, which, I have to tell you, is not the direction I would have chosen. I notice he is wearing Crocs and not getting much traction on the dusty, rocky driveway. A word to the wise: If you choose a life of crime, invest in some good running shoes or cross-trainers. Never try to outrun the police in Crocs. We'll catch you and we will laugh at you.

"Stop! Now!" I shout, closing in on him quickly. He turns his head and tries to stiff-arm me. I'm a rugby player at this time and accustomed to dealing with stiffies—wait, I probably need to work on my phrasing. In any case, I just yank his outstretched arm and throw my legs out in front of me, forcing him to fold over backward. We hit the ground and tussle for a minute. I throw a jab that makes contact with his right eye and watch as the skin between his eyebrow and eyelid pops open like an unsealed envelope. I grab hold of his hair but have unfortunately under-estimated his fighting prowess and grit. He swings back with a windmill of haymakers from both arms.

The lieutenant comes flying in and slams the guy into the ground with all his body weight. I look down and notice a wad of broken dread-locks in my hand. The man absorbs the hit from the lieutenant, hits the ground, somersaults, and rolls straight back up to his feet, like some kind of parkour lunatic! Without missing a beat, he takes off running again. I spring to my feet and take off right behind him. I see Bruno coming in from the side and it looks like we finally have him, but the suspect sees him too and changes direction toward a two-story house—in fucking Crocs!

He flies over the railing onto the front porch like it's nothing! More parkour! *I can do that.* As I hit the porch and attempt to jump it in the same manner, I learn that I cannot, in fact, do that. My weight and gear collapse the railing, and I end up crashing through it like the Kool-Aid Man, leaving me splintered and on my stomach. The suspect whips open the door and runs into the house and up some stairs.

Bounding to my feet, I follow, and as he gets to the last step, he parkour-spins around and Spartan-kicks me in the chest. Since I am not holding on to the rails, I begin to fall to the void, tucking my chin into my chest so I don't brain myself on the way down. I feel someone catch me and push me back to my feet, and I realize it's Bruno as I bound back up the stairs. At the top, I find the suspect fighting over a bedroom door with the female homeowner. He wins, yanks it open, and slides into the room, attempting to slam the door behind him. I shove my foot in the crack to keep it from closing.

The lieutenant is behind Bruno and already has his pepper spray out. He lunges his arm forward and rests his wrist on my shoulder for stability as he shoots a burst of the spray through the crack and into the room beyond. Naturally, the side of my face is within the spray zone and my left eye closes instantly as the sting of a million bees sets in. The lieutenant hits his mark and the suspect lets go of the door that I am holding with all my might, sending me flying back again into Officer Bruno. This time he doesn't catch me but just lets me fall to the ground as he charges past and high-kicks the suspect through a flat-screen TV and onto the ground.

At this point this should be over, but like the Terminator, this guy won't go down. He shoots back up with a child's rocking chair in hand and swings it at Bruno like a baseball bat, connecting with Bruno's thigh. The chair breaks into pieces, so the suspect spins around and grabs a four-year-old little girl—the whole reason the homeowner is fighting like hell to keep him out. He holds the child up over his face and screams, "YOU WON'T SHOOT THIS KID! GET BACK!"

I can barely see from all the pepper spray that has coated my face, but I can see enough to know this isn't good. A hostage situation is the absolute worst-case scenario, and it's infinitely worse when a kid is involved.

Red draws her Taser and focuses the red dot on the suspect's forehead, and without hesitation pulls the trigger. The first dart hits him in the center of his head between the eyes, and the second dart lodges in his collarbone, a few inches above the child. He drops the kid and falls back, but as he lets go, the kid's flailing arms dislodge one of the darts, rendering it useless. He rips the other dart from his head and begins to stand up. I run up and kick him in the face, forcing him back to the ground, as Bruno dives down on top of him.

Finally we have him down! I move quickly to handcuff the man before he recovers, when I feel someone grab the back of my vest and pull me off. I turn around to see the homeowner launching a coffee mug at my head. I duck, just in time. She turns around and runs to another room, locking the door. *What the fuck is that about?*

I turn around just as the lieutenant gets the second cuff on. The man is bleeding from his eye and nose, and the surrounding carpet looks like a UFC mat. The homeowner reappears and launches a few more coffee cups at us, screaming that we had Tased her kid. She retreats again and relocks the door.

I am nearly overcome by the effects of the pepper spray, gasping for air and in desperate need of some water. I am choking and can't see shit. My pity party is interrupted by Bruno. "Tansey! Quit being a fucking little cheerleader bitch and help us get this asshole down the stairs." I hear Red laughing out loud next to him. I want to tell him to fuck off but I am choking half to death, so I just start moving blindly toward the sound of Red's laughter.

I make it over to Bruno, and the two of us lift Eric L., the sovereign master of parkour, assault, and kidnapping, to his feet. He suddenly swings his legs off the ground, making us fall over from the unexpected weight change.

"Damn it, Leroy! Pull your shit together and help me lift this ass-hole!" Bruno shouts.

"Bruno! [yack, cough, yack] I'm gonna [yack, cough] murder you when this is over!"

Red pipes up. "Leroy, you want me to help them, since I'm not being a little bitch right now?"

"Fuck you, Red! Why don't you go Tase another child?!" I say, some-how finding a smile through the pain.

"Shut the fuck up, I didn't Tase that kid!" she says, knowing that she will be accused of Tasing this kid forever.

"All of you be quiet and take him down the stairs!" the lieutenant commands.

We pick him up again and move to the landing. Bruno and I are car-rying his full weight, trying not to lose our grip on his sweaty and now blood-soaked arms. We make it down three stairs before the front door flies open and a gang of Downtown District officers floods the bottom floor.

"Thank God, someone help me get this guy down the stairs. Leroy is being a little bitch right now!" Bruno screams so that everyone in a three-mile radius can hear.

"I swear to God, Bruno!"

Red erupts in laughter again as the DTD boys make it up the stairs and take custody of Eric L. EMS arrives and Eric L. begins to yell and scream that we are all under arrest. When an EMS worker reaches out to put a blood-pressure cuff around his arm, he leans down and bites her thumb, hard. She screams out in agony. Officers pounce on him, punch-ing him until he lets her go.

The man is now even more irrational, screaming and flailing about. It takes half a squad to subdue him and several shots of voodoo to sedate him. When a toxicology report comes back, it turns out the man has everything in his system. Cocaine, marijuana, alcohol, and viper semen (just kidding) are all coursing through his veins.

We charge Sovereign Eric with felony assault on EMS and LEO, as well as kidnapping and breaking and entering, but months from now the jury somehow finds him not guilty on nearly all of it. The witnesses (the domestic-dispute folks and the lady whose house he broke into and whose child he held hostage) will not come to court. The defense will claim that the defendant saw the police, was afraid of police, and ran from police, which caused the police to illegally chase him and then use unlawful force against him. He will claim that we then invented a story about a kidnapping and child hostage. The jury will believe all the bullshit, and the man will be set free for time served with only a few misdemeanor charges.

When I return to the station the following night, I find some cheer-leader pom-poms on my desk. Jayce and the boys are all snickering as I throw them onto the floor and sit down, ignoring everyone in the room, especially Red.

"Bruno left those for you," she says with a smirk.

"Eat shit, Red."

"They're pom-poms."

"Oh damn, I figured it was just the stuffing that fell out of your bra?"

"If it was, you could stuff it in your pants to hide your micro dick. What are we getting into tonight?"

"Nothing with you! You're bad luck for me! I'm gonna lay low-key tonight."

Thankfully, after all the action we have seen over the past couple of days, this night is looking slow and not much is going on in the district. We take advantage of the quiet and decide to have squad dinner together at Chick-fil-A. About eight of us show up and sit at a large table, sharing some lighthearted banter until dispatch interrupts us at 9 p.m. "South-east Units, be advised, multiple shots fired in the vicinity of New Bern and Cross Street."

A rookie officer who is just off training chimes in and says he will take the call, but we know that he can't take it alone. We pack up our ruined dinner and head outside.

"Raleigh, this is 411-David. I have one victim who appears to be . . . SIR, GET ON THE GROUND!" The radio goes silent. We run to our cars and jump into them like a bunch of Bo Dukes. The wailing sirens scream through the night as everyone speeds toward the call. Every cop in the city is trying to get there first . . . except me. If I was the only guy answering, I'd be speeding just like them, but since we're all showing up at the same time, I hang way back. I've seen enough humans shot this week, and my batting average for their survival is not great.

When I arrive on scene, about eight cops are trying to corral a rather tall black man. I exit my car and as I approach the gaggle, I finally grasp the totality of what is happening. There, at the end of a long line of cops, is a completely naked man who is bleeding from several holes in his chest. The man is about 6'4" and jacked, with chiseled abs and enormous arms. The blood is flowing down his chest, past his stomach, and off his fairly large penis like a small waterfall.

"Sir, lay down and let us help you! You're losing a lot of blood! You are going to die!" the rookie yells.

The man paces back and forth, smacking his chest with an open hand. Each whack sends a wet thud through the night air, causing blood to splatter in the direction of the wall of cops. Yeah, I'm staying out of this. A naked dude covered in blood, with like three bullet holes in his chest? Fuuuuuuck no. Whatever is keeping him going, I want no part of it.

"Sir, please calm down and let us help you!" "Sir, your heart can't handle this. Please sit down for us!" They're all pleading and begging this man to just take a beat, but he paces more frantically than ever.

Suddenly the man stops. He points his finger into the sea of cops. As his finger lands on them, each cop points at themselves, wondering if they are the one being pointed at. He just holds his stiff finger out, frozen in midair, as the cops look back to see who he might be pointing at. All eyes stop at me. I turn around to see who he is pointing at behind me, and realize that I am the last cop in the line, and I am a good ten yards back.

The man locks eyes on me and yells, "BEYONCÉ!" Again, I look behind me to see if I am missing something, because while I have been confused for many people in my life, there is no confusing me with Her Majesty, Beyoncé. "NO, YOU!" he yells. I point at myself, questioningly. "Yes, you, BEYONCÉ, come here." With that command, he starts to walk toward me. The crowd of cops parts like the Red Sea before Moses.

What the actual fuck is this?

"Hey, man! Hey! Hold up! I ain't Beyoncé," I say, practically pleading. It has no effect. The man continues to walk toward me as every cop stares, just allowing this naked, bloody maniac to come after me, because this week hasn't sucked enough.

I begin to shuffle backward. "Sir, I am not Beyoncé. I can't sing! I can't dance! I look terrible in a dress!" *He's hearing none of this.* The man begins walking faster, so I turn my shoulders and begin to run away. Although I was always taught never to turn and run from a dog, I am hopeful that running from a rabid man might play out differently. It doesn't.

He takes off after me. I make my second mistake, which is looking back instead of just running. There he is, gaining on me with a ten-inch, semi-erect, bloody dick swinging in the wind. I realize at that moment that I definitely have no interest in finding out what he wants to do to Beyoncé. Without regard for my own life, I sprint across all four lanes of New Bern Avenue, running like mad away from Pepe-le-I'mgonnafuckyou.

I circle back to where we started, Pepe in hot pursuit. The sea of cops wave me in, shouting, "Run, Leroy, ruuuun! Bring him back this way!!!" As I run through them, they close in behind me to form a wall and slow the man down. Out of breath and scared to death, I hide behind the other cops and the EMS truck that has just pulled up. A SWAT truck pulls in right next to it.

The EMS worker jumps out. "He's overdosing!" he shouts. "This is called excited delirium! He'll die soon if we don't inject him with drugs to slow him down. We need to get him and we need to get him right now!"

A SWAT guy, fresh off watching me run away, smirks, throws up his hands, and says, "Fuck it, I got him." He dives down at the man's legs in an attempt to take him down, thinking this will be an easy tackle, but the drugged-up stud must have wrestled at some point, because he instinctively sprawls his legs out, leaving the SWAT guy on his knees with a swinging, bloody penis bouncing off his face. I mean, there it is, just bing, bong, smack, slap, and finally resting across his face. Props to him for keeping discipline, because despite have a dick lying across his cheek, he keeps his arms wrapped around the man's thighs. "Fucking help me!"

No one else moves, still in shock at the dickstravaganza we are witnessing, so I run through and jump-kick the guy in the side of his knee, trying to knock him over, but the man doesn't even flinch. My action kicks the other officers into gear, and they all start grabbing appendages as we try desperately to get the man down.

It's important to note that you cannot Tase someone in excited delirium because their heart is already on the verge of exploding. But fuuuuck, even with all of our strength, we cannot get him down. The medic yells, "Just hold him still, and I'll poke him!" This seems as good a plan as any at this point.

We hold the man up with his arms outstretched like Jesus on the cross, and his legs spread out like the bottom half of an X. It looks terrible to the crowd of onlookers, who have no idea what is going on. People are filming with their phones and cursing us as they pull up to the red light where we are fighting. The medic, after an epic battle, manages to get the shots in and slowly, very slowly, the man begins to slump down. Finally, we get him onto the gurney and to the hospital.

In the end, we find out he has not been shot. He was jacked up on PCP and marijuana and has been stabbing himself with broken glass, trying to get imaginary bugs off his back and chest.

Don't do drugs, kids.

As for me, I know the jokes are coming, and I am dreading my return to the station. But to my surprise, not a single joke is told in the locker room. The next night at roll call, it comes up as an incident but no one makes any jokes. Finally, I can't take it anymore and have to say something.

"Okay, what's going on, who has the jokes?"

The rookie speaks first. "Jokes? Shit, I'm just so thankful he chased you and not me. That shit was beyond fucked-up."

"Holy shit, Tansey, I didn't realize you were so fast!" another rookie adds.

I don't know what to do at this moment. It feels weird not to be shamed for the work I did on the street. Isn't that part of the job? For the first time, it is becoming more evident to me that I have gained a little respect over the years. Roll call ends and Sarge calls me into his office.

"You made some good decisions last night."

"What? I didn't really do shit last night, except running from that crazy dude," I respond, perplexed.

"That's what I'm talking about. You just got issued a Taser. Most cops with a brand-new Taser would have just Tased him, but you remembered even in that crazy moment that Tasing him was off the table, and you chose to run instead. The old Leroy would have tried to go toe-to-toe with him or would have Tased him, but both of those decisions would have been dangerous gambles. Running was the smart move." He shakes his head. "Look at you now, Tansey." I stand there confused and a bit bewildered. "Your decision-making last night is why I am giving you the next rookie."

He is saying all those nice things and then the music in my head stops. "Wait, what? Tom, I don't want or need a rookie."

"Well, you don't have a choice. He starts next week. Enjoy."

His tone assures me this is not up for discussion, but I opt to be a little bitch about it anyway. "So, what you're saying is that if I do a good job, I get punished for it?"

"Training someone isn't a punishment. You should take it seriously. And Tansey . . . don't let him die."

Fuck.

I take a deep breath and assess the situation. Well . . . it could be worse. At least I'm not the guy who had a dick on his face.

20

MY ROOKIE

The giant clock tower rings, reverberating through the entire city. Men line the streets in robes of white, cloaks shrouding their faces. Golden braids cinched together adorn their waists, and they kneel as I pass them down the long red brocade. As I reach the end and slowly turn, they all rise, clapping. Thunderous applause. The bell strikes nine.

"Release him!" I bellow. With that a young man exits through a wooden door. The chosen one has been given a master. They begin to chant my name: "Tansey! Tansey! Tansey!"

Just kidding.

But that's kind of how it feels as I show up to roll call, about to pass the torch of knowledge and wisdom to one lucky young man.

Lightfoot, my rookie, strolls into the squad room thirty minutes early to his first shift, with the same shiny brass and polished uniform I flaunted on my first day as a cop.

"Hey, man, I'm Eric. You must be Lightfoot, I'm guessing?"

"Yes, sir, I'm Lightfoot. I'm supposed to be training with Officer Tansey? Do you know where he might be?"

"Yeah, that's me. I'm fucking Tansey." Lightfoot is surprised to hear that and his eyes run up and down me, and I can tell he's kind of questioning his luck and life decisions. In his defense, I am standing here in jorts, letting my luscious legs just hang out. *Jorts, for those of you who aren't into high fashion like I am, are jeans cut into shorts, not to be confused with pre-sewn jean shorts.*

He stares at me, confused, but slowly regains his composure, contemplating his next move carefully. I'm starting to think he had a different vision for a training officer.

Bored with the silence, I jump in. "Hey, homie, what kind of name is Lightfoot? I'll be honest, I thought that was a nickname."

"It's a Nipmuc name," he answers.

"I am not sure what a Nipmuc is, but it sounds racist as shit, and we do not tolerate racism here!" I snap at him, obviously joking . . . to me at least. He is less sure.

"Um, yes, sir, my name is a Native American name."

"That's better. 'Native American' sounds much more PC than fucking 'Nipmuc.'" I keep a straight face during this diatribe while he looks back at me, still trying to figure out if I'm joking or not.

When I realize we're not in the same headspace, I clarify: "I'm fucking with you, bro. That's a cool name you got there, Nipmuc."

"Oh, ha, well, it does sound racist now. I get your point."

"Hey, if you get dirty on shift can I call you a dirty Nipmuc?" I ask him.

"Shit, Tansey, are you trying to get an HR complaint?" another officer chimes in.

"No, but I feel like these are boundaries that need to be established sooner rather than later. We're gonna be in the same car for a while." I stretch out my hamstrings in my jorts while maintaining solid eye contact.

Lightfoot nods sheepishly to the other officer. "It's fine. I've already been warned about Tansey. I wanted to be paired up with him."

"Oh shit, homie, really? Why? You're my first rookie, and full transparency here, I'm a train wreck. So get ready," I say with some real excitement in my voice.

"Oh, I'm ready. The training staff said you would humble me up."

Now I'm confused. "Humble you up?"

"Yeah, I graduated top of the class, so they said you would bring me down a notch."

I laugh and shrug. It's funny that I have a reputation outside of just the SED. Regardless, I know how I'm going to raise my little rookie. I'm going to train him to be a much more confident, and frankly, a much better, rookie cop than I was. I'm going to teach him all the ways not to fuck up, since I'm an expert on how to indeed fuck up. I'll go easy on him from a training officer's standpoint; I'm not interested in all the bullshit hazing games. But I'll make him put in the work.

"Lightfoot, I only have three rules for rookies. Are you ready to hear them?" I ask, allowing him to swim in the gravitas of the moment.

"Yes, sir," he answers.

"Rule number one: If you do anything that results in me getting shot, you fail."

"Understood," he replies.

"Rule number two: If you wreck our car, or do anything in our car that results in me getting killed, injured, or mildly shaken up, you fail."

"Got it. No shooting or crashing, sir."

"Finally, you are not allowed to die. If you die during your field training, you fail. What are your questions at this time?"

"No questions."

"Excellent. Then we have a deal, Lightfoot."

"We have a deal, Tansey."

I guide him outside and show him our car. I let him figure out how to load his shit into it while I go and get changed into a proper uniform. We go to roll call, where I receive another new surprise, a new sergeant. Our second-shift sergeant is retiring and the new sergeant (whom I'll call Sergeant Young Gun) is taking his place. Young Gun is quiet, but he has an "I'm gonna prove myself as a hard charger" type of attitude. He is coming from the northeast side of Raleigh and has never worked the SED before. Tom briefs us on some new gang activity on Corey Street, and after roll call, Young Gun asks me to show him that street and its surroundings.

Smart move, Sergeant.

The area is a notorious Crip gang member hangout. With my new rookie in tow, we patrol the area with him for a bit. He drives his own car and follows us to the area. Once there, we cruise slowly past the clusters of gang members who are posted along the road like a bunch of cliques in a high school cafeteria. Young Gun notices a group hanging around a house and sees one of them slink away as we pass by. He tells me that the man is walking toward some woods just behind the house.

"Oh shit, he's probably the one holding. I bet he got nervous when we creeped by." I hadn't noticed the man myself because I was too busy talking to the new rookie. "He'll pop out on the other side—on the next street over. We could drive over there and then get out and walk—to see if we can talk to him. If he is holding, he'll most likely just run, though. Keep that in mind."

Lightfoot speaks up. "Wait, he'll run? What do we do if he runs?"

Top of his fucking class?

"Um, you fucking chase him."

Realization strikes. "Yep, got it. Just run him down and tackle him," Lightfoot says.

"And?" I ask.

"And . . . don't get shot?" he finishes.

"Correct. Let's go."

"Geez, they said my time with you would be wild, but I didn't think we would be doing this in my first hour."

"Dude, your career here in the SED will be the same every night, every day, every minute: things will get crazy and change from chill to fighting for your life on a dime. Show up every shift ready to rage. If not, you'll get hurt. As Lightfoot nods, I look to Sergeant Youngblood. "Sarge, why don't you get in the front seat of my car, and Lightfoot, you get in the back seat. But don't shut your door. Keep it cracked so if he runs you can just swing it open and get to work. I'll drive up on him slowly, and we'll see what happens. If he's holding, he'll run. If not, we'll just do a voluntary encounter with him and see if he'll chat with us. Does that sound like a good plan?"

"Sounds good to me," Young Gun replies.

We get situated and head to the next street. As we round the corner, there he is, about fifty yards away. He's just standing in the middle of the road like a deer in headlights. I speed up slightly, continuing in his direction. "Get ready, Lightfoot, annnnnnnd . . ." Sure enough, the suspect takes off running. "GO!"

Sarge and Lightfoot both bolt out of the car like two cheetahs trying to catch a gazelle. They are in what civilian television would call "hot pursuit." I slam the car in park, run around to shut their doors, and then lock the car up. I look up just in time to see them close in on the suspect. They leap to tackle him and disappear into a plume of dust that poofs up into the air on the side of the road as they drag him to the ground. I begin to jog in their direction.

Sarge lifts his head up and shouts, "Tansey, grab that gun! He threw it somewhere back there where you are!" This just got serious. I halt my jog and begin scanning the area for a gun. After a few moments, I find it. With the gun controlled, I walk over to my two compatriots and find them both out of breath. I can see the adrenaline pulsing through Lightfoot. He is amped. He has only been at work for an hour and he's already chasing down armed gang members.

We walk the suspect back to the car and run his information. He is wanted for questioning in a murder investigation, and the gun he tossed during the chase comes back as stolen. We drive him to the detective station, where, after a few hours, and much to our shock, he confesses to the homicide and admits that the gun he threw is the murder weapon. As if murder weren't enough, he has other extraditable violent-felony warrants in a neighboring state. Lightfoot has hit a home run on his first night, and on his first arrest. A foot chase, a stolen gun, a murderer, felony warrants, the murder weapon, a use of force (an item on the checklist of graduating field training) . . . it just doesn't get much better than that!

The news spreads through the department like herpes at a fire station. It is not just department news, but literal news. Local reporters pick up the story and it airs on the late-night news. Lightfoot's phone blows up with other rookies calling to hear the story. "What's it like to get into a foot chase?" "Did you really catch a murder suspect?" "How did you get a stolen gun?" I listen to him tell that story over and over again. He is on cloud nine, and to be honest, I am feeling pretty good too. The new sergeant also seems pretty pumped, excited now to be on our squad.

And it doesn't slow down. The next night when I greet Lightfoot, he has a twinkle in his eye. It is apparent that he is hooked on the action. He is ready for more, but with all good police work comes lots of paperwork. We have some typing to do.

"Now, you had your fun and you had lots of it. Here is lesson number three hundred and forty-five: the more fun, the more typing." He has to type out a felony investigative report, a departmental report, evidence notes, and then the use-of-force report, which repeats all the information he has put in the other reports, but in painstaking detail. After three hours of pounding the keyboard, he isn't even halfway done, and I see the twinkle in his eye beginning to dim. I remember feeling that same dimming, and I don't want it to take control of him.

"Okay, let's take a break, it's coffee time, *mi amigo*." He shoots out of the seat like a kid who just found out school is letting out early. He gives a big stretch and heads for our ride. I am excited too—watching someone type and trying to help them find the right words to use is exhausting. (Just ask my wife what it's like to watch me write this book.)

We make it to Starbucks just in time to be interrupted by the radio. "South units, be advised, we have an active stabbing in progress at 1615 Hardee Street. Suspect is still on scene and there now appears to be a larger fray."

We aren't close to the call, but I can tell Lightfoot wants to go. He has those "Daddy, can I please go play?" eyes.

"Do you want to drive fast, homie, or do you want coffee?" I ask him.

"Will you hate me if I say drive fast? I know coffee is important to you." Coffee is important to me. He's right. But not as important as stopping a stabbing, and I'm actually enjoying his enthusiasm.

"Do you remember my three rules?" I snap.

"Don't wreck the car, don't get you shot, and don't die," he replies quickly. He's a fast learner.

"Correct. Hit those blue lights and let's fucking drive, homie!"

Lightfoot pounces into the car as I slide into my seat. He takes a deep breath and hits the lights and sirens. Gripping the wheel tight, he swings out of the drive-thru, tires spinning. He looks over at me to check if he is doing okay.

"Don't look at me, look at the road! And don't wreck this car!" I snarl.

I direct him toward Hardee Street as the radio blows up with other units getting on scene and trying to make sense of some chaos. "Raleigh, the suspect was seen running east, we have multiple victims here, and we need additional units to search for the suspect."

I throw the radio at Lightfoot and tell him to tell them we are on the way. He keys it up and says, "We're on the way!" and then drops the mic.

"What the fuck was that?! Is that how they taught you to use the mic?" I ask, realizing that even though Lightfoot is a good rookie so far, like all rookies, he is dumb.

"Oh, no, um, sorry?"

"Watch out for that car! What are you doing? Drive around these ass-holes, they are pulling over for you, dumbass!" I shout, because Lightfoot seems to have lost the ability to function.

"Last unit, what was your last transmission?"

I grab the radio. "Raleigh, it's 424, we're having a learning moment here. I apologize. Can you show us 424D en route to the stabbing call? We are about five minutes out."

"Ten-four, 424 checking in."

I continue to shout at Lightfoot as he drives through the city like Evil Knievel's weird cousin, whom the family doesn't like to talk about. We finally make it to the area and begin to patrol through it slowly, scan-ning for the suspect. A neighbor flags us down. "He's in that house over there, Officer!"

I recognize this house. The homeowner's son has been admitted to the local psych ward a few times. I tell Lightfoot about the kid. "He's about twenty-three years old, and he loves 'riding the boat' or just straight PCP. He's a problem." "Riding the boat" is a term used to describe marijuana dipped in PCP. People on PCP are not fun to deal with, so I welcome the arrival of another car. It's another rookie who has recently made it off training. Recognizing him, I snap out some direction: "Hey, bro, go to the back. We will secure the front and wait for more units. Let me know when you get back there, and I'll start to knock."

He nods and heads around the side of the house. Minutes go by, and nothing.

I radio. "425, are you at the back door?"

He replies quickly, "Um, can you come back here real quick?"

"Not really, I have a rookie and I can't leave him here alone at the front door."

"I can't get to the back door." His voice has me concerned, so I need to check it out.

"Okay, stand by, I'm coming." I turn to Lightfoot. "Listen to me, I have to go help the other officer real quick. You watch this door and if anyone comes out, you point your gun at them and tell them to get on the floor. If they don't listen, you either run the fuck away or you shoot them, your choice."

"What?! Are you serious?!"

"Yes. This guy stabbed multiple people, and if he comes out and comes toward you, point your gun at him and tell him to show his hands and hit the floor. If he doesn't listen, shoot him or retreat. Remember, you are not allowed to die."

His eyes are wide-open, and he doesn't know what to do with me. Finally, he stammers, "Those are the most fucked-up instructions I've ever received!"

"Godspeed," I say, patting him on the shoulder and picking up a jog to the back.

As I get around the back of the house, I find the other rookie just standing at a closed gate. I'm not sure what's happening, so I ask him. "What? Is it locked or something?"

"No, but it's closed. Are we allowed to go back there?"

What in the actual fuck?

"Are you fucking serious? Who the fuck trained you?! A man stabbed several people and is now hiding in this house, and you're asking if you can walk through a closed gate? Go watch the front door and send my rookie back here." The kid hangs his head low and walks back around the house. Lightfoot comes running up and we open the gate, heading into the backyard. The back door of the house is open and there is a thick trail of blood all over the porch. The shape of the splatter suggests that someone has left through the back door.

"Shit, did he stab someone in there and they left, or has he been injured himself and left? That's a lot of blood. Whoever it belongs to can't have much left in them. We need to get more units over here." Suddenly we hear the rookie at the front door yelling and giving commands. "Stay here, Lightfoot, and the same instructions apply as before."

"Best instructions ever!" he quips.

I run to the front to see what the rookie is yelling at. As I round the corner, he aims his gun at me. "Hey, fucker! Don't point that shit at me!" I shout. The last way I want to go is getting shot to death by some untrained rookie. That's just embarrassing.

"I hear something in that shed." He gestures to a shed a few feet away.

"That shed right there?" I ask.

"Yes, what should we do?"

I roll my eyes. "What in the fuck is wrong with you?! You are a fucking cop! Act like it! Seriously, I'm having a chat with whoever trained you. You need to go back to training. Are you scared or just dumb? I can teach you if you're dumb, but you seem to be afraid. If you had gone to that back door like I told you, we might still have our victim or suspect on scene! Now you're yelling at a fucking shed!" I walk over to the shed and rip the door open with my gun pointed into the darkness. It is empty, other than a few tools and a push mower. "Was that so fucking hard? You're a cop, and there's a bad guy somewhere close by! Do your job." If I sound pissed, I am. I have no use for scared cops in the SED. I don't know where this kid has come from, but he obviously doesn't belong here.

As I walk back to Lightfoot, another officer chirps up on the radio. "Raleigh, I think I have the suspect. Can I get a check-in." The officer's tone is a bit confused, like he isn't sure if he actually has a suspect.

I respond, "Hey, unit that has the suspect, I don't have access to a map, but can you blow your whistle so I can hear where you are in relation to me, and we'll start your way."

We hear the whistle blow. He is literally one house over. "Okay, we are coming to you." Lightfoot and I jump the fence and head around the front of the next house. A man is lying face down on the front porch in a large pool of blood. The officer has his gun pointed at the person, giving him commands to show his hands. Lightfoot seems confused and is inching toward the body.

"Stop, Lightfoot. He might be dead, or he might be playing possum, or it might not even be the suspect." He looks even more confused. "It's okay, we're going to work through this. First off, he matches the suspect description, or at least the clothing does. So given that, we'll treat this like he is likely the suspect." I look back over to the other officer, who nods his agreement. "Okay, here is what we are going to do. This officer will continue to hold his light on him. I'll move over there and point my gun at his head. You will follow me and roll him over to check his hands. If he's playing possum and has a weapon, you yell 'possum' and move back, and I will shoot him. Quickly. Do you understand?" I look him in the eyes to make sure he gets it.

"Shit! Um, yes, I got it."

I raise my voice. "HEY, SIR. This is your last chance to show me your hands, or at least moan if you can understand me." He doesn't answer, so we put the plan into action. I squat down and put my pistol to the back of the man's head, pointing outward so as to direct the shot away from adjacent houses. Lightfoot rolls him over to expose his face and hands. The suspect is unarmed but blood is flowing out of his forehead like someone has turned on a faucet. It is coming from a nickel-sized hole in the man's skull.

"Shit, he's been shot in the head!" Lightfoot exclaims.

"Raleigh, we need EMS. It looks like our suspect has been shot in the head. He is not conscious but is breathing very shallowly. The scene is secure." There is already an ambulance staged a block away because of the stabbings, so EMS rolls up within minutes to assess the man. They lift him onto a gurney to begin transport to the hospital. One medic works on the exit wound at the back of his head, which gushes like a spigot now that he is on the gurney, while another works on the relentless flow of blood spurting out of his forehead.

Lightfoot and I climb into the ambulance, and off to the hospital we all go. The man flatlines twice; he needs some serious help. At the hospital, orchestrated chaos ensues. Nurses and doctors hustle about like a swarm of worker bees. They move the man from the gurney to the surgical table. A chunk of skull and brain matter falls onto the floor, with the smacking sound of raw beef hitting tile. A nurse comes by and scoops the chunk into a petri dish like it is no big deal. *The things we all get used to.*

I look over at Lightfoot, and his face is pale. I can tell he is about to pass out. Now, this is what makes me just a little different than other training officers. Most would let him hit the floor and then deal with it later, jokes and all. But I feel that we have already endured enough stress for the night, and his performance so far is just fine. No further learning moments are necessary.

"Hey, homie, go back to the car and grab some evidence envelopes." He turns slowly toward me, his expression sickly. "Go get me some envelopes." He shakes his head to regain composure and hustles out of the room. I don't need envelopes, but he needs a purpose and a job to do or else he is going to embarrass himself.

It's not that I want to let him off easy or anything. I have no intention of coddling him. But I got put through the wringer, and I'm not so sure that the level of shit I took was a value-add. I also had the luxury of a military background, so a lot of the carnage wasn't new to me. Lightfoot, though, is a babe in the woods, and I want to walk him right up to the line of breaking, but never over it.

He returns to me just as the CT scan of the man's brain comes back. To everyone's surprise, no bullet has entered his skull. After hours of medical examination, the doc determines that someone has punched a hole in the back of the man's skull, and that someone is most likely wearing a ring.

Well, shit.

Meanwhile, back at the crime scene, detectives are questioning witnesses. I know that they are probably trying to find out who the shooter is, when in fact there is no shooter. I call Sarge and give him the update.

"Hey, man, you won't believe this, but there is no bullet in homeboy's head. Someone punched a hole in the back of his skull, and the fracture in front is from his head bouncing off the asphalt. They found asphalt in the wound."

"No shit! They were telling the truth?! Hot damn! The uncle is adamant that he didn't shoot him, and that he did that damage with his fist."

"Yeah, can you check to see if he has a ring on?"

"He already showed it to me. It is a Marine Corps ring, but it doesn't have any blood on it. He told me it had brain or something on it and that he has already washed it off."

"Holy shit! That is badass. What happened exactly, or what are they telling you happened?"

"The suspect is unknown to the family. He wandered up while they are outside barbecuing and starts hitting on the niece. They said he was high as shit or drunk or something, and so she tells him to go away. Allegedly, he makes a sexual pass at her and she responds with 'eww.' The suspect pulls out a box cutter and attacks the girl, slashing her up pretty good until the uncle gets him off her and apparently beats the brakes off him."

"Damn, how's the girl?"

"Lots of stitches and staples, but she'll live."

"Well, the dude isn't as lucky. He's in a coma right now, and I don't think he'll be chatting anytime soon."

"Ah, that's probably the best thing for him. How's the rookie?"

Lightfoot lowers his head in embarrassment. He knows he had been seconds from passing out at the sight of the brains on the floor, and he knows I am going to drag him to the Sarge.

"He is incredible. Follows directions to a T, and handled the brunt of the night like a real warrior. He'll be a good one, I think."

"Good, because 425 just put his shit in a box and dropped his badge on my desk. He says he's evidently not cut out for this stuff."

"Oh damn. I kinda yelled at him for being a pussy tonight. Honestly, though, if tonight was enough to break him, it's good. He will just get hurt or get someone else hurt. I hope he finds his path somewhere else."

Lightfoot puffs his chest out a little as we walk out of the hospital and back to our vehicle. He's already a better cop than a guy who has passed his current phase of training. And he knows it.

Three weeks later, it is time to do my first rookie evaluation. I write down all the things he has done in the course of three weeks. We have already checked nearly every requirement needed to pass him, and we still have six weeks to go. I turn the paperwork in, feeling pretty proud of how far Lightfoot has come in three weeks. It's not that I think I've made him or anything. He is his own man. But I do think I've made the right choices for his personality to get him to where he is now. I'm actually enjoying this training-officer thing.

Shortly after turning it in, Sarge walks over to me and says, "I need to see you in my office." I drop what I'm doing and walk in. He starts right away.

"Hey, man, I just read this eval, and I am going to have to talk with Lightfoot. I just wanted you to have a heads-up so you don't think I'm doing something behind your back."

"Oh, okay, is something wrong? The kid is killing it," I say, confused.

"No, no, everything is okay. It's just that he has done so much in a short period of time that I am honestly worried about his mental health. I know we don't let rookies burn comp time, but I'm seriously thinking about making an exception. Based on this report, he is far ahead anyway, and he's seen more and done more in three weeks than most cops will do in their career." He chuckles and shakes his head in disbelief. After I leave the office, he calls Lightfoot. I go back to the locker room and start putting my gear on for the night.

A few minutes later, Lightfoot walks in. He looks at me, puzzled. "Hey, what are you doing? Sarge says he wants us to take a few nights off."

"Actually, he wants you to take a few off, and for good reason. I've probably pushed you a little too hard," I tell him.

"No way, man! I've had the best three weeks of my life. I can't wait to get back out next week and do it again. I didn't even want a few nights off, but he said I had to. Sarge says you are taking two off also, so it works out."

That sounds promising. "He said that, did he?" I walk back down the hall and tap on Sarge's door. "Hey, Lightfoot says I'm taking two days off too?"

"Yeah, I figured you would unless you want to just go back to the line and hump calls with no rookie," Sarge blurts out in that Sarge kind of way.

It's actually been a crazy three weeks, and I have acquired tons of comp time. I am not unhappy at the thought of some downtime with my wife and kids. I have not been home on time since Lightfoot's training began, plus I always get to work early. I definitely have leaned way too far toward work on the work/life balance scale as of late. Cops notoriously create family problems by not keeping tabs on how little they are around at home. We get so caught up in the job that we forget there is life outside of it, usually until it's too late. I love my wife and kids too much to end up there.

After our time off, we return refreshed and ready to go. Lightfoot cruises through training and grows up fast, and I'm really proud of him. Training a rookie is like raising an infant all the way up through puberty over the course of nine weeks. They start off useless but kinda cute, until they shit on everything. Then they get to the terrible twos, where they want to run around touching things they shouldn't. Then there's the most fun part, where they still look up to you but they know enough not to get themselves hurt or killed. Finally there's the pain-in-the-ass part—the teenage years—alternatively known as the last three weeks of training. They start to think they know everything, because they've been at this job for a month and a half. They're embarrassed to have you around, and start thinking they'd be better off on their own. They even develop a little attitude, and to top it all off, they start to stink. Just like with teenagers, you need to remind them that hygiene is important and that Febrezing their vest goes a long way.

The cycle is the same with every rookie. And Lightfoot, even though he has been a great rookie, is no exception to the rule.

Lightfoot and I are cruising the beat when a Gang Unit officer comes over the radio, calling that he is in a foot chase following a search warrant service. The chase is only a few miles away in what can only be described as the worst neighborhood in the city. Lightfoot doesn't even ask: He just reaches down, hits the lights and sirens, and whips a U-turn. He is looking straight ahead out of the window, making it clear that he isn't asking for, and doesn't need, my permission to get involved. He is a full teenager now, and He. Knows. Everything.

I stare at him intently as his hands tightly grip the wheel, his eyes laser-focused on the road before him. He must feel my stare, or maybe we have been together long enough that he thinks he can read me like a book.

"I know, I know, don't wreck the car," he mutters with some serious sass that makes me want to beat him about the head, neck, and shoulders.

"No, you're fine, I trust you, but where are we going?" I ask like the Librarian in *The Matrix*.

"To that foot chase! Weren't you listening to the radio?" he snaps, aggravated to have to explain himself.

"I was listening to the radio, but let me ask you something: Why are you driving to where the chase started? Why aren't you looking at the map to see where they might be heading?"

"Um . . ." He's got nothing.

"Exactly. Turn here!" I say firmly.

"But this is Peterson Street. The chase is on . . ." He waffles.

"TURN HERE NOW!" I shout.

He slams on the brakes and yanks the wheel hard to the left, nearly flipping the chariot into a sideways slide down Peterson. Well . . . at least he listened.

"What the fuck, man! Why are we turning here? The chase is three more blocks that way!" he complains.

"Turn off your lights and sirens, and calm down. Those apartments run east to west and parallel the greenway. They're most likely hitting the greenway and heading east to— Turn right here!" I command.

"Into this field?!" he asks, confounded.

"TURN!" Again he slams on the brakes and jerks the wheel, sending us careening into the grass. "Now slow down and drive slowly through that little trail over there. Roll your window down and take your seat belt off."

"How do you know they went east and not west?"

"West is uphill and heads into downtown; east is downhill and heads into a nature preserve. Where would you flee? Now pay attention:

There's a forty-foot ravine alongside the greenway that separates it from the reserve. If they see us or hear us, they'll jump down into the ravine and run up the other side, and we'll never catch them. We've got to see them first and get them quickly, so they don't ditch us in the . . . well . . . ditch."

On cue, we see two heads pop out from behind a tree. Before I can get a word out, Lightfoot slams the car into park, jumps out, and yells, "Stop! Police!" He takes off running. I climb clumsily out of my door, which is pinned up against thick foliage. This is exactly what I didn't want to happen. But here we are—about to be involved in a very long and muddy chase.

I sprint after Lightfoot, about twenty-five yards behind him, as he runs directly at the suspects. Of course, they break right and head down the ravine.

Fuck me. I don't want to be muddy.

Leroy Jenkins would have been right beside Lightfoot. Hell, he would have passed him. Officer Tansey has a different plan.

"LIGHTFOOT, STOP! I'M RELEASING THE DOG!" I scream at the top of my lungs.

Now, Lightfoot knows I don't have a dog, but when you hear a dog is being released, everyone pays attention. His head whips around and he stops dead in his tracks. I let out the loudest and realest bark I can muster.

"ARUFF RUFF, GET DOWN BEFORE I LET THE DOG GO! RUFF RUFF RUFFFFFFF!" The two suspects dive to the ground like Pete Rose sliding headfirst into home plate.

"Don't let the dog go!" they cry. "We good! We good! Please, Officer!"

"RUFF RUFF ARRRRRUUUUUFFFF!!! Lay face down and don't fucking move! RUFF RUFF RUFF! This dog will eat your ass, do you hear me?!" I scream.

"Yes! Please! We all good!" they beg.

I glare at Lightfoot, motioning with my head for him to go put cuffs on them as I continue to bark like a crazy person. I don't stop until he has taken both suspects into custody. My throat is hoarse.

The gang officer finally makes his way to us by following the sound of the barking. Lightfoot is bringing both suspects up the ravine when the gang officer gets to me.

"Damn, Tansey. Good work. When did you get a dog?" he asks.

One suspect chimes in, "That dog was crazy! He was looking right at me! The meanest dog I ever seen!"

The other joins the conversation, adrenaline forcing his mouth to run. "Shit, yo! I didn't even see that mofucka! I just hit the dirt and prayed to Jesus he didn't eat my ass!"

Everyone seems confused when they don't see a dog with me, so I bark loudly. And then everyone gets it.

The first suspect's eyes go wide. "Wait. What! There wasn't no dog!? Nah, bruh, I seen that shit!"

"Nope, no you didn't, there was no dog. It was just me. Two points police, zero points the streets today, boys. We are two-for-two," I say with a smirk.

The second suspect has an actual smile on his face *while being arrested.* He is genuinely impressed. "Man, that is crazy as hell. You should be an actor or something. That was real as shit, dog . . . Literally, bruh, you a dog!" I'm convinced that he would have given me a high five if he wasn't in cuffs.

We load up in the car and Lightfoot frowns, nodding, hating his life right now. Closing his eyes so he doesn't have to look at me, but knowing he has to acknowledge the situation, he says, "Okay, okay, you win. You were right."

"I know, son. Daddy's always right."

21

LOST SOULS

"Okay, what is everyone putting in for, so I can start typing out your recommendation letters?" Sergeant Tom barks at all of us, huddled around his desk. I am now one of the more experienced senior officers, eligible to begin the process of applying for a supervisor role or a detective position, and Tom has all of us seniors in his office trying to figure out how to best set us up for success. He's a fantastic boss like that.

These guys all have a plan. One by one, they spout off what positions they are applying for, as I slowly and discreetly make my way out the door and back into the squad area. I don't have a rookie right now, and we have a squad full of younger cops to take tedious calls, so I am at the point in my career when I can cherry-pick my calls, which, I have to tell you, is nice.

It's especially nice tonight. It is night shift, and it is Friday. The radio is relentless with calls going out every few minutes, and everyone is back-logged by about three calls each from the very start of the shift. I've been surrounded by death lately, and even though the nickname "Grim Reaper" hasn't stuck the way Leroy Jenkins did, I have been asking myself a lot of questions lately. The SED is always full of death and pain, but more and more, I feel like I am the gravitational force around which it orbits.

We have a solid seventeen officers working tonight, but half of those are rookies, so the workload is brutal, even for us senior guys. There isn't even time to take a piss or fill up your water bottle. By about 2:30 a.m., I have responded to fifteen or so calls and been to jail once. Finally, I take advantage of a brief respite in calls and head to the squad room to grab a bite. Apparently, every other cop has the same idea, so there is nowhere to sit. I'm a little aggravated, and I know it's silly. Back in the day, a rookie might have offered up his seat to the senior officers. But for better or worse, President Obama's "Pillars of Policing" protocol got rid of most training hierarchies, and the rookies have been trained to think of themselves as equals with little respect for those who came before them.

On the one hand, I don't think rookies should back down if a senior is doing the wrong thing. That part is good. But the overcorrection is an issue because inexperienced officers believe that their experience and training are equal to that of those who have done the job for years, and it's causing problems. But that's an issue above my pay grade.

Besides, I don't have too much time to be frustrated because the radio chirps up again, and this time it is for a Nature Unknown, referencing a young, white male sitting on the steps of a duplex on Leonard Street. Description: a pink polo, khaki shorts, and boat shoes.

This is unquestionably an odd place for a white male to be at 3 a.m., especially since he's elected to sit on the steps of the home of one of the most notorious criminals and gang leaders in the area, dressed like he's going to a fraternity kegger. The notes in the call make it seem like the 911 caller has tried to make it clear that this isn't just some crackhead loitering outside. The fact that anyone in that area has even called 911 is odd. Problems in that neck of the woods tend to be taken care of . . . without police assistance.

No one else seems eager to take the call, so I key up my mic. At least a suspiciously out-of-place white frat boy will be less drama than the other Friday night calls sure to go out at any moment.

I drive to the address, and sure as shit, there he is: a twentysomething white male wearing a salmon-colored polo tucked into Dockers shorts and wearing boat shoes. Motherfucking boat shoes. He's slumped over on the steps of the porch. I walk up and shine my light on the young man.

"Hey, man, what's up?" I nudge him with my boot. He sits up and leans away a bit, taken aback by my presence.

I try again. "Hey, bud, what are you doing here?"

"Uhhhh, am I being detained?" he slurs drunkenly.

"Excuse me?"

"Am. I. Being. Detained?" he says in a way that makes me think he has rich parents and is used to getting his way.

"Well, kinda, yeah. You are trespassing on this property, which is clearly posted right there above your head." I shine my light up on a black sign with orange letters that reads No Trespassing. "Look, homie: I'm not trying to mess with you or be a dick, but I need to know why you're here and where you came from because honestly, you're lucky that you aren't face down in a ditch with all your shit missing. Speaking of which, do you have your wallet and phone on you?"

"You aren't getting my wallet and my phone. I know my rights."

It's good to see that rich preppies and gangbangers go to the same law school.

He sits up now, swaying, staring at me with bloodshot eyes, trying to be a confident alpha male.

"Fair enough, big fella. I'll tell ya what. It's almost three a.m., and you're obviously drunk, so tell me where you came from, and we'll get you back there free of charge. I'll put it on the city's tab." He stares at me, bewildered and frankly too drunk to process my sarcasm. He takes my comments as earnest.

"My friends are on Glenfield," he slurs.

"Cool, that's about three miles that way," I say, pointing toward Glenfield Lane. "How about I drive you back there?"

He takes a few seconds to think about it and then stands up. He wobbles as he lunges his hand outward to shake my hand, as if we are making a gentlemen's agreement.

Staring at his hand, now in mine, I regain my composure. "Well . . . okay . . . cool. Let's jump in the car, and I'll drive you back." I guide him to the back seat of the car, and just before I open the door, I ask, "Hey, man, before I put you in the car, it's my department's policy that I have to put your info in my computer so I can change my status to taxi driver. Can you help me out?" He blinks at me, then slowly reaches into his pocket and hands me his wallet.

I guide him into the back seat of my Explorer, then run his info. He has a previous underage DUI charge and another separate drunk-and-disorderly-conduct charge. He has only recently turned twenty-one, and his drinking seems to already be a big problem in his life. I hear him sniffling in my back seat.

"Hey, bud, you good?" I ask him.

"Yeah (sniff), I'm fine. My girl left me tonight, and my friends and I got into a fight." He goes on to call them all some nasty names. I'm sure it is the alcohol talking, but at that moment, he seems to hate everyone in his life. He has some very vicious things to say about them. He's got kind of a Gollum-versus-Smeagol thing going right now, where he vacillates between wishing his friends were here and lashing out at them in a way that makes me think he would be violent if they were.

"Where are they now? If you're angry at them, should I just take you home? I don't want to leave you with someone that you are just gonna fight with."

"No, I ain't going home. I'm going the fuck away! I'm gonna move to Apex," he says with thunder, as if Apex, a growing North Carolina suburb about twenty minutes away, was the solution to all of the world's problems. I mean, I guess according to *Forbes* it is ranked the third-best place to move to, so maybe he's on to something.

"Well, okay, but where can I take you tonight?" I ask.

"Anywhere but home."

I am too tired for this, and there are two more domestics holding in the call logs. Drunk kid who can't hold his liquor is not a cop problem. Drunk kid who can't hold his liquor in a place he might get killed is a cop problem.

I can't bring him to jail, because they no longer accept drunks who haven't committed a crime. I can't bring him to the hospital, because being drunk in and of itself is not their problem. But I have to drive somewhere, and it has to be far away from here. I decide on the safest place I know that is near Glenfield, and that is the city gas pumps. It is well lit, cops and detectives are in and out of there constantly, and if he doesn't want to go back to his home, it has a nice bench where he can sleep it off. I need gas, anyway.

I pull up, let him out of the car, and escort him to the bench. There is a maroon Buick at the pump where an undercover cop is pumping gas. He watches me explain to the kid where he is. I then hand him a business card with my cell number on it. "If you decide you want me to drive you home, please call me, and I will come pick you up, okay?" He nods. I check the kid's phone, and it is 70 percent charged with full bars of service, so I know he will be fine.

I walk back to the pumps, and the undercover cop asks me about the strange, drunk kid. When I tell him the story, he is as surprised as I am that he hasn't been mugged. I explain why I've chosen to leave him on the bench, and he agrees that it is the most logical way to solve the problem.

The night goes on, and I respond to some shots-fired calls and a domestic before closing out the night at 6 a.m. and heading home. Saturday night is almost as crazy, and then Sunday night ends the weekend with a stabbing that takes up most of my shift. I sleep all day Monday and wake up Tuesday to a call from the city of Raleigh. It is always fun seeing the city number pop up on my phone.

"Officer Tansey? This is Detective Mann."

"Hey, what's up, Mann?" I giggle to myself at the dad joke.

Ignoring me, he continues: "Can you check your email and see if you recognize the gentleman in the latest BOLO?"

I open the email and see a mug shot of the young man I dealt with on Friday. "Oh yeah, I recognize him." I tell Mann the story and explain exactly how I handled it. I can tell he is taking notes on the other end and hear him turning pages as we talk. "Is everything all right?"

"Well, yeah, probably. His parents reported him missing. No one has seen him since Friday. So far, you are the last person to have contact with him."

"Huh, well, he specifically told me he was never going back home and that he was moving to Apex, so maybe he was serious. He is twenty-one, so he doesn't have to tell Mommy and Daddy where he is."

"Yeah, I agree, but he hasn't been to work either. I'm just trying to put some things together for the family before I close this out. Could you write a supplemental report stating that you saw him, and what happened on Leonard Street?"

"Sure, no worries," I reply. The not-going-to-work thing is a little concerning, but the dude also didn't exactly have his shit together, so who knows?

A few days later, the detective calls me again. "Hey, can you meet me at the station?" My heart sinks. Detectives handle almost everything over the phone. They only bring you in for the bad shit. I drive to the station, and he is already waiting in Tom's office. I walk in, and they shut the door. The mood is somber.

"You aren't in any trouble, but I have to ask you some important questions. Did anyone see you drop off the missing man at the gas pumps?"

"Um, actually, yes. There was an undercover detective."

"What was his name?" he asks sternly.

"Shit, I don't know his name, but he was in a maroon Buick. It's the city gas pumps. There are cameras everywhere, so I'd just go look at them," I answer, solving their problem in the most obvious way possible.

"I will, but first, be super honest: If I go and pull that tape, will it show you dropping him off and leaving him on that bench?"

I know he is doing his job, but it gets exhausting always having everyone assuming that you are lying or hiding something. "Yes! I dropped him off at the pump, and that was it! He had broken no laws, and the jail doesn't take drunks because of liability reasons . . . they make them go to the hospital. But the hospital is too busy with real problems, so they kick them to the curb if there is no medical reason for them to be there. They don't need to deal with a drunk dude going through a breakup. Why are we wasting time on this asshole, anyway? He got drunk, walked into a bad neighborhood, got rescued by police, and dropped off safely. Wherever he went from there is his problem, not ours."

The detective leans over the table toward me, overpronouncing his words the way the Agent talks to Neo in *The Matrix*. "Well, it is our problem because he's dead. They found his body on the side of the highway this morning. A road crew found him."

I feel the blood drain from my face. "Oh. Shit. How did he die?"

"I'm not sure. Maybe a hit-and-run. The body is really decomposed. It's rough to look at. Birds have taken his eyes, and the bugs and critters have torn the rest of him to pieces. I'm just here to clear you of anything and to make sure your story matches up."

As I think about the poor unhappy bastard I met that night, I hope it was at least quick. I hope he didn't die alone and scared, like the Mexican framer who haunts my days and nights. After an uncomfortable pause, I muster, "Well . . . go check the cameras. My story doesn't change. If you have any more questions, just let me know."

A few hours later he calls back to confirm that he has verified my story with the cameras and found the other detective who had witnessed the whole thing. "Can I connect you with the family?" he asks. "They want to talk to you, as you are the last person who spoke with him before he died. Can I give them your number?"

I think for a minute, quietly.

"Tansey, can I give them your number?"

"I'd rather you didn't. I'm not going to lie to them, and the only things he had to say about them and his friends were terrible."

"Um, okay, Tansey," he says before hanging up. I know most people would soften the blow and just talk to them, but I don't know them or him. Even if I tried to lie, I'm terrible at it. I'd rather just leave them with whatever happy memories they have of him, and not make them think they contributed to his demise.

News soon spreads through the department, and the dark humor that we use to deal with all the death in our lives births the joke that I murdered a poor, drunk kid. My phone is now blowing up with dark texts. "Hey, can you give Jammari a ride? He's a real asshole." Or "Hey Tansey, can you give my ex-wife a ride to the gas pumps?" The rookies are calling me the Grim Reaper, again.

Outwardly, I laugh it off, but at the same time, I feel a little annoyed and very disheartened. I took a guy out of a dangerous situation and he still ended up dead. Another lost soul. Would he have been better off being mugged? Am I making any difference at all?

The bodies keep stacking up, and I need them to stop.

"All units be advised, Garner Police Department is in a vehicle pursuit, headed toward Raleigh on Gamer Road." It's day shift, which is a welcome respite from nights at this stage of my career. I am about to turn on Gamer when I look up and see a black sedan blow through the intersection going well over 100 miles per hour. A few car lengths behind him is a Garner cop who appears to have slowed down significantly after passing by me. The road is virtually empty. It is a four-lane road that leads to a highway on-ramp about three miles farther on. They have recently changed the departmental chase policy, and we are not allowed to chase cars anymore. I just stay stopped at the intersection so my GPS won't alert any of the Karens from IA that I am in a chase.

Officer Bruno comes on the radio. "Raleigh, I have Garner Police's suspect vehicle. He has wrecked right here at the highway underpass. We are gonna need EMS quickly, please." His voice is shaking, but oddly calm. I cue up my mic: "I'm thirty seconds from your location. En route."

When I pull up to the scene, I see a large plume of smoke consuming a black sedan that is slightly off the road and up the grassy hill that leads to the overpass. I jump out and hear yelling from the Garner cop who passed by me, but I don't see Bruno. I assume someone has jumped out of the vehicle and run, and that Bruno is in a foot chase, so I move up to the wrecked sedan.

The Garner cop has his weapon drawn and is screaming at the car, "LET ME SEE YOUR FUCKING HANDS! I swear to God, I'll shoot you! Stop moving!"

I pull my pistol and tactically move up just off his left shoulder, then pause. He is target-fixated, and I can tell tunnel vision has set in. He is repeating himself, shouting again that he is going to shoot whoever is in the car. I speak calmly: "Brother, I'm coming up on your left side, okay? Please don't shoot me."

As I approach the vehicle, I see that the back window is covered with a duct-taped trash bag, leaving me unable to see the threat. I pull my baton out with my left hand, while holding my pistol in my right, and bust out the makeshift window. The Garner cop is still yelling in circles, "Stop moving! I will shoot you! Stop moving, I will shoot you!"

I peer into the car. The driver has been partially ejected and is lodged in the windshield up to his torso. He isn't shooting anyone. The GPD officer is still yelling. I try to get his attention.

"Hey, buddy! Hey, man! This guy is dying, okay? He's twitching. He can't stop moving." The cop doesn't acknowledge me, and instead just stands there, gun drawn, staring at the bloody chaos in the car. The passenger is under the steering wheel, folded up between the pedals and the driver's feet. I can tell the GPD officer is condition black; he has completely checked out.

I take a more forceful, in-charge tone. "Hey, man, lower your gun. I got this. This man is done. He is not gonna shoot you, or anyone else. He's dying."

Finally, the young officer looks over at me with eyes as wide as saucers. His pupils are enormous; I can't even see his irises. "Hey, man, lower the gun, I'm gonna start working on this guy. Okay?" I ask.

Finally, he lowers his gun, and I run around to the door to try to open it. The driver stares at me. His head, arms, and stomach hang out of the glass, and his hips and feet are mangled on the driver's seat. He is blinking slowly, gargling, and choking on his own blood. I put my full weight behind ripping those doors open, but neither will budge, so I call for the fire department. The smoke is annoying me, especially because I think I am still babysitting the GPD officer.

Looking around, wondering when the help is coming, I suddenly see that I am all alone. There is no Bruno, and no GPD officer. I move out of the smoke to get my bearings. As I turn back to the street to see where everyone is, I notice the GPD officer leaning on the hood of his car, obviously distraught, and I see an ambulance, fire truck, and blue lights about a hundred yards up the road. I realize then that this car had hit another car, and we have two scenes. "I need the Jaws of Life over here!" I yell.

"We're using them already, but there's another truck on the way," a cop I don't know screams back. Minutes later, it pulls up to help me while several other units pass by me and continue up the street to the other wreck. I am not sure what is going on—why isn't my scene the priority? I mean, these people are fucked. I need help! I also get hit with anxiety, worried that Bruno has been hurt. I haven't felt that in a while, and I push the stomach-turning feeling inside me to the back. I have work to do.

The firemen and I use the jaws to pry the door off, and there on the seat is a woman's head, just under the driver's ass. Without missing a beat, the firefighter says, "Yikes, in my house, it's usually the opposite."

"What?" I ask, dumbfounded.

"Usually my wife sits on my face, not the other way around," he says, cold as fuck.

For the first time ever, I am speechless. There's a guy dying here. "Fuck, man, that is dark as shit!"

"Yeah, well, fuck these pieces of shit," he murmurs as he starts to work on the guy hanging out the window. Again, I am shocked at how strangely everyone is acting. I've literally never seen a firefighter be this aggressive.

"Hey, copper, you know there's a gun in the car, right?" he suddenly says, stopping.

Nodding but unfazed, I say, "Yeah, I can't get to it. That door won't open, and there are two bodies between me and it, so—"

He interrupts me. "Yeah, I can't work on this guy with a gun right there. Safety protocol. You know the deal." He steps casually back a few steps, making it clear that he doesn't give a fuck about this suspect. I know then that whoever the driver hit is in bad shape, and everyone is putting this scumbag last. "Okay, well, what do you want me to do?"

"If you get the gun out, I'll go back to work, but I can't do it with the gun in there. You understand, right?" I don't know what they know, and it sounds like that's probably for the best right now. What I do know is that it is my job to save these people, even if they are assholes. I don't get to make the call about who to save any more than a doctor can decide who to operate on.

The only way to get the gun out is to move homeboy out of the window. I ask the firefighter and a medic who has just arrived for advice, and they tell me to pull him back through the window and out onto the ground. The medic is willing to talk me through it, but not help me. I'm frustrated.

"Okay, Tansey. You need to grab his arm and yank him back through the window, but the slower you go the more the glass is gonna work its way into him, so just pull as hard as you can." The firefighters are actively extinguishing a fire that is burning under the crushed hood, so smoke and chemicals are blowing in my face. I reach in and grab the driver's arms. The bones are so shattered that it feels like I'm grabbing a bag of corn flakes. I pull and tug as hard as I can for what seems like forever until his near-lifeless body tumbles out like Gumby over the chick's head and out onto the grass. EMS scoops him up and takes him away. The girl who was underneath him has a massive hole dead center of her head, between her eyes, where the bridge of her nose once was. She is definitively dead.

I crawl in and get the gun out. Once it's out, the medical staff take over.

I start walking to the other wreck scene, and as I get close, I see Bruno. Physically, he appears to be fine, but he is visibly and excruciatingly upset. I walk up to him. He shakes his head, stopping me with his palm, and whispers, "It's a church van. There are two dead little girls in there, and the driver is dead."

My heart drops. I have three young children at this point, and Bruno is also a father. As any parent will tell you, a child's death crushes your soul irreparably. No amount of career experience eases that anguish. "Oh fuck, man. No. Goddamn it. What the fuck?"

"Is the suspect dead, at least?" he asks, his eyes steeling, exposing the human imperfection we all carry.

"Probably. He is in real bad shape, and his girlfriend is dead. So at least there's that to sleep with tonight," I say for no good reason, other than to try to cheer up Bruno. I don't want him dead. I don't want anyone dead, least of all these kids.

"I am never sleeping again," Bruno murmurs, and walks away.

The GPD officer sits on the ground, slumped against his car. His head hangs mournfully to his chest, with his hand gripping his badge, pulling on it. He didn't do anything wrong. He didn't break a policy. He was chasing a violent suspect, and once the speed exceeded the department rules, he slowed down. I saw it with my own eyes. But looking into that car and seeing those dead little girls has broken him. I know what he is going to do before he does it.

He drives straight back to his station and resigns.

After we clear the scene, I check out for the rest of the shift. I park behind a church and take the time to pray through my own tears for a while, before finally passing out and sleeping in my car until the night passes.

No matter where I go, and what I do, I can't escape death. It follows me. No matter how fast I run, I can't escape it. It always settles back on top of me. Soul after soul after soul has vanished before my eyes. Some innocent. Some very much guilty. I feel for them all. I don't know how much more of this I can take.

22

SEARCHING FOR THE END

never apply for any promotions.

When Tom asks why not, I explain that I'm a line guy and I always want to be a line guy. I have no desire to be a detective, and definitely not a supervisor. I just want to chase bad guys, mediate family problems, and clean up neighborhoods. My kids are coming into their best years, and I want to focus on my time with them and my wife.

I've watched supervisors and detectives for a while now and I see how their workdays extend as they try to solve problems, or take care of cops in crisis, or need to stick around across shifts when bad things happen. The job is so important, it is easy to justify the added time devoted to it. It's easier to ask the family to deal with it because you are serving a "greater good." And I can tell you what the result is: Many cops I know have terrible home lives. If you don't turn off the job when you get home, everyone suffers, and if you constantly trade family time for cop time, you never really can turn it off.

What you devote your time to is what you end up living for. I don't want my kids to deal with any of that. I am determined to be a good father and a good husband.

To preserve my health and the health of my family, I've shifted my mindset from the job being a battlefield for achievement to a job that I care about, show up for, perform highly at, and then leave behind. It's not easy to do that, and I know that my only pathway to finding the right balance is to totally commit to not climbing the political ladder, the financial ladder, or the commendation ladder. I am content with where I am and who I am.

I also decide, after watching other cops who have done it the right way, to pursue other passions. I begin moonlighting a few days a week, teaching wine classes, hosting wine parties, and being a private somme- lier to some high-end fancy folks. I also start a wine blog, and all signs are pointing to eventually opening a wine shop of my own. But that isn't where my heart is either; I'm a doer, not a salesman. My real dream is to own and operate a vineyard—to make the wine.

Since making wine in this region is tough, I am starting a business plan for a distillery. As a cop, I can't own a bar, but after checking with all of my supervisors, a distillery that only sells wholesale is perfectly fine.

Studying wine, immersing myself in wine culture, and developing my distillery idea keep my mind off the job on my days off, and entertaining with wine is something that makes me happy. It gives me something to think about other than dead babies and domestic violence. I need some- thing more than policing to be whole.

I need to ensure my mental health is rock-solid so that I can be there for my coworkers and my family. A lot of "tough guys" like to roll their eyes at the term *mental health*, but more and more, I see the effects of poor mental health on society. In fact, a lot of an officer's job is showing up for people in crisis: people who have allowed a temporary problem to feel like there is no escaping it, so they seek a permanent solution.

I am dispatched to a call with Officer Quiet, the low-key Brazilian jiujitsu brown belt who is also an Army veteran. Unfortunately, he is coming from the opposite side of the city, so I arrive a full twenty min- utes before him. A woman who runs a group home made the 911 call. There's a twenty-eight-year-old woman named Lisa locked in a room and the manager is worried that she is in there hurting herself. When I arrive, she ushers me over to the door the woman is locked behind. I thank her and approach, knocking lightly.

"Hi, this is Eric. I was called here to check on you and see how you're doing," I say gently.

"Are you a cop?" she asks with a lively but muffled voice.

"Do I sound like a cop?" I ask, grinning.

"Yes, you sound like a douchebag."

"Well, damn, ma'am! That just isn't polite, but to be honest, I am a cop. I'm not really here as a cop, though. I'm here as more of a crisis intervention negotiator . . . and I just want to ask, are you having any thoughts of . . . or are you actively hurting yourself?"

"Maybe I am, and maybe I'm not," she snaps back with a whole lot of sass.

"Don't say that, Miss Lisa, or I'll have to end our nice conversation and be forced to break this door down to come rescue you."

"Why would you break the door down? It's not locked. You could just open it . . . not like a cop, but like whatever you said you were."

I reach down and jiggle the handle. Sure enough, not locked. *Well, shit. Probably should have started with that idea, Tansey.*

"May I open the door, Miss Lisa?" I ask, bringing my gentle voice back.

She's not impressed with my attempted niceties. "You're a cop. You said you were gonna break it down, so I'm figuring if you can kick it in, you can also just open it."

To be honest, I appreciate her sass. "Well, I'm gonna open it so we can chat face-to-face, okay? You aren't gonna shoot me or stab me with anything, are you?" I ask, dropping the overly sweet tone, which I absolutely know is unappreciated.

"Maybe I will, or maybe I won't."

Given her answer and tone, I can't take any chances. I pull out my Taser with my left hand and aim it through the door as I turn the knob and creak it open to see what I am working with on the other side. My eyes focus, and there she is, standing up butt-naked in the bathtub, shoving a large shard of glass into her wrist. Her hands are positioned low against her torso, just in front of her vagina.

"MA'AM, STOP CUTTING YOURSELF!" I yell. When I see her double her commitment to self-harm, I pull the trigger on the Taser.

Now, they always say that in a stressful situation, you shoot where you are looking. I am looking at her wrist, because that's where her weapon is and that's where the blood is flowing, so that's the direction the barbs fly. The two darts connect with their target and her body seizes up, stiff, and falls face-first out of the tub, barely missing the sink. Her nose hits the floor and blood explodes outward as she continues to ride the lightning for another four seconds. When it is over, she moans loudly.

"Ahhhhhh shit! Shit! Did you just TASE ME IN THE PUSSY?!"

My face goes ashen at those words. I roll her over, trying to dodge the blood that is gushing from her nose and lacerated wrist. I see the two prongs sticking out of her labia.

"Holy shit, I did. I did Tase you in the vagina. I am soooo sorry about that," I say, meaning it with every fiber of my being. I was not trying to do that, nor was I looking at her vagina when I Tased her. I really want her to understand that!

"What the fuck, man! I want to kill myself, so you Tase my pussy?" she snarls.

Just then, Officer Quiet enters the room and drinks in a naked bleeding woman with Taser darts in her junk. "Whoa, Jesus, what is going on here?!"

She answers for me. "He Tased my fucking pussy!"

"Haha, yes, he sure did, didn't he?" Officer Quiet grabs a rag and makes a quick tourniquet out of it and his handcuffs to stop the blood spilling out of her arm while I call for an ambulance. And . . . we wait while Lisa curses me up and down for being so stupid.

"This dumbass first tries to pretend he's not a cop by telling me his name is ERIC, or some faggot-ass name like that, and then he wants to kick a fucking door in THAT'S UNLOCKED, and then that dumb bitch TASES my fucking PUSSY to keep me from slitting my fucking wrist?! What sick fuck does that?! I am gonna sue the shit out of ALL OF YOU!"

"Ma'am, I can assure you that I . . ."

As I start talking, EMS arrives in the blood-soaked bathroom and sees the woman lying there with two Taser barbs lodged in her vagina lips. "Ouch! That looks like it hurts. So, what can we do for you?"

She answers for me again. "Well, aside from wanting to kill myself because my life is shit, this asshole tries to make it better by TASING MY FUCKING PUSSY!"

The EMT chuckles nervously. "Ha, yeah, I see that. Okay, well, here's the issue. The policy is that we can't remove the barbs from a victim because they're evidence unless there are extenuating circumstances. So"— he gestures uneasily in my direction—"he has to remove them."

She and I have the same reaction, but she voices it first. "What?! I don't want this dumb fuck anywhere near me!"

I back her up completely. "Um, yeah, I'm going to be honest, I don't really feel comfortable doing it either. Aren't these extenuating circumstances?"

The EMT dodges this problem the way politicians dodge responsibility for their actions. "Sorry, cupcake, it's your responsibility. You Tased her, so you collect the barbs."

I look at him, then at her, then at him again. He nods at me. I look back to her. She glares at me, but finally nods. I reach down and, reminiscent of trying to gently remove a fishhook from a baby bluegill, I pull the darts out as she screams and curses me up one side and down the other. "YOU PUSSY-TASING MOTHERFUCKER! FUCK YOU! YOU LYING DOOR-KICKING PUSSY-TASING PIECE OF SHIT!"

Finally, when she's had her fill of screaming at me, she gets up and limps out to the ambulance, yelling to all the other women in the house about all my unsavory attributes.

"Girls, if you are gonna kill yourself, do it before this asshole shows up, because he will Tase your pussy on your way out!"

I follow awkwardly behind her, through the house and past the other women. I can feel their scathing eyes on me, disgusted by my unintended target. I can't just stop and explain the psychology behind my barbs landing where they did; all I can do is scurry quickly out the back door to my car.

———

It is four o'clock in the afternoon, and I have wrapped up all my reports for the day, which is a fantastic feeling. I am lying low behind a church, trying not to get into anything that would make me get off late. I am supposed to teach a wine class later this evening, and have some studying to do to make sure I am at my best for my students.

But God and the universe have a real sense of humor about cops who try to make plans just after their shift is supposed to end.

Like clockwork, a domestic call goes out on the far end of the district. I slam my hands on the steering wheel in frustration, take a deep breath, and head for the call. I try to calm myself down, but damn it, I really want to get off work on time tonight. While on the way, an alert comes over the radio: "All units, be advised, we have a suicidal subject hanging her legs off an overpass on Florence Street. The responding officers suggest that she must be deaf by the way she is trying to verbally communicate with them. If there are any officers that know sign language, please advise."

As luck would have it, I'm from St. Augustine, Florida, home of the Helen Keller School for the Deaf and Blind. I am very familiar with American Sign Language and the deaf community. The high school I attended is the first school to accept ASL as a foreign language, and I took all four years of classes that they had to offer. My first apartment was only a few miles from the school and my neighbors were deaf, so I had lots of extra sign practice even after high school. That was years ago, and I have probably forgotten a lot, but after many moments of no one responding, it sounds like I am the only option in a city of seven hundred officers.

I key up the mic and tell the entire city that I know sign language. The dispatcher sends me the call, and as the reality of the situation begins to set in, I get nervous. It has been so long since I have signed regularly. I start going over signs in my head while driving like a madman through the busy rush-hour traffic.

My phone rings, and it is Tom.

His voice is gruff. "Tansey, do you really know sign language? Because so help me God, if not, you need to tell me right now. This chick is about to jump, and she ain't letting us get anywhere close to her."

Four o'clock traffic is heavy in this part of the city. By five it will become gridlocked, but at four it is busy. The girl is posed above a rush of moving cars.

"I'm not completely fluent, Sarge, but I'm pretty good. I know sign language," I assure him. There's a pause on the other end, and I can imagine him being really surprised that good ol' Leroy has levels to his game, not unlike an onion or an ogre. "Okay, get here fast," he says, hanging up.

I hit my lights and sirens and drive through the traffic as fast as I can. When I arrive at the overpass, they have already blocked off both sides of the bridge, so the girl is the only one out on it. I can see her sitting on the railing, dangling both legs off the edge. She's a tiny thing—very much a kid. I walk over to Tom and the gaggle of other leadership that have gathered at the south end of the bridge.

"Here he is," Tom mutters to the group, still somewhat concerned that he is being punked.

"Okay, Tansey, I hear you know sign?" a hostage negotiator asks.

"Yep, I know a little," I respond.

"You either know it or you don't," he snaps back at me.

"I know enough to understand it and sign back loosely," I explain.

They pause and look at each other. Not a person here, myself included, wants me to be at the heart of a sign-language negotiation with a kid, but we are all out of options. It's time to make lemonade.

"I guess that's good enough. I don't see another choice. Turn your radio to Tac Two and keep me informed. She doesn't want me on the bridge at all; she made that apparent. So you are going out there alone. Good luck." He looks at me awkwardly as I stare back, expecting more instructions.

None come.

"Wait, that's it? You're a hostage negotiator, and you're telling me to just go out there and good luck?"

He stares at me for a second and then answers me. "You're a good cop, and honestly one of my favorites. I was relieved when I heard it was you. I have confidence in you. Now go out there and be all you can be. Is that what you wanted to hear?"

I know he is full of shit. He's literally never met me. But fuck it. Here we all are. As an adult, it's amazing how many times you figure out that most of life is really just winging it.

I look to Sarge to see if he has anything to add. "Tom?"

Sarge wants nothing to do with this. "What? Don't look at me. You're the one who keyed up the mic. Looks like you're in, so step up to the plate and swing away . . . and hey, don't strike out."

I shake my head at them and then turn toward the bridge. A lump has formed in my throat. I push the dizziness away.

I edge out onto the bridge with my hands raised. She begins to mumble loudly at me, as deaf people do when they don't have an implant in. I don't know what she is saying, but her tone is not friendly. I begin signing right away to show her that I'm not like the other cops who have previously approached her.

I start signing the best I can with anything useful that pops into my head. My hands are trying frantically to follow my brain's commands, "I'm Eric. I am a cop. I am sorry you are here on this bridge. I am scared for you. Don't fall, please."

My radio is keying up with the noises of other officers and medics responding to the scene. I reach down, turn it off, and begin to sign again slowly, deliberately.

She is shocked to see me using American Sign Language. She lets go of the railing to sign back to me, then lunges hastily back to grab it before she falls backward, suddenly remembering that she is hanging off the side of a very tall overpass. My heart leaps when she almost falls; that abrupt movement knocks the reality right into me.

A moment before this I was annoyed about being late for class, and then about having to do sign language when I'm hardly an expert, but now I am completely present. This is serious. This is very, very serious. She clenches the railing, white-knuckled, her eyes on me. Her silent communication is deafening: "Oh shit, that was close."

I sign gently, saying that she should just swing her legs back around the railing so that she can sign to me safely. The sun is behind me and shining directly into her eyes. She lets go of the rail with one hand and uses it to shade her eyes from the sun.

I am terrified that she is going to fall backward again, and I desperately want her to move onto my side of the railing. Seeing her that close to the edge is giving me wild, weird anxiety. I beg her again, and with one hand still shading her eyes, she shakes her head no. This is going to take time. She has to trust me. I have to slow everything down.

I turn my radio back on. "Raleigh, she can't see me because the sun is silhouetting me. Can we get her some sunshades?"

"Um, ten-four, 424. We can try, but real quick, what are sunshades?" he asks.

I take a deep breath. *Come on, man.* "I'm sorry, Raleigh. Sunglasses. Can we get her some sunglasses?"

Officer Professor chirps up: "I got 'em, Raleigh."

Officer Professor drives his car past the barriers and begins inching onto the bridge. She becomes panicked. I can tell she thinks I am trying some trickery; she looks right at me and begins to stretch her leg off the bridge, letting me know in no uncertain terms that she is going to jump if he comes any closer.

I look around. I can see other cops down on the highway, trying to stop traffic below her, and a news helicopter is flying over us. I watch her noticing all these things too, and the reality hits that this is a huge deal, and the world is now watching her. I sign to her, "He is bringing me sunglasses. I am not trying any funny business."

She juts her chin out defiantly and sticks her leg even farther off the bridge.

I put both hands up and then bring them to my chest, pleading that I'm not being tricky. I guess the Professor can sense her volatility because he drives very slowly, flapping the sunglasses out of the window to prove his purpose. He stops about thirty yards shy of us, then climbs out with his raised hands and the sunglasses above his head. The tension is palpable. He throws that snazzy pair of sunglasses as hard as he can, but they land short of where I am standing. He gets back into his car and retreats off the bridge.

I sign, "Please, calm down. No funny business. I am going to get the sunglasses for you." I slowly stroll over to the sunglasses and pick them up, showing her there is no game here. I gesture to her that she can have them. She still thinks this is a ruse, so she shakes her head no again while grasping the rail, one leg stretched precariously into the air.

I shrug and throw the glasses, which land next to the concrete barrier that holds the railing. She mumbles angrily at me again, so I turn and walk to the opposite side of the bridge and sit down on the ground. Now there is no way I would have even the slightest chance of rushing her if she gets off her perch to grab the glasses.

With my most unassuming posture possible, I sign, "Please, take the glasses so you can see me and don't have to squint." She hesitates a moment, still looking at everything going on around us—fire trucks, news choppers, a highway full of onlookers, and the horde of police and negotiators. I just hold eye contact with her and sign persistently from my side of the bridge. She can barely see my hands but squints at me, seemingly very interested in what I have to say. She slowly, methodically, carefully brings her leg back up to the solid surface, giving me a moment's respite from my anxiety. She then quickly grabs the glasses, dons them, and jumps back to straddle the railing.

With the glasses on, she starts signing aggressively, but I am so far away now, I can't keep up with what she is saying. I keep nodding my head, signing to her, "slower, slower, please."

Even though I can't make everything out, it is clear that she is angry. I try to piece together what exactly she is saying, but all I can pick out is "took my phone," something about a tiger, "embarrassed," she hates "hearing school," and she hates her implant because she doesn't feel pretty. I know there is a lot more, but I just can't keep up. I stand up and ask if I can come closer, which makes her swing her leg right back over the railing.

This is getting repetitive, and just like when a cop loses control and gets stuck in an action loop, I can't allow myself to get stuck in a verbal loop. I sign for her to "please stop" and just "help me understand you." There is no way I can mediate any of this if I can't see exactly what she is saying.

She pauses and looks at me. I edge just a little closer.

I sign: "Look, I am a cop [I point to my badge]. That means I am not a good student. I am dumb. I am not good at sign, and I am sorry. Please, I am scared. I can't screw this up. Do you see all these people? If you die, I am messed up. I don't know what to say to you, so you have to help me.

Please, help me talk to you. I don't know what is wrong. I don't know why you want to die. If you let me talk to you, without being scared you will fall, I promise not to touch you, or tackle you, or try to rescue you. Just please move to this side, and I will sit here, and we can talk."

I don't know if anything I just said was the right thing to say, but I put myself in her place, and I know I wouldn't want to be bullshitted in this moment. She looks confused that I call myself dumb and insist that I don't know what I am doing. She must feel sorry for me, because she slowly moves her leg back to just straddling the bridge again. She signs, "You are dumb? Why?"

I feel a wave of relief when she responds directly to me, her hands slow and deliberate. If she is willing to give me a shot, I will not let her down. I sign back, "I don't know why. I was born that way?" I say, smiling.

She rolls her eyes and scoffs at me, signing, "You are a cop, but you are not dumb."

"Thank you, but I feel dumb right now."

"Why?"

"Because everything I sign or do makes you want to jump off this bridge, and I can't understand you because you sign so fast."

She lowers her head, shakes it back and forth. She signs again, even slower now. "I don't want to jump because of you. I am mad at my mom. She took my phone for texting boys, but it is fake. They think I can hear. They don't know I am ugly and deaf. I hate my implant, so I threw it. My mom is angry. I hate hearing school, and I miss Tiger."

"Who is Tiger?" I ask.

"My cousin who knows sign. My family doesn't sign. No one signs to me except Tiger. Do you want to write notes to me?" she asks.

"What?" I say, confused.

"Do you have paper and pen?" she signs.

"Yes!" I pull out my pad and pen and show her. She gestures for me to throw it to her, so I do. She writes, "Thank you. You are not dumb. I don't want to die. I just want Tiger. I will go with you, but only if Tiger is with me, and my mom is not on the bridge. Can you get Tiger and tell the helicopter to go away?" She throws the pad back to me. I read it and then point to the helicopter. She nods and waves her middle finger at it. "Got it. I'll see about Tiger and your mom, and I will ask the helicopters to leave," I sign. I turn my radio on and key up the negotiator.

"Hey, guys, I think I'm getting close. She has a few requests, though." I relay her message, and they oblige.

"Tansey, we talked to Mom and she gave us Tiger's info. We have a unit going to get her, and Mom is now off the bridge."

"They are looking for Tiger. The helicopters are leaving and you can see your mom has left the bridge," I sign. She seems pleased by these developments.

We continue to talk on that empty bridge, using a mixture of notes and broken ASL. She tells me a story about how terrible her mother is—that she is a crackhead who hates her. She often leaves the girl and her siblings home alone for days while she goes out whoring and smoking crack. The kids knock on the neighbors' doors for food. Her siblings don't know sign, so she never gets to talk with anyone at home.

Imagine, in an already desperate family situation, being unable to communicate with the people around you. For her entire life, this is all she has known.

I listen but really have nothing to say. Soon Tiger appears at the end of the bridge, waving. When she sees her, she lights up, and then looks at me, sheepishly. "I think I am ready to get down, okay?"

"That makes me really happy," I answer, meaning every signed word.

She signs, "Can I ask one more favor?" I nod. "Can you not tackle me, and not put me in cuffs?"

"I promise."

She points to the horde of cops and signs. "They will tackle me and put me in cuffs. But you, please don't, okay?"

"They won't touch you, and I will make sure there are no cuffs. I promise. Hey, you want some pizza?"

She signs a question mark at my last comment.

"Okay, look, if I tell them you request pizza before you go to the hospital, they will have to give it to you. Then we can go eat it at the station with Tiger before they take you there."

She ponders the idea. "Really? I am not hungry, though."

"Well, do you want to hang with Tiger for a few minutes?" I ask.

"Yes, please!" she answers excitedly.

"Okay, I'll tell them you want pizza." I wink at her. "Plus, I am hungry, so if you don't eat it, I will."

She rolls her eyes and shakes her head, now understanding that she is dealing with a man-child. Still, she smiles.

We walk to the end of the bridge, and she runs and embraces Tiger. The two teens cry on the bridge, signing back and forth rapidly until we are able to escort them back to the station for some pizza. When we get there, a high-ranking officer from the Admin Division asks what kind of pizza she wants.

I reply, "I don't know, just ask her." I am kidding and my tone is obviously sarcastic, but this office nerd doesn't catch it. He bends down, inches away from her face, and yells, "DO. YOU. WANT . . . SOME . . . PIZZA?"

I'm dumbfounded. "What the fuck! Sir! She can't fucking hear you even if you yell as loud as you can. What are you doing?"

"Oh well . . . I . . ." He stands up straight, his face beet red. Everyone in the room stares at him like he is a nut job. "You said to ask her." The room is full of cops, medics, and hostage negotiators. The officer is obviously embarrassed, but I can't help myself.

"Well, that was fucked-up, sir." I sign "2 Legit 2 Quit" from the MC Hammer video to no one in particular and without even looking at her say, "She would like a thin-crust pepperoni, stuffed-crust sausage, breadsticks, and a side of wings with ranch. And Tiger wants a large cheese with regular crust, and a side salad with ranch . . . actually, make it three side salads." The guy is so focused on getting the order right that he doesn't even notice that the two girls haven't said a word. I am just listing whatever shit I want. He jots it down and leaves the room.

The girls don't really want any pizza, but they grab a few slices, and the rest is just so there'd be enough to feed the squad. The girls talk for a few minutes, crying and signing excitedly. Finally, she looks at me and signs, "I am ready to go to the crazy house," and winks.

Then she turns back around and waves to make sure she has my attention. I confirm she has it. She signs, "Thank you. You are not dumb. You got them to buy you pizza." We both laugh.

Lieutenant Queen Bee, who magically showed up when the news chopper arrived, asks what she had said. I look her dead in the eyes and say, without an ounce of emotion, "She said to mind your own business. This is a private conversation . . . Just kidding, she said I'm awesome and deserve a raise." The lieutenant huffs and glares at me, then looks at Tom for some backup. But good old Tom, well . . . he doesn't care. That's what she gets for driving all the way to our district to get involved with our calls. Don't you have some No Trespassing signs to hang a hundred feet in the air or something?

With the girl's departure, the horde of people leaves the station, and thankfully leaves our squad to enjoy the pizza in peace. Tom walks over while I am stuffing my face and asks to see me in the hallway. I savagely bite the crust off and follow him out, chewing obnoxiously.

He holds his hand out for me to shake it. Is he serious? I am confused, but that has never stopped me from being a smart-ass, so I wipe both hands childishly down my pants and then shake his hand.

"I am proud of you, Tansey. You handled that perfectly. You've become a halfway-decent cop. Enjoy your pizza."

Holy shit. He is serious.

This is a huge deal for me. I can't prove it, but this may have been the nicest thing Tom has ever said to someone at work. I hold my chin high when I walk into the room and see my squad mates smashing the pizza and wings before heading home for the night. For that brief moment, I allow myself to feel proud to be a police officer in the city of Raleigh.

I check my watch. *There's still time!* I leave the office and drive straight to my wine class. When I walk into the shop, everyone stares at me. The shop owner walks over and gives me a big hug. "We saw you on the news! On the bridge! We couldn't believe it! I just assumed we would cancel the class for tonight, but here you are!" People start shaking my hand, rubbing my shoulders, and patting my back.

I hate every second of it.

It's not that I am not proud. I just told you that I was. But this is my place away from work, and it brings me back to the fact that I know her life isn't going to be better until she can get out of that home situation, and that will be a while. One of the struggles of being a cop is that when you see people, especially kids, in terrible situations, you want to help. You want to get more involved. But you really can't, or I would have adopted about 53 kids by now. And she'd be No. 54.

The mom goes on the news the next night with her makeup done and her hair finely coiffed, talking about the seriousness of mental health. But I know this isn't a case of mental health problems. It's a case of having a shitty mom. Your daughter is deaf and you haven't learned to sign? Fuck you.

And in case you think I'm being overly judgmental because there are complexities in this world, when I spoke with the mom after the incident, I let her know in no uncertain terms that her daughter is lonely, and that taking her away from deaf school has isolated her even more. "Ma'am, is there a reason that you have never learned sign? I can point you in the right direction."

Her reply sent ice through my veins. "Why the fuck would I do that shit? I got three other kids who are normal."

So how do you deal with that?

The department wants to put me out front as a poster child for good policing, but I turn down all media requests, ask for my name to be redacted from all stories, and ask the media department to stop running any stories about it. I know the higher-ups love feel-good stories, but I just happened to be the guy that knows sign language. How many times a day does a Spanish-speaking cop help Spanish speakers? Or a Russian cop helps Russian speakers? Arab? Chinese? I'm glad I had the skill set. The next day, I won't.

Besides, we just threw a girl back into a bad situation. Celebrating this is like taking a piece of shit and coating it in chocolate. We don't need to profit off the worst day of her life, especially after we're just sending her back to have more of them.

I try my best to erase it from my memory.

Months later, I receive a call that I am being named Officer of the Year for my handling of that incident. I go to the ceremony, but I refuse to speak, doing nothing to help my relationship with the chief or her minions. When the public relations officer comes up to take my photo, he asks me what my name is again. "Tansey," I reply. "Oh right! I chose you for this award! That story made the department sound really good. Great work."

When I leave, I stuff the award under the seat of the patrol car, and I leave it there. Three years later, I receive a call from a city garage. They are cleaning the car out for auction and find the award under the seat. I tell them to keep it, but they drop it at the main station, and it makes its way back to me. When it does, I pray that she is doing well and has escaped them all.

My radio buzzes. "424D, a fire alarm has been activated at a home in Idle Pine Village."

Idle Pine is a large neighborhood in my district with houses packed in on each other like sardines. Since the houses are so close together and there are so many, any fire alarms immediately notify the fire department. They get tons of calls out there, and they are fake 99.99 percent of the time. It's like the neighborhood that cries wolf.

Today the alarm has been activated twice, and twice the fire department called the residents, who stated it was all clear. When the activation happens a third time, the dispatcher rightfully decides a cop should go see what is going on—but I am not aware of any of that information. All I know is that I am going to a fire alarm.

I roll down the street and find the address. There is no fire, and no smoke. All I can see is a family getting out of their car with bags of Bojangles breakfast. I say good morning and ask if they have smelled or seen a fire, or if they know the reason for the alarm. "No idea, Officer. We haven't seen anything," they say cheerily and head into their house.

I begin to walk up the driveway to the adjacent address when a little boy opens the door and darts past me as if I'm not there. I call after him about the alarm, but he ignores me, scurrying away without so much as a nod. I look on as he rounds the corner toward a neighbor's house. Bewildered and a bit curious, I turn back toward the house and come face-to-face with a man standing in the doorway, a large revolver pointing right at my head.

It's over.

I shoot my hands up over my head and let out a frustrated "Fuck." I can't believe it. He's got me dead to rights. I have no options. I've seen people in their last moments more times than I would like to remember. They never saw it coming, and neither did I. It's been a normal Sunday morning, but now I am about to die. An image of my family flashes through my mind as I start to walk backward toward my car, my hands still raised.

"You got me, man. I don't know why you want to shoot me, but let me say this: Whatever it is you got going on, I'm out of it. I got a family and I hate this fucking job, so you let me go and we are good."

He keeps the gun aimed at me, his face completely emotionless as I continue to move backward. While I'm sure my backing up takes mere seconds, it feels like forever, and I am more upset than I thought I would be in the face of death. I'm not sure what I expected to feel at this moment, but I am pissed. I finally feel the bumper hit my leg, and with a sudden move of panic, I spin around, drawing my gun and sliding onto my knees behind the tires. "Drop the gun, sir!" I scream.

A moment goes by and I hear footsteps moving away from me. I pop my head up for a quick peek just as the man disappears back inside the house. I stand up and move around to the A-pillar of my vehicle and get on the radio. "Raleigh, this is 424. I need backup. Suspect is suicidal and has a gun in his hand." I hear sirens around the city sound off as the blue wave begins to head in my direction.

The man walks back out of the house and begins to yell at me. "You gonna shoot me, bitch, or are you gonna just hide behind that car?" He throws an Army medal out onto the grass. "I'm ex-military, asshole, and if you don't shoot me, I'm going to kill you!"

I yell back, "I'm military too! You had your chance to kill me and you didn't take it, so good luck! I don't even think you want to kill me. Just put the gun down!"

He comes off the porch and starts walking toward the driveway with the gun in one hand and a bottle of Crown Royal in the other. "Kill me, asshole! Just fucking doing it, you pussy!" he screams.

"Come on, man. This isn't the answer. Just chill, brother," I say.

He opens the door of his truck and looks right at me. "You gonna stop me, bitch?!"

"No, I told you that already! You could have killed me and you let me go. You and I are good. I suggest you put the gun down, or at least the booze, and just chat with me for a second."

He pulls the door shut and starts the truck. He lowers the window and backs down the driveway, staring intently at me as he does it. He stops just shy of my car and asks me again, "Are you going to stop me?"

My gun is pointed right at his face as I say, "No. You wanna leave? Go ahead. I'm not asking you to stay here and fight me."

With tears in his eyes, he takes a swig from the bottle of Crown, then pulls out onto the road and drives out of sight. The horde of police cars flood the streets with weapons drawn, moving to points of cover. I tell them that he has left in a truck seconds earlier. Everyone gapes at me, wondering why I am not in pursuit.

A supervisor approaches me. "Hey, man, you good? You okay?"

I am standing in the middle of the road, my gun hanging down by my side. "Yeah, he left that way in a blue truck with a bottle of Crown and a .357 Dirty Harry–style revolver," I say quietly.

Perplexed but not angry, he asks, "Why aren't you in pursuit of him? Tansey, why did you just let him go?"

"Let's just say we had a gentleman's agreement."

"A what?" he asks and then just walks away.

It isn't just the agreement with him. I realize that I'm scared to make the decision to chase him. I don't want another church van incident, where the act of pursuing a suspect, even at low speeds, leads to dead innocents. I also don't want to have a gun battle with a depressed veteran. Both options sound terrible to me, so I just decided to take neither one. The supervisor, now fully ignoring me, rallies the troops and leaves to go find the guy while I drive back to the station to cool off.

I walk into Tom's office. He is a week out before retirement and his give-a-fuck meter is at an all-time low.

"What happened on Idle Pine?"

"Some asshole pointed a gun at me and I retreated. He left in a truck toward Garner."

"Why didn't you shoot him in the face?"

"He didn't shoot me when he could have. I felt like I owed him one."

"How did that work out for you?"

"Well, they're out there chasing him down, and I'm sitting in here waiting to see how it all plays out."

"I would have emptied his brains out and taken my vacation, but you do you."

I stay there quietly in his office while he sits on his computer, looking at lake houses or fishing boats or whatever retiring old supervisors look at on their computers. I am done. I am exhausted from the job, and peering down the working end of that gun puts into perspective that I am risking my life for nothing. Suddenly, I loathe being a cop. I decide, right then, that I am done.

But I don't want to be done. I look up at Tom, my eyes yearning for wisdom, hoping to find something from him that I am missing, something just out of reach that will make me understand it all.

"Hey, Tom, how did you make it twenty-five years?"

He pauses, taking me in. "It was a different time. The calls were the same, but the stress of how you dealt with them was different. You're coming up in a time when you are damned if you do, and damned if you don't. I would never do this job now if I were a young cop."

"Thanks, Tom."

"Go home, Tansey."

Driving home that night, I have a lot on my mind. I've been seeing more and more suicides lately—attempted and completed. Suicidal people are at their lowest points and often feel like they have nothing to lose. You have to be extra careful of falling into complacency and getting too comfortable. It's hard not to sit there and get lost in their story, empathizing with their pain or depression. But they share one common thread, whether they are teenage deaf girls, angry women cutting themselves, or depressed veterans—they have lost hope.

Today, there was a moment when I thought I was going to die. I didn't see it coming. I wonder if they saw the moment when they tried to take their lives coming, or if it surprised them the way the gun surprised me.

I wonder if I still have hope.

THE END

Even from down the street, I see the blood spurt into the air and hit the sidewalk. A full melee breaks out, and I see five or six people swinging wildly at each other. I push my car forward, and as I do, they all go running, disappearing into the neighborhood like cockroaches fleeing from the light. All, that is, except one, who appears to be the latest victim of the surging gang violence that has enveloped the city.

As I approach the victim, I notice two things: she is pregnant and there is a growing glow of blood emerging from around her on the pavement. Whatever wound she had has only been in place for seconds. There shouldn't be that much blood. Before my car is even stopped, I'm ripping a tourniquet out and getting ready to go to work.

I jump out and sprint over to her, taking a quick battle assessment. They fucked this girl up good. She's been slashed with a box cutter or an X-Acto knife from her vagina to just above the knee, and she's dumping blood from an arterial wound. I know I have seconds to work before this is too late.

Without putting gloves on or anything, I jump in there with my tourniquet. I'm instantly covered in her blood. Every time her heart beats, more blood spurts across my chest, legs, and crotch. Kneeling in front of her, I rip the tourniquet open. Knowing time is short in this kind of bleed, I desperately try to get the tourniquet clamped down above her wound. Most of the spray is hitting me in the gut now, and I can feel it traveling down my stomach, leaking down under my belt, and running down my groin. As I cinch the tourniquet down more and more, the spray gets less and less, but I'm not sure if it's because she is running out of blood or because I finally am getting it under control. I hope it's the latter.

Thankfully, an ambulance pulls up quickly since I am only two minutes away from the nearest hospital. When the EMT hops out, he looks at the ground, and at the blood covering me, and says, "Did it hit the femoral artery?"

"I don't know, man. I think so. I just know that there's too much blood. I don't have the training for this. That's all you guys."

They quickly load her up and we head to the hospital. They call it in as a femoral artery bleed and get to work on cleaning her up. By the time we arrive, you almost can't tell that she almost died mere moments ago. I still look like Carrie.

As they roll her in, with me a few steps back, they are greeted by an Indian doctor. She immediately starts yelling at the EMTs. "How many times do I have to tell you guys not to call in femoral bleeds when there isn't one present! Look at her! She's not bleeding at all! And whoever put this tourniquet on," she says, glancing at me, "should know that with her being pregnant, this can cause serious complications!"

At this point, I'm salty. I don't want to hear it. I look at her and squint my eyes, deciding not to speak. To prove a point, she maintains eye contact with me and then the EMTs, then leans over and nonchalantly releases the tourniquet. The second she does, blood sprays to the other side of the room. It's worse than any movie I've ever seen and the walls of the operating room are doused with blood splatter in a way I couldn't replicate if I tried. She changes gears immediately, realizing how bad she just fucked up. "I need a surgeon!" she screams as she pushes me out of the room. In seconds, six people are in the room working feverishly to keep the woman alive.

I hang around until she is in stable condition and then head back to the station. I throw my uniform into the trash—I don't want one that has seen this much blood. I spend an hour in the shower, slowly cleaning every bit of blood off me, and keep soaping myself and rinsing until no more red is running down the drain.

After two years, my distillery is really coming together.

I filed for permits, garnered investors, found the necessary equipment, and found the perfect location. Tons of cops volunteered their time and effort to help me—it almost became a department project! For all the bad things about the job, there really is an irreplaceable brotherhood and sisterhood in the Thin Blue Line that I will always love and appreciate.

It wasn't just my RPD compatriots who helped me with my dream. My fellow rugby players, friends, and family from every corner of my life pitched in. Everyone volunteered their time to help make my dream come true. The distillery build was a community effort, which I remain touched by. I think the business retains a familial community vibe because it would not have been possible without the community.

We are weeks away from opening when I hear that the city manager might have an issue with the distillery. I don't know how that is possible since I asked my chain of command about it, and confirmed it was not against any rules or laws. Moreover, I ensured it was built in a neighboring county, and not one where I worked.

Because no one has brought it to my attention, I assume it is just griping. Besides, who would have an issue now with a project that the whole department has known about and helped with for years?

"Come on in, Tansey!" Tom says from behind his desk. He's only got a few weeks left, but true to form, he's doing his job to his fullest. "What's up, boss?" I ask.

"Great news. The doctor put you in for a lifesaving award and she'd like to come down here to apologize to you in person. She wants you to know that if just about anyone else had been on scene, that girl would have died."

"Tom, that's not necessary. Please kill this, and she definitely should not come here."

"Why? What's the problem? She said she yelled at you and you didn't deserve it, so she wants to make amends," Tom says, weighing my odd reaction.

"First, she has a stressful job where people are dying all the time and every split-second decision she makes matters. Like us. I can't count the number of times I was a dick when I shouldn't have been. I don't run around apologizing every day. No one has time for that shit. She's a good doc. We all know the drill. Neither one of us owes anyone anything. Second, you know we don't do these awards here."

Tom knows we don't do awards, and I am wondering why we are even having this conversation. The SED does not acknowledge lifesaving awards unless it's an amazingly huge deal like saving the fucking president. These awards are a big deal in the suburbs where nothing happens, so when a cop saves a kid from choking or something, they have something to celebrate. Here, though, we have someone dying or almost dying every day. If you get one and you don't really deserve it, everyone shits on you. I've saved dozens of lives and this is the first one we are even talking about.

"Nothing I can do about it, Tansey," Tom says matter-of-factly.

"Don't give me a lifesaving award, Sarge. Please."

"I didn't. She did it through the city. You're going to get it," he says, pausing, "and there's nothing either of us can do to stop it."

Fuck.

"You're going to have to make a choice, Officer Tansey. You can either abandon your plans to open your distillery, or you can turn in your badge and gun," the city manager and chief tell me.

I'm numb. I can't believe this is happening to me. They had years to bring this up, and now, on the eve of my grand opening, after I've spent hundreds of thousands of dollars—my entire life savings and then some—on this thing, they are dropping this in my lap.

If I wasn't numb, I'd probably be mad that these two best friends and sorority sisters seem to be enjoying this moment. Not that I'm saying this was planned or that there is any nepotism involved.

"What are my choices, ma'am?" I ask.

"I laid them out for you already. You can get rid of your distillery and stay, or you can quit."

"And if I don't do either?"

"Then we will have no choice but to fire you."

"Okay, let's do that. I've never been fired before," I answer.

They are shocked! They very clearly thought that they could bully me into their way of thinking, but I don't care anymore. I haven't done anything wrong, and I'm not going to quit.

The next day, I am called to Internal Affairs to meet with the Karens.

McGinley, motherfucker that he is, immediately starts yelling at me and pointing at me with aggressive knife hands as he tries to tear me down and make it out that I'm some kind of piece of shit. I'm not having any of it. I launch right back at him immediately.

"I've done nothing morally wrong, ethically wrong, or legally wrong. There's no need to knife-hand me or use that tone. We can talk like adults, or not at all," I say.

My response is a kick right in his tiny dick and he loses his shit: "You're not going to tell me what to do! I'm in charge here! Do you hear me? I'm in charge?" he screams, beet red from head to toe.

"Yeah, okay, buddy. You look it," I say, grinning.

McGinley glares at me and growls, "We'll see, smart-ass," before storming off.

Within two weeks they move me to an unassigned department working a college beat. I have poured my heart and soul into the SED for seven years. This is an unprecedented move, especially for an officer with my service record. Clearly, the goal is to get me to quit. FUCK. THAT.

The abuse continues. McGinley and the Karens park outside the distillery and take pictures of it, of me walking into it, and of a whole lot of shit that everyone knows about, like they're some kind of characters out of a Jason Bourne novel surveilling me. I try to help and take some funny pictures of me in the distillery and offer the pictures to them. That decision endears me to no one in IA, which comes as a real shock to me.

Finally, the cowards all realize that I will not quit—that they cannot break me—and they suspend me. They declare that having partial ownership in a distillery is simply unbecoming an officer. Never mind that everyone told me it was okay, that my business is located in a neighboring county, and that it did not involve serving alcohol. Never mind that simultaneously, a Raleigh city councilman owned a brewery *in Raleigh*. Never mind that in the city of Fayetteville, just to our south, a police officer literally owned a bar with no issue. They have decided I am bad, and there is nothing I can do about it.

They take my badge and my gun.

McGinley shows up with a couple of the other Karens and is grinning from ear to ear.

"I need to get your shotgun out of your car. Sign this consent form so we can search your car," he barks.

"I'm not signing any fucking consent form," I answer.

"You have to sign it," he growls.

"I don't have to do shit. You can take the shotgun out of the back of the car, and that's it," I tell him.

Ignoring me, he goes for the handle of my car door to the back seat.

"Did you not fucking hear me?" I say, stepping between him and the door.

He snaps at me and tells me to get out of the way.

At this moment the captain walks over. "What the hell is going on?" he asks.

"McGinley is trying to search my car without my consent, because apparently he didn't go to cop school," I respond.

"I need to search his car to get his shotgun!" he almost cries to the captain.

"Just take his shotgun. You don't need to search anything," the captain says, ending it. He walks away.

As soon as he is out of sight, McGinley grabs my car door again.

"You're not going in there. The captain just told you, you're not going in there. What the fuck is wrong with you?"

McGinley says he needs to search the laptop he sees in my car.

"That's my personal laptop. It's mine, not the department's. The only things on there are stories I write about all the fucked-up shit that has happened to me on this job. I can't wait to get home tonight to write about this cocksucker that doesn't believe in following the law."

He moves to wiggle the door one last time.

"You're not going in there. Were you like this as a street cop? Did you just break the law all the time? I mean, if you're doing this to me after a captain told you that you can't, what did you do to kids on the street who had no one to back them up?"

He curses me under his breath.

I am on a roll now, and I don't give a fuck. "No, bro. We both know how this ends. You took my badge and my gun for bullshit reasons, and you're going to go jerk off to it tonight. So go fuck yourself. You're a piece of shit."

He's shaking. I hope he hits me. *What a piece of garbage.*

I can't help myself. "Are you shaking? That's hilarious. You're a fucking coward."

I pop the trunk and hand him the shotgun, then drive home.

Within twenty minutes of leaving, I get a call from Bruno. "Did you just call McGinley a fucking coward to his face?" Shortly thereafter, Sarge calls. Same question. I get about a dozen calls that night, asking me to relive the conversation.

Three weeks later, Sarge calls me to let me know that my lifesaving award has been approved. Fifteen minutes later, I am finally fired.

Even though I knew this moment was coming, it suddenly hits me: I am no longer a cop.

———

The event at the PNC Arena in Raleigh is beautiful. It's a who's who of politicians. The governor, mayor, several representatives, and of course, the sorority sisters—the city manager and the chief—are all here.

I'm adapting well to civilian life, and I'm looking at this moment as a nice way to close the book on a career that meant, and means, the world to me. I was able to bring my wife and children, as well as many of my friends as could get away. Tom, Jayce, Red, Quiet, Thor, Ralph, and a few others are all here, as are my new business partners.

We are all having a great time, laughing, eating, and drinking, when Sarah Rapp, the media person for all of Raleigh, nudges me on the shoulder. "Hi, Eric. My name is Sarah and I am doing the media tonight. I don't know what's going on, but I'm uncomfortable with it and I feel the need to tell you this: I've been told I am not allowed to take any photos of you or release any photos to the media of you today."

What the fuck?

"Thank you for telling me. I will get to the bottom of this," I tell her, immediately jumping up and walking up to the PR captain.

Unlike Sarah, who is a civilian government employee, this guy is a cop. He swears up and down that there is no such rule. "Listen to me, Tansey. I'm the PR captain. I'm telling you that what she told you is not true. I would never tell her to do that. It doesn't even make sense."

I believe him. I have no idea what's going on, but as I just heard it from the man himself, I opt to let it go and return to my table. Moments later, he appears again, looking uncomfortable. "Tansey . . . I don't know how to say this, but . . . the chief says not to take photos of you. I'm so sorry. I know this is unbelievable. I've never seen anything like this before. I need you to know that this is not me."

"Well, you wouldn't be a captain if you didn't do what they told you," I say, maintaining a smile.

"Come on, man, you know me. That hurts my feelings," he says sullenly.

"Well, dude. *This* hurts my feelings."

Not a person at my table can believe what is happening. I am about to walk out when Sarah returns, a look of action in her eyes. "Who wants to take pictures? Huh? I'll show you how to use my camera! I've put it on automatic, so it's really easy to focus." *She has more character than the captain.*

Sarah teaches my friends and wife how to use my camera and I start doing a series of poses as they snap away. The press are about to receive so many Tansey photos that if you flick them really fast, I'm animated.

When they call me up onstage, there is applause as they drape a big medal over my neck and an officer reads the citation aloud. I don't care about the citation or the applause, but I do care about the look my oldest son has on his face right now. He is so incredibly proud of me. It warms my heart and makes this whole moment worth it. My wife doesn't get the chance to smile at me, because she is snapping my picture. She also artfully captures a picture of the chief scowling as I get my award.

———

Riots fill the city and it seems like the whole place is burning to the ground from the news. I don't see any of that, though, because I'm happily working on my distillery, working hard to sell our rum.

My phone rings. I recognize the number. It is from the station. I answer.

"Hey, man, there's a guy here who wants to talk to you. He doesn't believe me that you're gone," comes the voice of one of the new guys, Charger.

"Sure, man, Put him on."

"Tanny, dat you?" comes a voice I instantly recognize as a homeless guy who used to give me information on anything really bad that was about to go down. We'll call him Jimmy.

"Jimmy, how you doing, man?" I ask.

"Tanny, is it true? They fire you?"

"Yeah, man, but don't you worry about me, okay?"

"They do you wrong, bro?"

"Ha, a little. You know how it is."

"Fucking cops, man. You can't trust any of them. Only you, Tanny. Only you."

"Hey, you can trust Charger, okay? He'll take care of you. You can tell him the truth."

"You sure, Tanny?" he asks, needing to know if I really mean it.

"I'm sure."

"You really not coming back, Tanny? For real?"

"I'm really not, man. But it's okay. Take care of yourself."

I end the call and sit down in a chair, just staring at the screen for a minute.

When I started as a cop, I thought the job would be easy. I learned very quickly that nothing is further from the truth. And when my career was ending, I was sure I wasn't making a difference anymore, and believed that maybe I never did. After all, crime continues and people continue to die, from addiction, from violence, and even at their own hands.

I can make a list of all the people I didn't help. I could start writing right now and that list would be five times the size of this book. But Jimmy needed me. The girl on the bridge needed me. The lady with the femoral tear needed me. I helped quite a few people, and I was the only person with several others when they passed.

I thought I'd be a cop forever, but maybe that was never supposed to be. Maybe the right thing for me, like so many other men and women over the years, was to serve my community for a time—to give it all I had, in mind, spirit, and body, until I had nothing left to give.

I was wrong about being a cop forever, and I was wrong about something else: I didn't expect to gain the friends, mentors, and bosses that I would encounter who would change my life forever. From day one with Jayce until the bitter end, I repeatedly encountered heroism, selflessness, and grit unlike anything I ever thought possible. Even as it ends, I am so unbelievably grateful to all of them. They are, no matter what anyone else tells you, America's best.

I know now that none of us can save the world. None of us can even save our city. But we can all serve our communities. And maybe, just maybe, the world would be a better place if more of you, for a couple of years, or for seven years, or for a career, donned the blue. Unlike so many jobs and careers you might choose, as a cop maybe you too will have that rare opportunity to save someone's life, to protect a child, to catch a criminal, to make a difference. Perhaps you might even be lucky enough to be subjected to the never-ending taunts and good-natured insults and ridicule of your brothers and sisters, and learn just a little Pig Latin.

I can't tell you what journey you'll endure, but I can promise it will be absolutely worth it.

ERIC TANSEY
ACKNOWLEDGMENTS

How do I even start acknowledgments? I guess I'll start with thanking God because, well, that's obvious. Next, I'll just say thank YOU for reading my book. You're awesome, so give yourself a pat on the back. To my wife, Ashleigh Tansey, for helping me get these stories on paper and doing the first big edit: I'll thank you more later . . . wink, wink.

To my squad and coworkers:

Tom, you were a hard supervisor, but you were fair and just. Without your patience this book would have been a lot shorter. To the supervisor that read most of my reports (I'll call him Doc), thank you for being such a grammar Nazi and always encouraging me to become a better writer. Thank you Jayce and Detective Hans for being awesome field training officers. Thank you to all the men and women of the Raleigh Police Department—except for the Internal Affairs Department, Chief Antoinette, her deputy chief, and Lieutenant Queen Bee. Way to sell your souls to the political elites.

To my family:

First, I have to thank my mom, Patsy Tansey. She taught me to see the good or the funny in every situation. She is a great storyteller, and maybe one day we can write a book together about her life and her crazy, sad, but very funny childhood. Thank you to my dad, Darby Tansey, for giving me thick skin as a child and raising me to be a real man. Thank you to my little brother, James Tansey, for always encouraging me and keeping me accountable. Thank you to my cousin/orphan sister Katie Hopkins for sharing my dark sense of humor and for always just being a part of my family. Thank you to my mother-in-law, Lynette Davidson, for buying me a different cop book to help keep me motivated to finish this one. Thank you to my aunt and uncle in-laws, Jay and Heather Wolf, along with Grandmère Hope for always asking about the book and being super supportive throughout the long process.

To my friends:

Thank you, Dr. Dardin Pyron, for listening to my crazy stories and then demanding that I write a book. You are a great listener and a great human being. Without that special dinner and wine in the mountains this book would never have gotten started. Thank you to Andrea Gibbs for reading my stories and listening to them over and over again, and for being a part of the first edits of this book. Thank you, Jonathan Bates, for the artwork and for all the encouragement and dedication to the project. This book would not have gotten the steam it got without your creativity and passion for art and the career field. Thank you, Noel White, for also demanding that the book be finished, and for reading the very first edits of the book and still just loving the project. Without your encouragement as the first "reader" of the first draft, I would have quit the project, so thank you.

To the book team:

Thank you, Nick Palmisciano, for believing in me and for taking on this project. Thank you for putting up with me during the edits and thank you for fighting alongside me with the editors to make sure the integrity of the book was maintained but stayed funny. The Funny Police are real and they should be defunded immediately. Boo to the people who lack a good sense of humor. Thank you, Dan Milaschewski, for being a great agent and negotiator through the whole process.

To my kids:

Thank you, Duke Tansey, August Tansey, Elkin Tansey, Sunday Tansey, and Birdie Tansey. I started writing these stories when I was still a cop and some of you weren't even born yet. I wrote them because I thought I might die before you were old enough to hear these stories firsthand and I wanted you to hear them from my perspective and not just from Uncle "Thor," "Bruno," or "Red." They would not tell these stories accurately anyway. In fact, please don't even listen to Red's and Bruno's sides of these stories. They will tell them differently, but my version is the right version. They just don't remember them properly. You kids have always been my "why" and I hope you can learn from my journey. Life is hard but you have to just keep putting one foot in front of the other and you have to just keep smiling. I'll end the book how I started it. With a quote from Herman Melville. "I know not all that may be coming, but be it what it will, I'll go to it smiling." Cheers.

NICK PALMISCIANO
ACKNOWLEDGMENTS

I had no intention of writing this book with Eric. In fact, I had no intention of ever writing a police book. But what a ride this has been, and I'm so thankful for it.

I met Eric Tansey when he came on my podcast. Some mutual friends had talked about him for a couple of years, and he had worked on the *Drinkin' Bros* podcast for a while. I knew he was a soldier that had done a lot of work with the special operations community and I knew he had become a cop. What I didn't know is that he was a larger-than-life human being who wears his heart and his emotions on his sleeve, and has somehow ended up in the wildest situations imaginable.

Every story he told was funnier than the one before, and the more we enjoyed hearing his stories, the more animated he became, and the bigger they got. I told him at the time, "You should write a book!" And then his wild-man smiling face got serious. "I mean . . . I kinda did," he replied.

With that, Eric sent me a collection of short stories that he had written for catharsis over the nine years he had been a police officer. There were <u>so</u> many. Some wild. Some deep and poignant. Some really fucking dumb.

I reached out to my editor from *Scars and Stripes*, Amar Deol, and asked him what he thought. I felt like there was something here. A few weeks later, he came back to me and said, "I think this could be something big and I'm in . . . but only if you write it with him."

I was very surprised. He and I had actually been talking about a very different book project. I was just trying to hook a brother up with a great editor. But now that plan was derailed and I had to think about this. *Could I do a cop book justice?* While I served in the infantry, and many people see military service and police work as similar, I knew enough cops to know that wasn't the case, and I <u>certainly</u> would learn that through the process of writing this with Eric.

I told Eric what Amar had said, and he looked at me with big doe eyes and said, "So . . . I mean . . . will you?" Just like that, I became part of *Pig Latin*. And as we put pens to proverbial paper and finished our first chapter, Amar got hired away by another book house!

Thanks for nothing, Amar! (Just kidding. Love you, man.)

So, we wrote this book on an island. Eric and I jotted away, while my dad and my wife checked our work and cleaned it up. The due date came from our agreement with Amar, and we turned it in. And I think the fine folks at Atria were surprised, not only that we had knocked it out on time while they were in the process of bringing on a replacement editor, but also that we had written one of the craziest books in human history. They now knew they needed to find an editor that shared our level of, well . . . unbridled insanity. Enter Seamus McGraw, who called me no fewer than a hundred times asking me, "Does Eric really want to say this? Does he really want people to know this?"

And the answer was always, "Yes."

So I want to thank Amar for believing in Eric and me. It was a huge leap, and I know Eric and I will always be grateful for the opportunity. I also want to tell Amar to fuck all the way off, because he abandoned us like Warner abandoned Elle Woods for Vivian in *Legally Blonde*. (Still kidding, man).

I want to thank Seamus for coming in and working with us on a very challenging project. I appreciated how detailed you were and how much you cared about making sure the story was told the right way. There were a lot of moments and chapters that required a lot of work, and it was very easy to take them from good to great with your unwavering support.

As always, thank you to my father, the elder Nick Palmisciano. My dad has always been my first editor, from middle school until now. He's a better writer than I am by a wide margin, and I'm still hopeful that he writes his own incredible story sometime soon. But that won't happen if he doesn't take better care of himself—like this year, when he ignored major pain in his stomach so as not to inconvenience anyone and then had to have his gallbladder removed in an emergency surgery that almost cost him his life. Am I using Eric's book to do a personal PSA for my dad? Yes. Yes, I am.

To my mom, thanks for the homemade pasta, the guidance, and the grit. I needed all three to survive writing a book with Eric Tansey. I love you.

To my wife, Suzanne, thank you again for your thoughtful commentary as we worked through the book. You made every chapter better, and you're the only person other than me that knows the emotional range that Eric Tansey brings to a project. This was a very hard book to structure with all the available stories Eric had on paper and in his brain, and you helped me get to what I think is a great picture of Eric's life and character. I also enjoyed watching your British self have secondhand embarrassment at 90 percent of his stories.

To my kids, JD, Leo, Siena, Katalina, Jack, and Max, don't become a cop! Or at least if you do, don't work the Southeast District of Raleigh! I don't think my heart could handle the stress of knowing what you're up against. Thank you all for tolerating the long nights while Dad stared into his laptop or sat in his office.

To my agent, Dan Milaschewski, thank you for seeing this through. Your guidance is unmatched. Your passion is obvious. You're a consummate professional, and it's an honor to be represented by you.

And now to Eric Tansey. You are a pain in the ass. And you're amazing. Your ability to argue and get fired up by every little thing that isn't exactly the way you want it (even the shape of the ears on the neon pig's head on the book cover FFS!) made me want to choke you to death on many occasions. It was very easy to understand why so many people wanted to fire you!

But listening to your stories, talking to the men and women who served with you, seeing your generosity in your everyday life, whether it's giving all there is to give for your kids, your fellow veterans, police officers, or volunteering for hurricane relief are why I'm proud to call you a friend, and proud to have played a small part in telling your story.

I hope I helped represent you and the Thin Blue Line in the way that you all deserve.

No matter what any politician says, <u>you were a great cop</u>.